WALKER COUNTY HIGH SCHOOL ATHLETICS 1920–2000

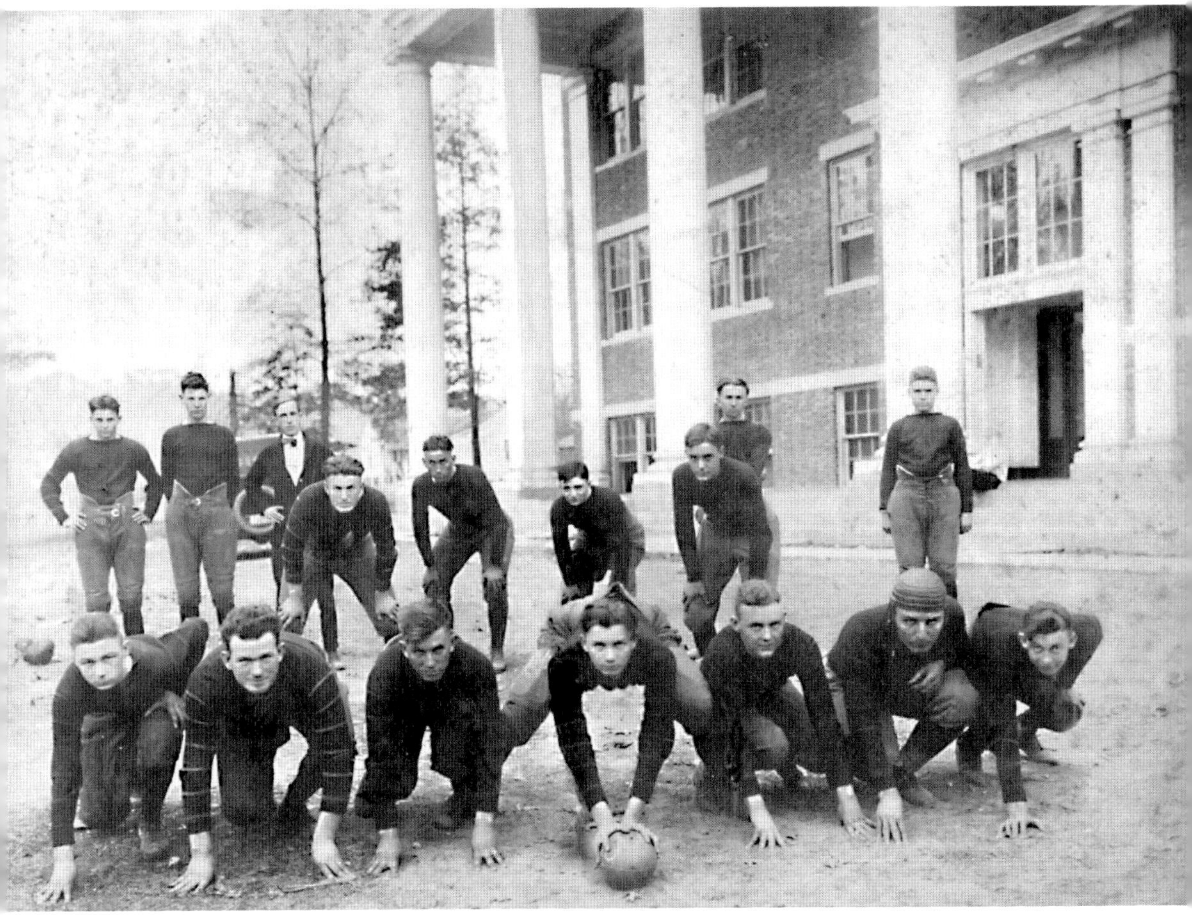

STARTING ELEVEN, 1920. The first football team in the history of Walker County is shown in front of the old Walker County High School, built in 1916. From left to right are (first row, linemen) Stanley Freeman, Lawrence "Moxie" Brown, Harold Kilgore, Colis Watts, Willard Brown, Cupe Perry, and Joe Legg; (second row, backs) Lacy Brakefield, Jim "Bear Tamer" Sparks, Bill Grey, and Pervy Dodd; (third row, standing behind the starters) Lee Hamilton, Bruce Jones, coach Cranford Robinson, Jimmy Gallager, and John "Slick" Lollar.

FRONT COVER: The front cover shows Danny Gambrell; see page 29 for his full story. (Author's collection.)
COVER BACKGROUND: The background photograph is of the 1976 football squad, which was the area champion. (Author's collection.)
BACK COVER: This photograph shows the 1996 girls' softball team, which won three straight Alabama State Championship titles; see page 8 for this story. (Author's collection.)

WALKER COUNTY HIGH SCHOOL ATHLETICS 1920–2000

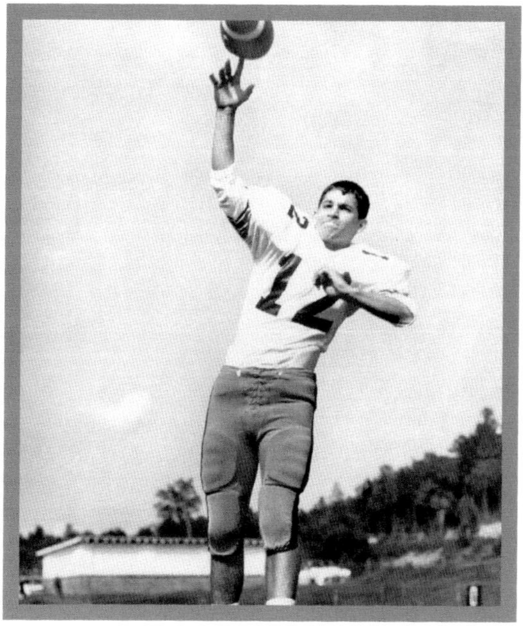

Pat Morrison

ARCADIA PUBLISHING

ISBN 978-0-7385-4434-2

Published by Arcadia Publishing
Charleston SC, Chicago IL, Portsmouth NH, San Francisco CA

Printed in the United States of America

Library of Congress Catalog Card Number: 2006940455

For all general information contact Arcadia Publishing at:
Telephone 843-853-2070
Fax 843-853-0044
E-mail sales@arcadiapublishing.com
For customer service and orders:
Toll-Free 1-888-313-2665

Visit us on the Internet at www.arcadiapublishing.com

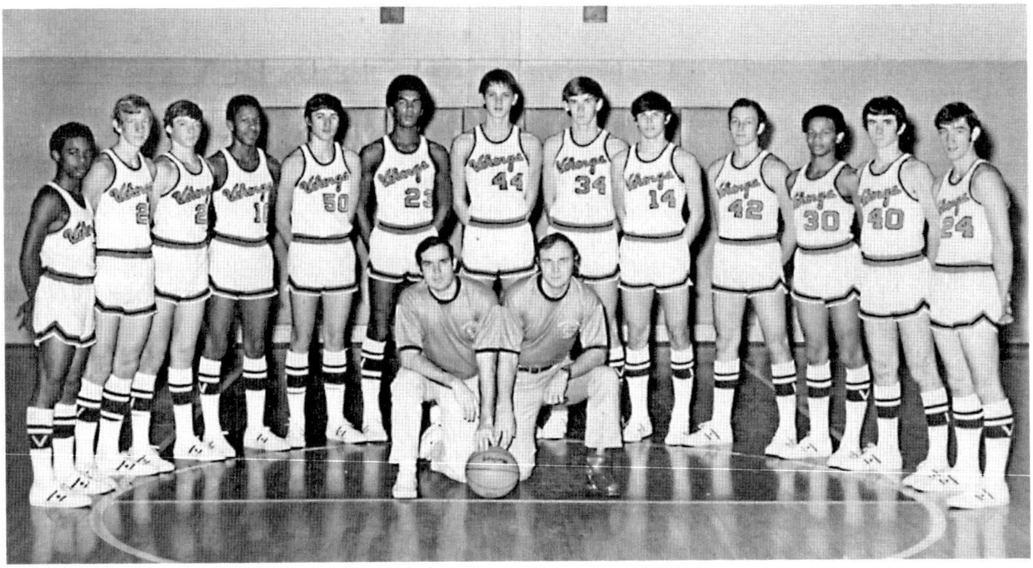

WALKER'S ONLY UNDEFEATED BASKETBALL TEAM, 1972–1973. This Herbert Greene–coached team is the only undefeated basketball team in the 80-year history of Walker High School. Pictured from left to right are (first row) coaches Herbert Green and Pat Morrison; (second row) Leon Harton, Buddy Woodley, Al McAdams, Darrell Davis, Henry Wood, Robert Paige, Ronnie Shaw, Sammy Lee, Chuck Justice, Mike Hendon, Lee McElrath, Tony Price, and Ronnie Daniel.

CONTENTS

ACKNOWLEDGMENTS

This book has been both a labor of love and an emotional experience. First, let me express my regrets that I could not include every team and every player that has contributed so much to making Walker High School athletics such a respected program throughout this state. Due to the availability of photographs and space limitations, it is impossible to include everyone who deserves to be recognized in this work.

The idea for this book first emerged when I was given an old out-of-print book entitled My *Beloved Vikings* written by the Reverend Paul W. Stewart, a Nazarene minister, who also had a great love for Walker County High School. It chronicled the early years of athletics at the high school. From the moment I first read it, I knew that someday I would supplement it with photographs and bring it up to the end of the 20th century.

I want to thank my wife, Helen, for her support, love, and understanding not only during this project but throughout all phases of my life. Even though it is impossible to thank all of those who have contributed photographs, information, or other forms of assistance, I do wish to thank Walker High School principal Danny Gambrell for being an invaluable source of help and T. D. Norris for his first-hand knowledge of many teams, individuals, and events in Walker's past.

I also want to thank Bucky Mize (librarian at Walker), Paula Wade, Phil Schumacher, David Campbell, and June Hudson (all retired Walker teachers), Brenda Abner, Jimmy Alexander, Francis Ballanger, David Banks, Brenda Beard, Hilda Brown, Jerri Bennett, David Deason, Konnie Godfrey, Billie Hoobler, Shelia Kilgore, Linda Lewis, Al McAdams, Colleen Miller, Billyfrank Morrison, Geraldine Murray, Mildred Myers, Pat Nelson, Randy Panter, Skip Roberts, and many more who have assisted me in various ways. Unless otherwise noted, all the photographs in this book are from the author's private collection.

I hope the production of this book will pay back in some small way the monumental way my life has been touched by those thousands of former Vikings who will always hold a special place in my heart.

INTRODUCTION

A devastating fire on February 28, 1916, set into action a series of events that would begin a legacy still in existence today. The fire burned the original Walker County High School atop Academy Hill in Jasper, Alabama; it destroyed not only the building, but every book, paper, and record that existed. The high elevation prohibited water from being pumped to the top of the hill to extinguish the blaze.

Local entrepreneur L. B. Musgrove, who had given land to build the original school, stepped forward and gave 25 acres in memory of his mother, Elizabeth Cain Musgrove. This property was located on the east side of town at a much lower elevation than the previous school. On this new site not far from the original location of the Native American trading post established by Lorinza Dow and later named Jasper, a magnificent new three-story brick building with six large white columns was constructed and named Walker County High School.

Walker had fielded a basketball team at least as early as 1913, but no records remain of the team, which played its games outside on the grounds of the newly built Methodist church in Jasper. Walker administrators and boosters decided to organize a football team in the fall of 1920. Walker County High School Athletic Association was organized to promote basketball and baseball and to create a football program. With the help of faculty members, students, and boosters, the association raised money to purchase football uniforms, and a football team was born. With the development of this football program, young men came from all over Walker County. They came from such places as Eldridge, Nauvoo, America Junction, Saragossa, Gamble Mines, Pocahontas, and Jasper to try their hand at this new and fascinating sport, and since many were multiple-sport athletes, they also improved the basketball and baseball teams. This is where our story begins.

I came to Walker in June 1968, when classes were still being held in the old columned building. My life has been richly blessed by coaching with some of the top coaches ever to lead Walker's varied teams—coaches such as Vic Karabasz, Herbert Green, Larry Blakeney, David Campbell, Phil Schumacher, Danny Gambrell, and Bubba Davis. More importantly, I have been blessed to teach and coach some of the best young male and female athletes that this nation has to offer, and I will never be able to repay the experiences that I have had during those years. I was fortunate enough to know personally some of the great men of old who made a lasting impact on Walker, men such as Geddes Self, Bill Call, T. D. Norris, Harry Erwin, Judge Al Blanton, D. Joe Gambrell, and Bernard Weinstein.

Walker County High School became Walker High School in 1971, when the Jasper City Board of Education purchased it. These two names will be used interchangeably throughout this book.

I have known many of the men and women in this book and thousands more who have left their indelible marks on Walker County High School. This is a book about not only the great players, but also the average athletes who have contributed their blood, sweat, and tears to make Walker High School athletics one of the most respected programs in the state of Alabama.

I hope to give the reader an insight into the development of all areas of athletics at Walker. This book contains a collection of photographs, postcards, and stories of all sports (men's and women's), cheerleading, majorettes, parades, and pep rallies from 1920 to 2000. Read about the first touchdown in Viking history; a football player who was captain of an undefeated state championship team, an undefeated national championship team, and an undefeated world championship team; a male basketball player who personally scored more points than most teams of his day; and a female basketball player who never played high school basketball but was the all-time leading scorer for her college team. Learn about the development of the helmet and the face mask and the elimination of girls' athletics in the late 1920s.

Through the years, great and average athletes may come and go, coaches and administrators will develop new techniques and strategies, teams may or may not leave a winning legacy, but one thing will never change: Viking Pride. It is forever.

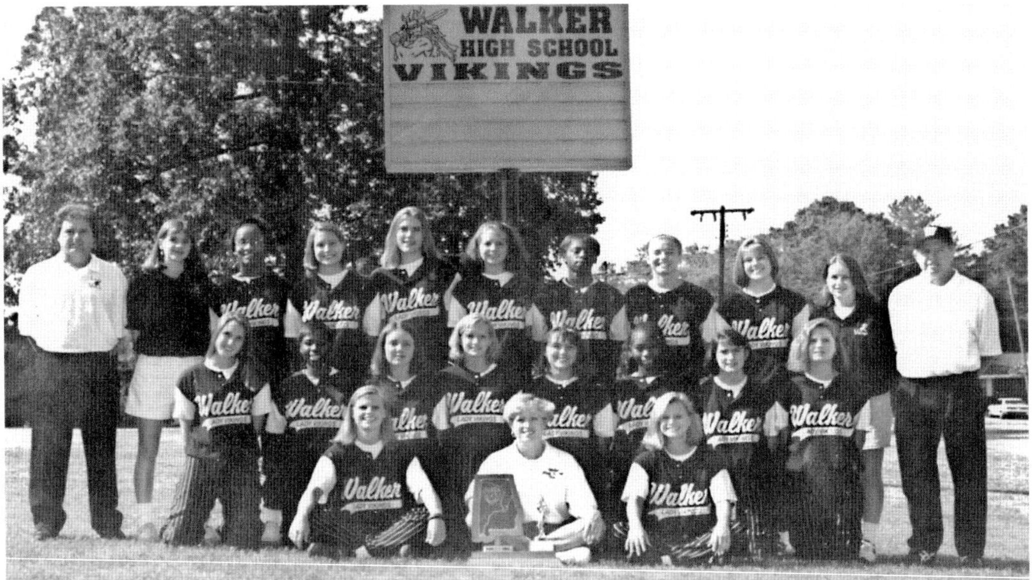

THREE-TIME STATE CHAMPIONS, 1996. Shelia Kilgore led these Lady Vikings to an astounding five-year streak, winning three state titles (1994–1996) and finishing second the other two years. From left to right are (first row) Heather Slagle, Coach Kilgore, and Jennifer Cain; (second row) Stacie Hice, Shayla Rodgers, Natalie Carmichael, Angie Sanders, Cassidy Anderson, Essence Satterfield, Jenny Kelly, and Ashley Sims; (third row) Coach Keith Anderson, Carrie Statham, Brandy Robinson, Amber Thomas, Jessica Waid, Mandi Thomas, Synesha Smith, Sandy Ivey, Brandy Brown, Amanda Sherer, and Coach Ronnie Kilgore. (Courtesy Shelia Kilgore.)

1

The Early Years

1920–1949

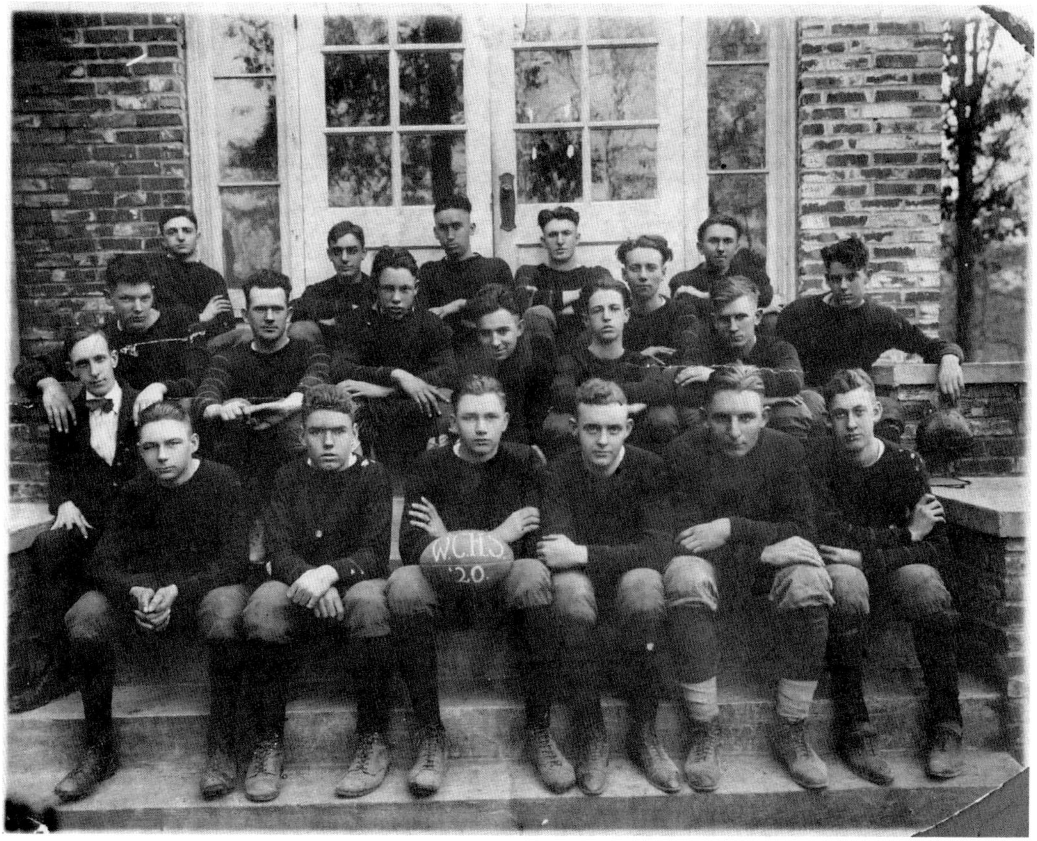

Walker's First Football Team, 1920. This, possibly the first official photograph of the Walker County High School football team, was taken at the back entrance to the high school. From left to right are (first row) Stanley Freeman, John "Slick" Lollar, Colis Watts, Willard Brown, Cupe Perry, and Joe Legg; (second row) coach Cranford Robinson, Bruce Jones, Moxie Brown, Earnest Broom, Ralph Kitchens, Harold Kilgore, Earl Christenson, Lee Hamilton, and John Whit Long; (third row) Bill Grey, Pervy Dodd, Jim "Bear Tamer" Sparks, Lacy Brakefield, and Jimmy Gallagher. Most of these young men played in the first football game they ever saw.

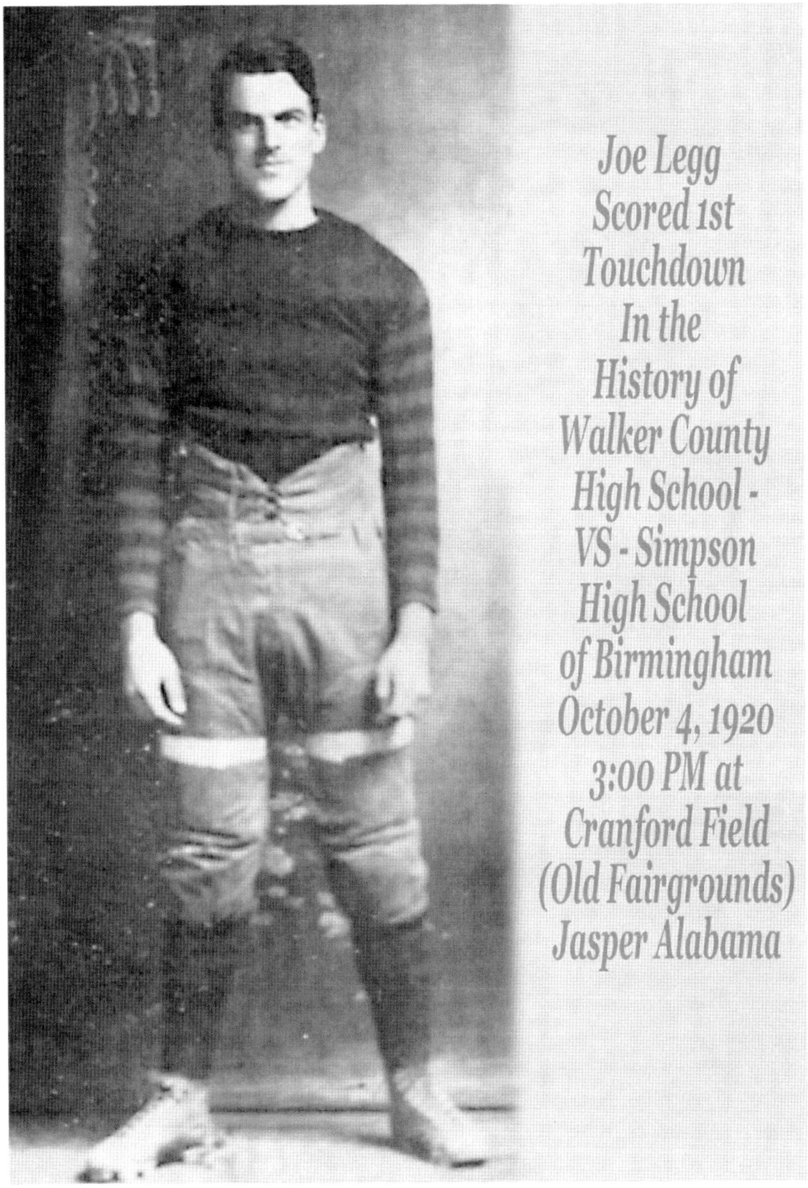

FIRST VIKING TOUCHDOWN, OCTOBER 4, 1920. Joe "Foots" Legg went down in Viking history for scoring the first touchdown. This game was played at the old fairgrounds in Jasper, then known as Cranford Field, in the vicinity of Murphy Manufacturing. The game pitted the Vikings against Simpson High of Birmingham. Legg intercepted a pass, having no idea what to do with it. The coaches were yelling for him to run, and finally he did. After crossing the goal line, he was required to touch the ball to the ground before the score counted; this is where the word touchdown originated. Joe had no idea he had to do this either. Finally one of his own players tackled him, the ball touched the ground, and the official raised his hands indicating a touchdown. Joe was to play on the first three teams at Walker County High School, including the state championship team.

Bruce Jones, 1920–1921. Walker's first superstar was Bruce Jones from America Junction. He was the captain of undefeated championship teams at Walker, the University of Alabama, and the Green Bay Packers. He gave up a Hollywood acting career with fellow teammate Johnny Mack Brown to return to Alabama and marry his sweetheart. This picture is featured on the front of the Bear Bryant Museum program.

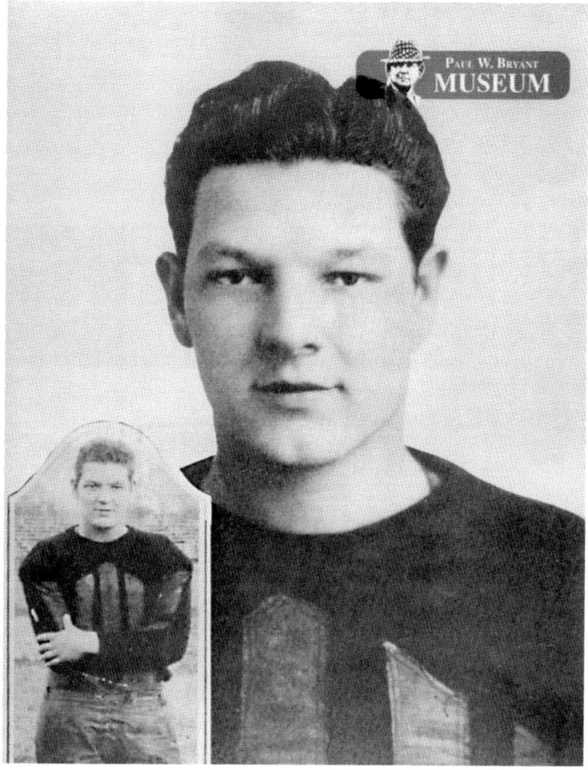

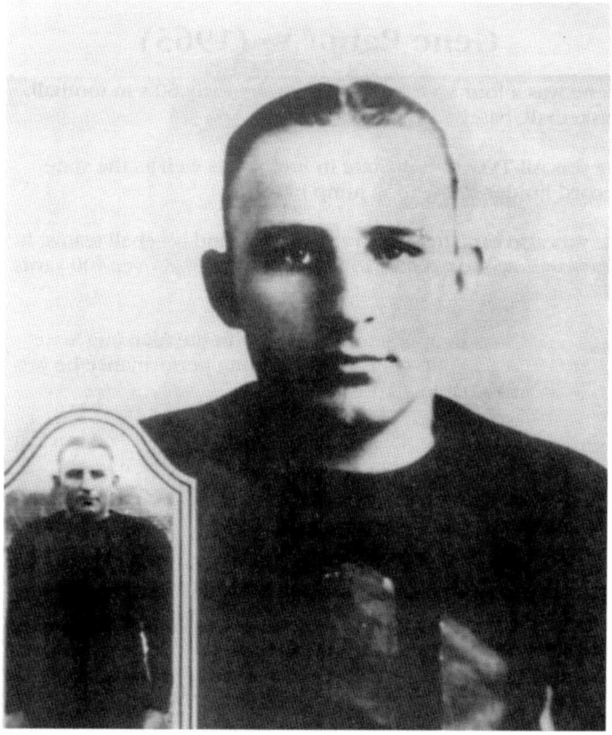

Claude "Cupe" Perry, 1920–1921. Cupe Perry's career was almost identical to Bruce Jones's. He played in state championships, national championships, and world championships with the same teams, and both were from America Junction. Cupe returned to Jasper after his professional career ended and began coaching at various high schools in the county. He became one of the first football officials in Walker County.

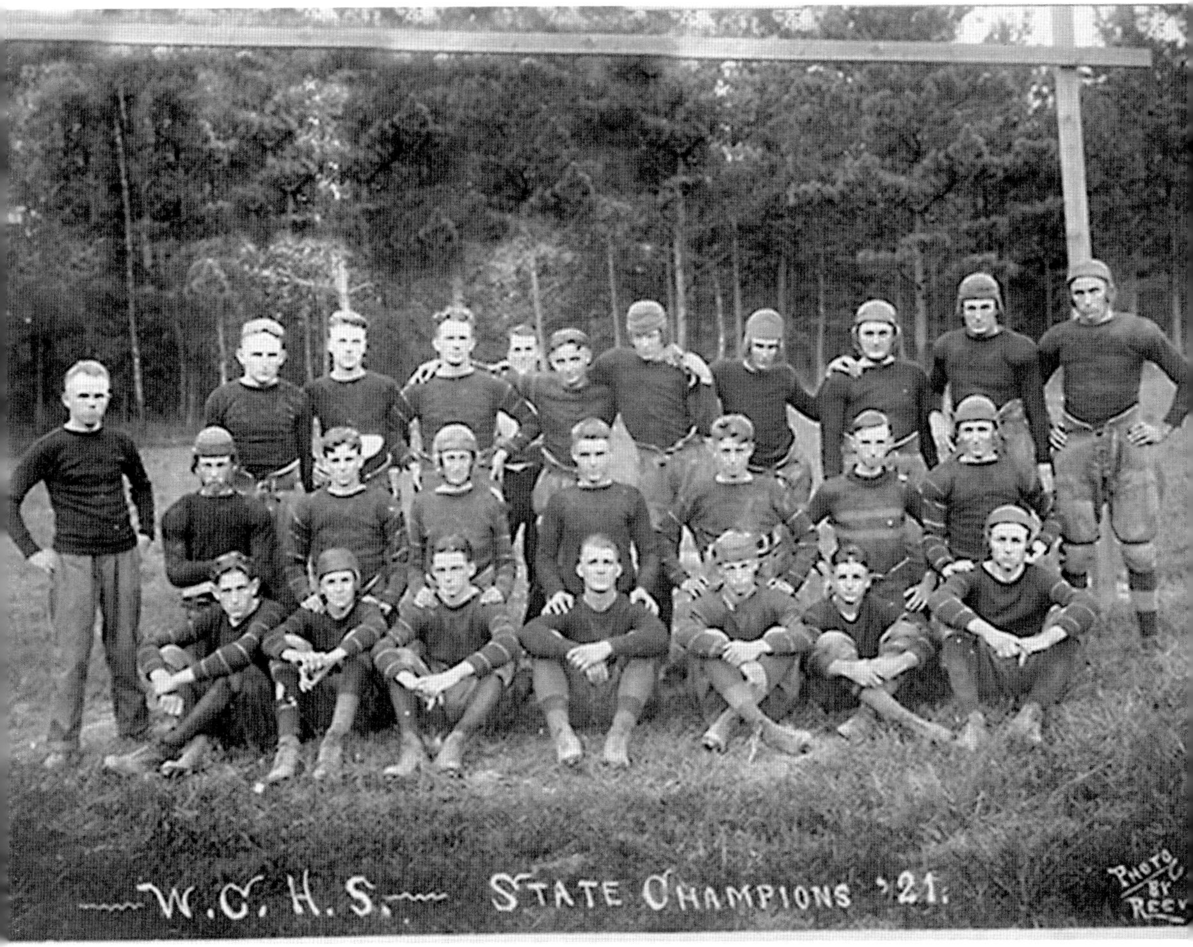

First State Champions, 1921. This team was undefeated and untied and was crowned as the Alabama state champions of 1921, becoming Walker's first state championship team in any sport. From left to right are (first row) Lacy Ellis, Charles Tweedy, Stanley Freeman, Sam Allison, John Whit Long, Earl Christenberry, and Exes Plylor; (second row) coach F. E. Christopher, Earnest Broom, Lee Hamilton, Jimmy Gallager, John Lollar, Cash Woods, Roy Crow, and Hansel Beasley; (third row) Cupe Perry, Pervy Dodd, Lawrence Brown, Joe Legg, Ralph Kitchens, Bruce Jones, Cliff Brown, Coleman Wilson, Lacy Brakefield, and Jim Sparks. This Viking team scored 293 points and gave up a mere two touchdowns all season. They defeated Central High of Birmingham, which later became Phillips High, by a score of 6-0 in the championship game. A Birmingham reporter called them "those giants and Vikings from the North." The name stuck, and they remain the Vikings to this day.

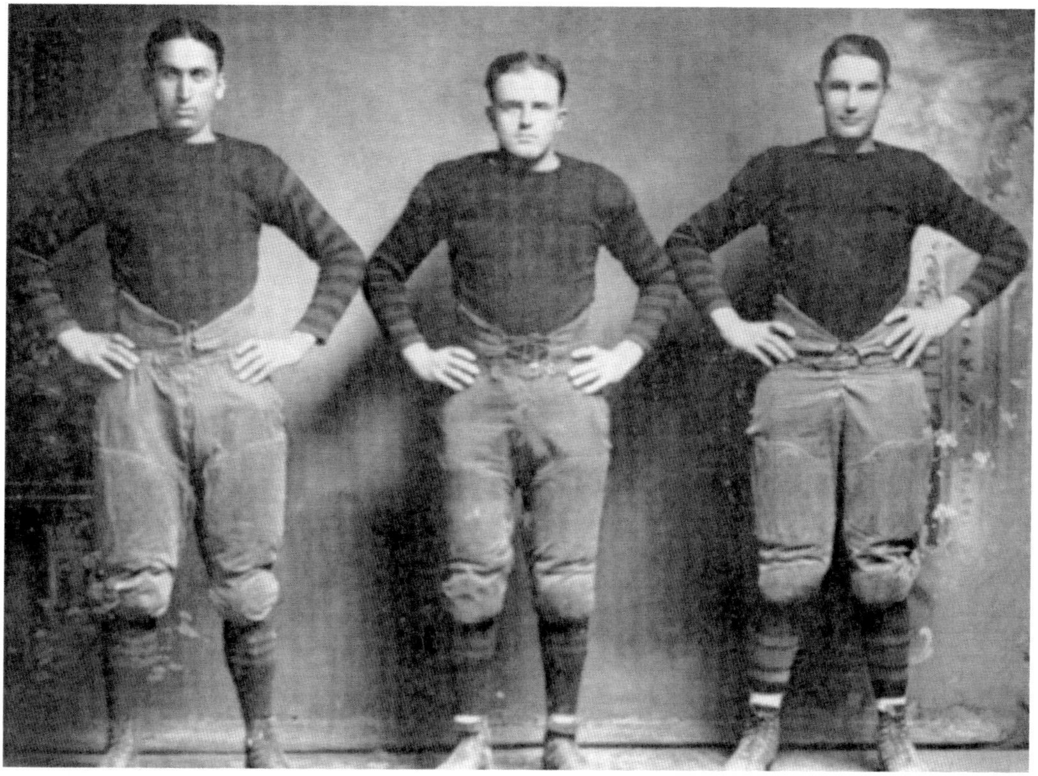

FOOTBALL CAPTAINS, 1922. From left to right are captain Jim Sparks, alternate captain Drew "Red" Gibson, and captain-elect for the 1923 season Cliff Brown. Sparks had played on all three teams at Walker, Brown had played in the 1921 state championship, and Gibson had played on the 1922 team. Notice that unlike today, these players wore little padding on the upper half of their bodies, and most wore no helmet.

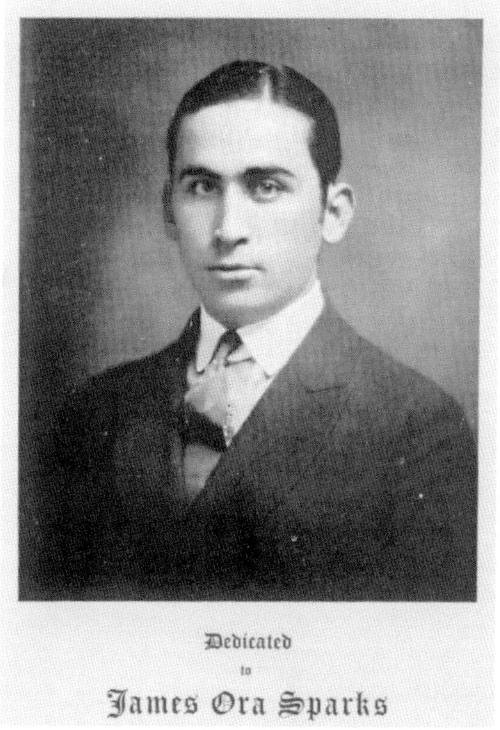

JIM "BEAR KILLER" SPARKS, 1920–1922. Jim Sparks played on Walker's first team and its first state championship team, was captain of the 1922 team, and was a star on the basketball team. He entered the University of Alabama in the fall of 1923 with the prospects of a great college career like his teammates Jones, Perry, and Lollar. Fate intervened when he died on the operating table at the university infirmary of a ruptured appendix.

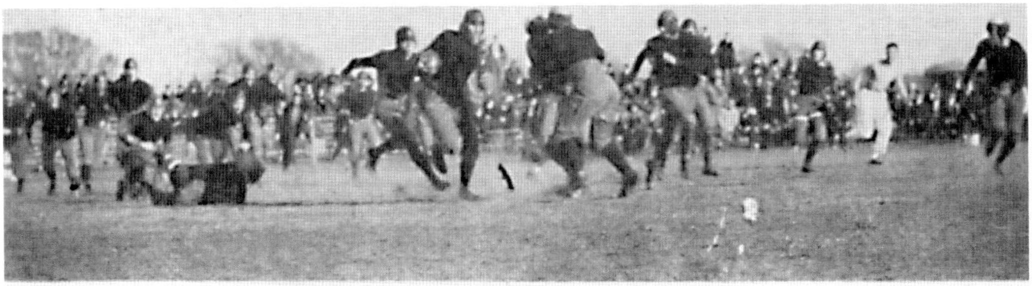

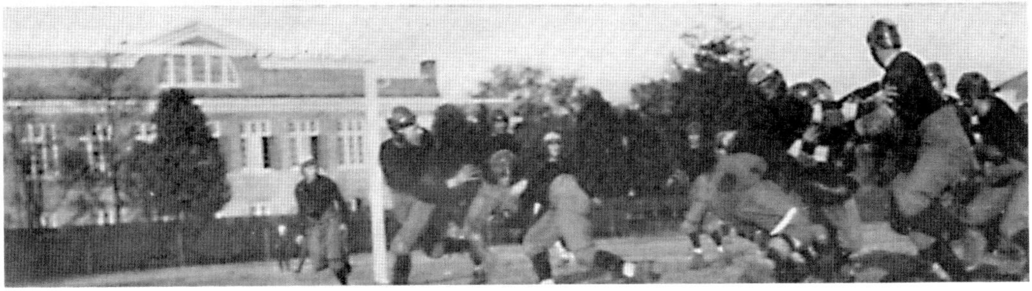

Action Shots of Walker Vikings, 1923. These pictures show the Vikings in action in 1923. The bottom photograph shows captain Cliff Brown breaking through the line to tackle the halfback behind the line of scrimmage. This is thought to be the Fayette game, which Walker won 7-0, handing Fayette their first loss in three years and providing Vikings fans a reason to celebrate homecoming.

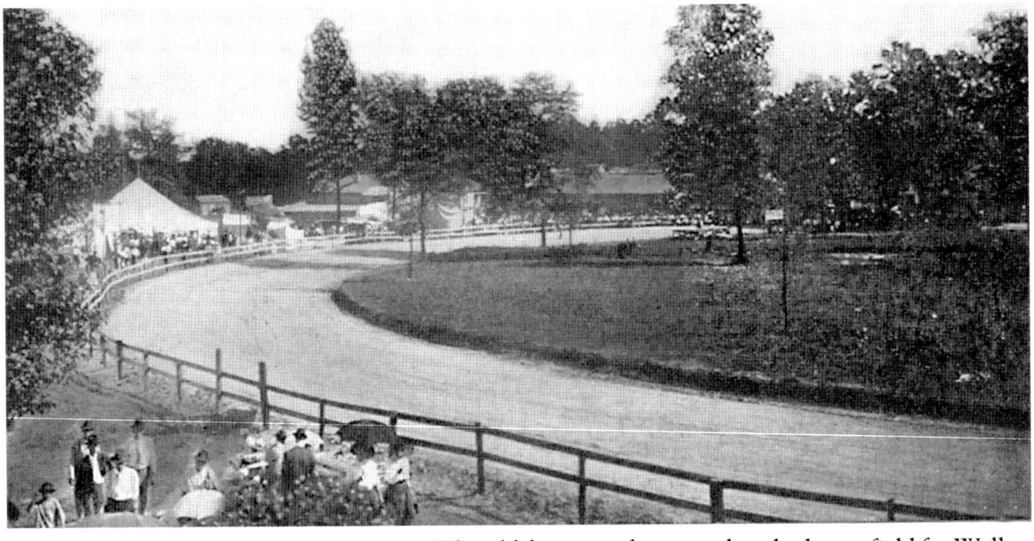

Cranford Fairgrounds, 1920–1923. The old fairground was used as the home field for Walker County High's football games during the early years. The field was named in honor of Capt. Jack Cranford, local businessman and former mayor of Jasper. The fairgrounds stood where Murphy Manufacturing Company is now located. These early games were played as day games because there was no field in Jasper with lights until 1936.

LON RICHARDSON, 1925. Lon, shown in his letter sweater, was a well-known player in the early years but is perhaps better known as the father of Billy Richardson, Alabama's great running back. Lon was known as "Little Lon" because of his short stature, but there was no one with a bigger heart or who took the game more seriously than he did.

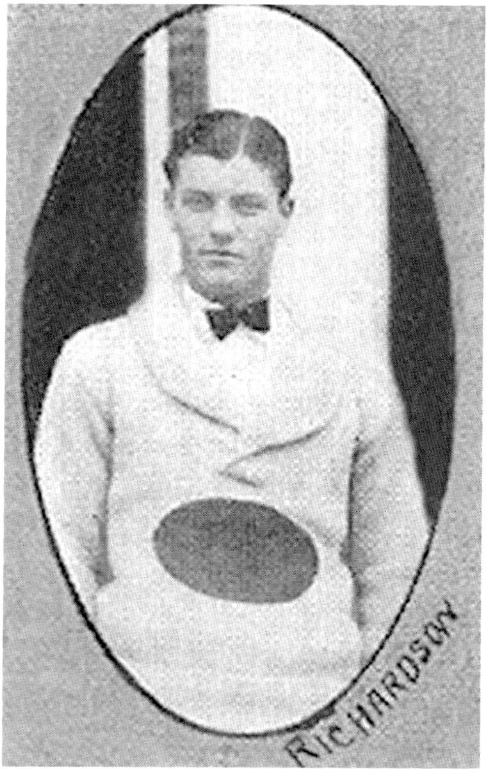

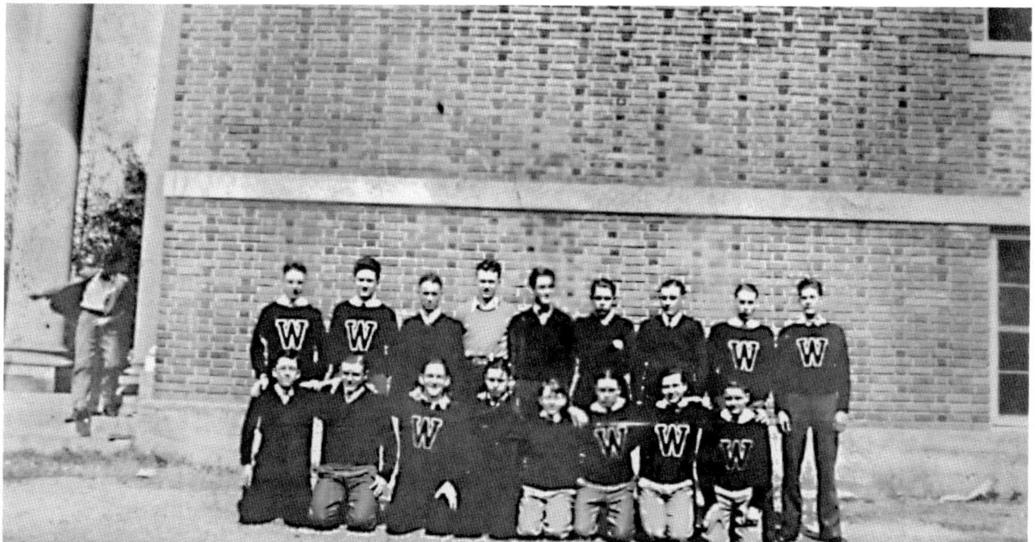

FIRST W CLUB, 1928. Charter members of the Walker County High School W Club are pictured at the side of the high school building. From left to right are (first row) Charles Huggins, Wallace Gibson, Bobbie Morrison, two unidentified, Paul Landrip, Doug Leake, and Harold Jones; (second row) Bob Hamilton, Woodrow Purcell, Claude Hall, Bert Simmons, Ralph Morrison, Hastin Savage, Lattis Bishop, George Bagwell, and Howard Randolph.

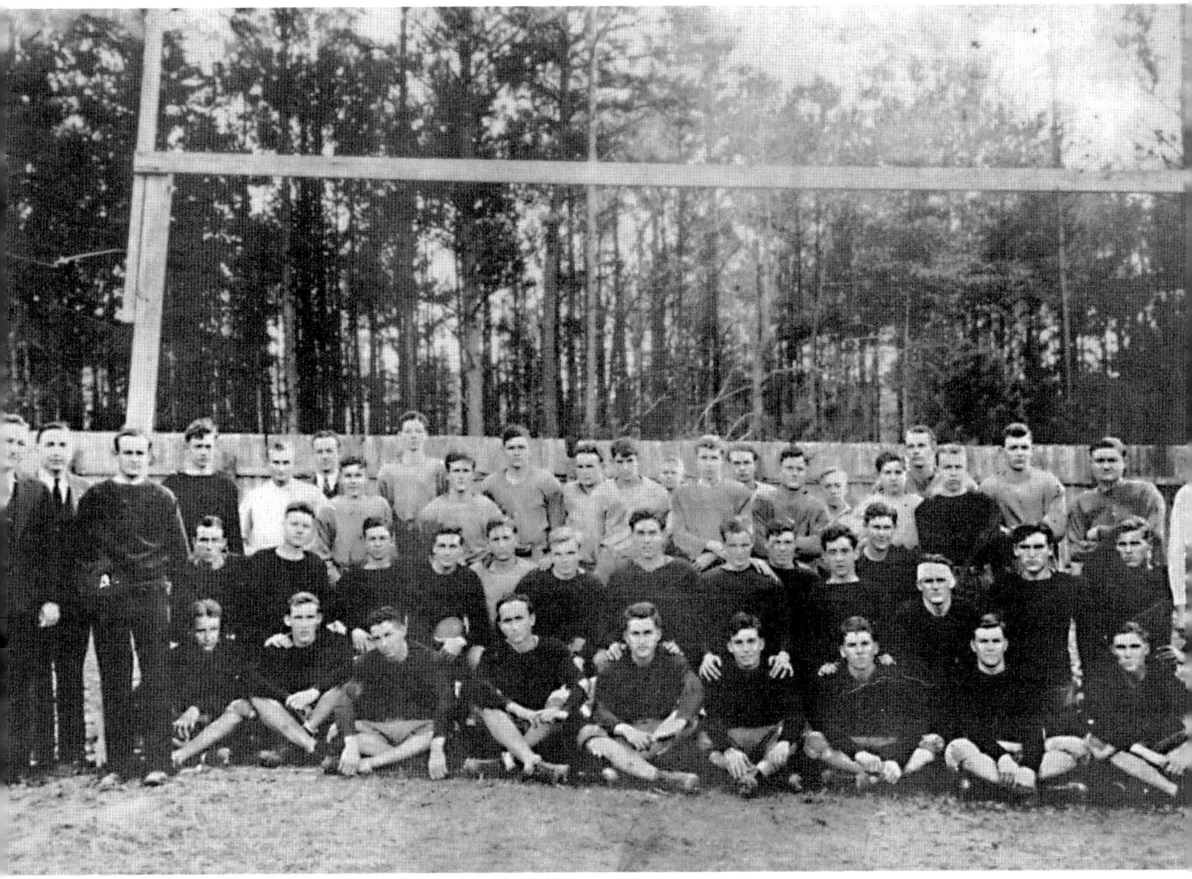

UNDEFEATED STATE CHAMPIONSHIP TEAM, 1930. Listed here are the members of the undefeated 1930 Vikings, who recorded Walker's second state championship. Pictured are, in no particular order, Principal W. P. Smugg; coaches Ebb James and Jerry Brown; managers Eugene Todd, Owen Pharr, Ivey Drewry, and John Leak; team members captain Barney Musgrove, Henry Ferguson, Woodrow Nichols, Paul Boteler, Louie Townsend, Euel Hambric, Jack Sherer, Lamar Miller, Fletcher Ferguson, Clyde Tirey, Marvin Estes, Clyde Westbrook, A. J. McDanal, Fred Hutto, Howard Sudduth, Welton Lockhart, Richard Tennent, Walter Pearson, Lecil Grey, Fred Swindle, Spurgeon Bishop, Robert Kilgore, Henry Sanford, Willie Pearson, David Boteler, Wilson Beaird, J. P. Best, Alga Hendrix, J. T. Simmons, Billy O'Rear, Chesley Barnett, Sam Gunter, Harry Short, Lloyd Martin, Coleman Salters, Woodrow Wilson, Maxwell Drewry, Jack Hall, Erbin Gardner, Auburn Argo, Junior Turner, William Thomas, Alfred Russell, Son Richardson, W. T. Brakefield, Junior Burton, Tommy Cairns, Auburn Jackson, and Scott Townsend. Ebb James was the twin brother of Gov. Fobb James. Barney Musgrove was to have a great career at Auburn, and A. J. "Jelly" McDanal was to do the same at Alabama.

A. J. "JELLY" MCDANAL, 1930. A. J. was unquestionably Walker's first great running back. Against a tough Hartselle team, Jelly carried the ball six times for five touchdowns and 249 yards, averaging over 40 yards per carry. He was selected All-County, All-State, and All-Southern. He received a scholarship to the University of Alabama, where he roomed with a tough young tight end named Paul "Bear" Bryant. (Courtesy of WCHS.)

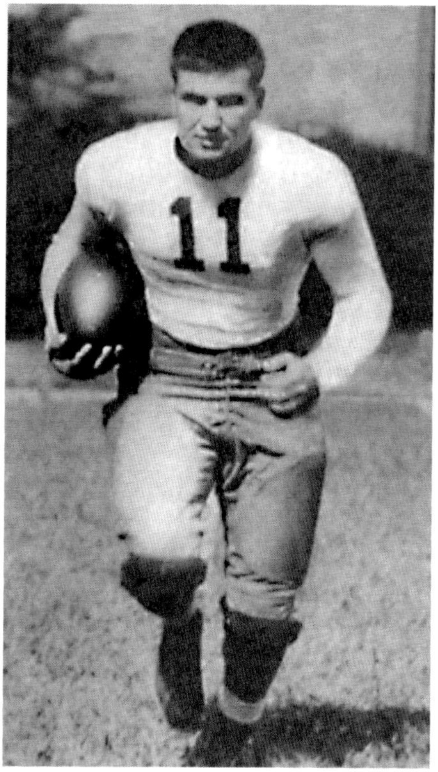

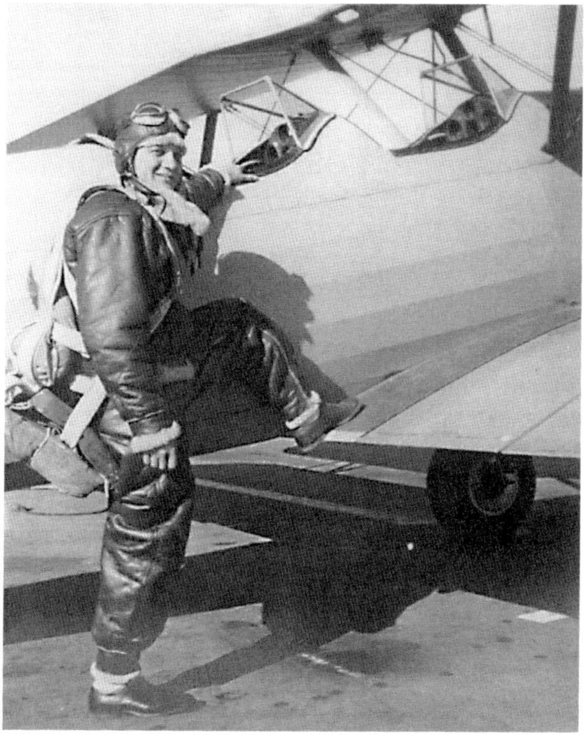

ALTERNATE CAPTAIN JACK HALL, 1934. Shown at the foot of his biplane in 1944 is Lt. Jack Hunter Hall. Jack was an outstanding athlete at Walker, and he, like many graduates of Walker, responded to his country's call when war broke out. Some even left high school to serve and then came back and finished school. Many did not come back at all, making the ultimate sacrifice for their country.

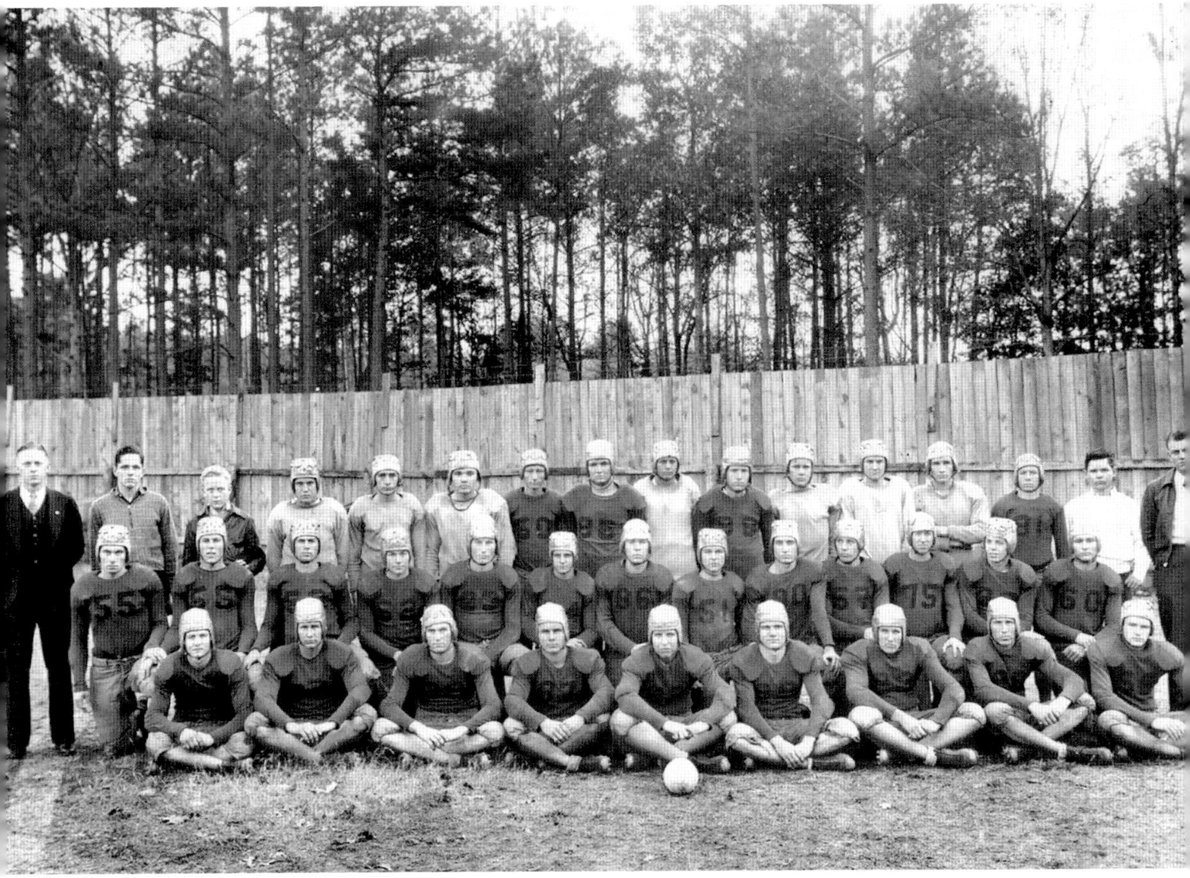

First Walker County High School Team to Play Night Games, 1936. The first game played at night (under lights) was against Winfield High School. Walker won the game 40-12 to christen the new electrically lighted field. This team was coached by ex-Viking and former All-Southern quarterback Al Blanton, who played for Howard College and later became a judge in Walker County. From left to right are (first row) Nute Barnett, Kelly Sartain, Fayette Sherer, ? Barnett, W. D. Kelley, Everett Hudson, Doyle Barnett, ? Sherer, and Lawrence Brakefield; (second row) Jack Maddox, Freeman Clark, Charles Rollo, ? Sartain, Arnold Jones, Max Sorrell, ? Sherer, Jimmy Cain, Arthur Sartain, Pete Sherer, Hap Butler, and E. C. Black; (third row) coach Al Blanton, Alfred Sartain, John Landrip, Robert Connor, Charles Wiggins, six unidentified players, Jack Cornelius, unidentified, Red Best, Ed Cain, and assistant coach Earnest Teal.

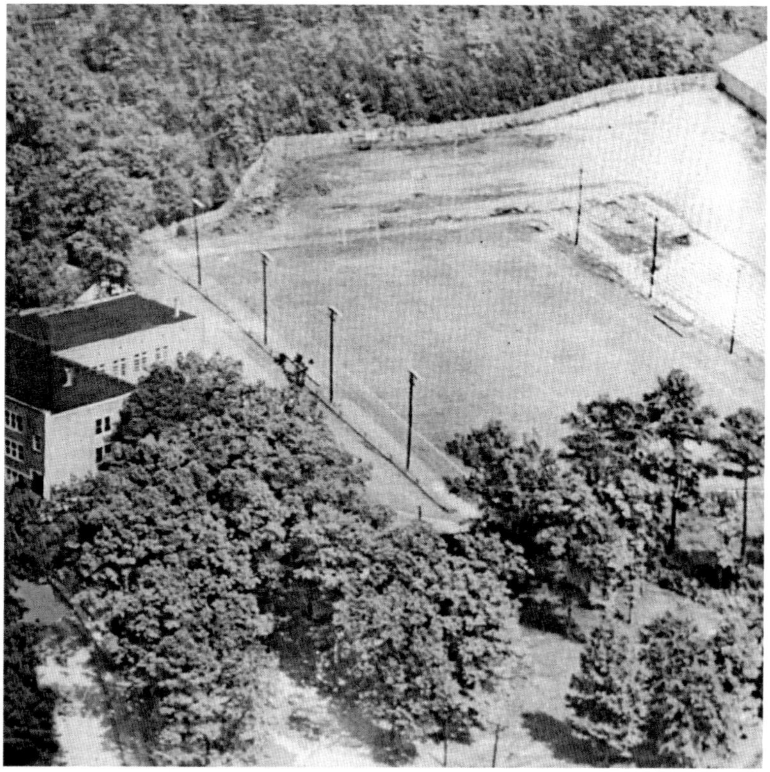

Aerial View of Walker High School, 1937. This overhead view of Walker's facilities in 1937 shows the high school on the left, the football field in the middle (with the new lights allowing the Vikings to play night games), and the field house on the far right. At this time, there was no track, practice field, baseball field, training room, weight room, D.O. parking lot, or gym. All these areas are only woods.

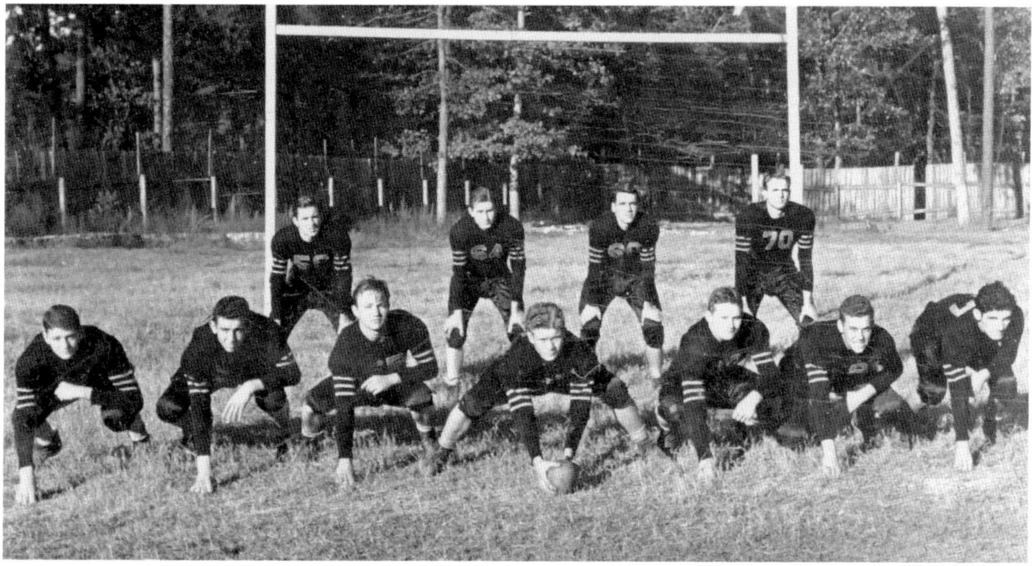

Starting Offense, 1941. This team, coached by Paul "Red" Hudson and assisted by Wick Hudson, had an unusual season, with a record of three wins, two losses, and three ties. They only lost three seniors to graduation. The players are, from left to right, (first row, linemen) Charles Tucker, Arben Drummond, Cliff Barnett, Fred Sherer, Dewitt Cooper, M. S. Snow, and Tony Lee; (second row, backs) Bobby Liddell, Ray Sherer, T. E. Segars, and Cleston Addison.

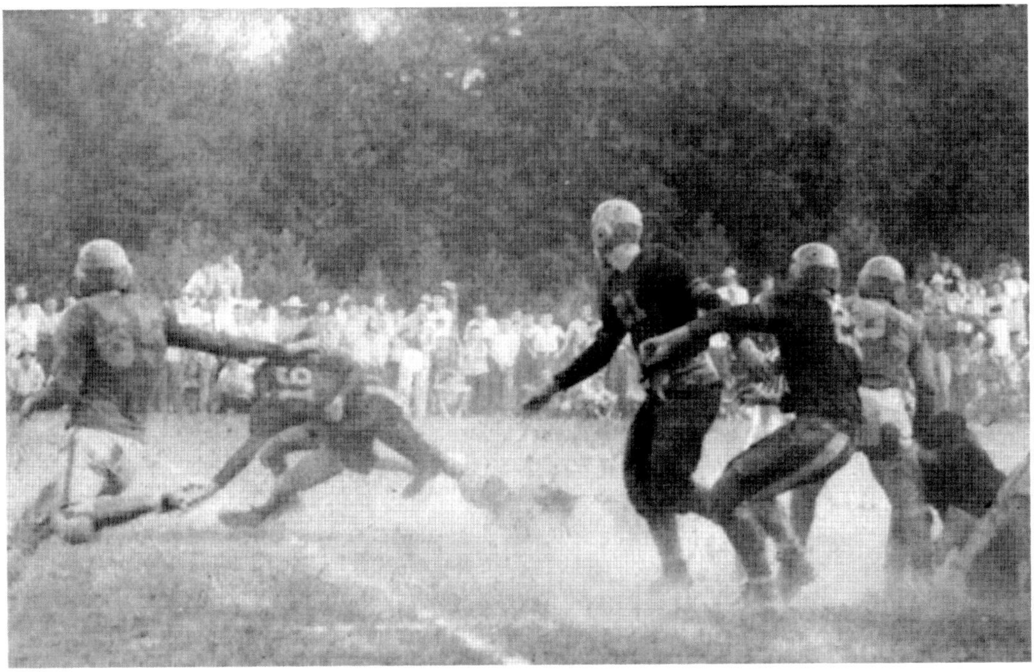

WALKER VERSUS CORDOVA, 1945. Ralph Hamner (16) rambles for yardage and is brought down after a short gain. Gerald Kilgore (21), Elvin Haygood (28), and Jack Best (41) look on. The Vikings beat the ever-tough Cordova Blue Devils 19-0 in this game. Hamner, Kilgore, and Howard Wilson each scored one touchdown in the game. Few bleachers were available, and many fans stood along the sidelines.

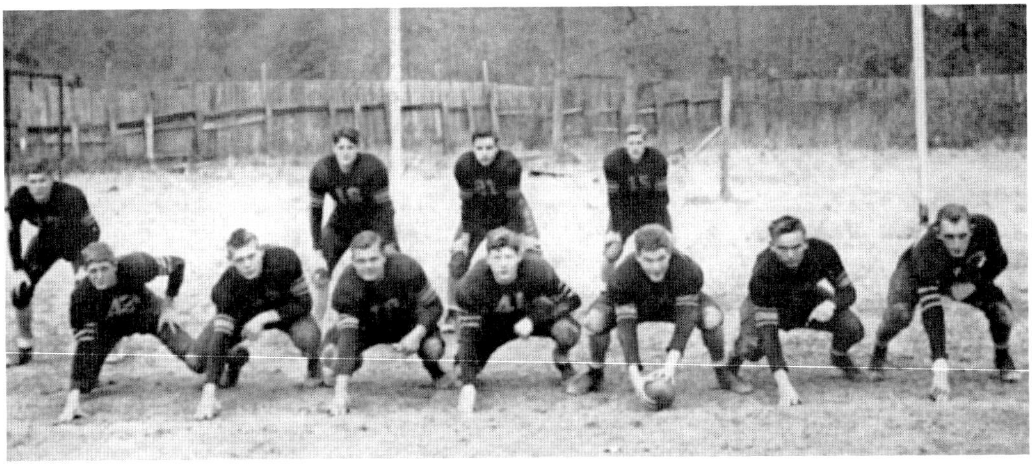

STARTING OFFENSE, 1945. This 1945 team was led by Ralph Hamner, a true triple threat. Ralph was to become Walker County's most decorated soldier during the Vietnam War. From left to right are (first row, linemen) Bill Allbritten, cocaptain Bobby Jones, John Wilson, Jack Best, George Pounds, Bill Williams, and Tuck Lum; (second row, backs) Jimmy Pounds, Ralph Hamner, Gerald Kilgore, and captain Howard Wilson.

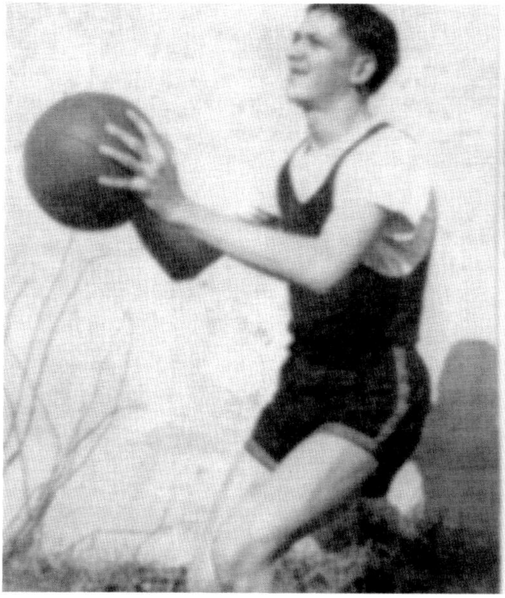 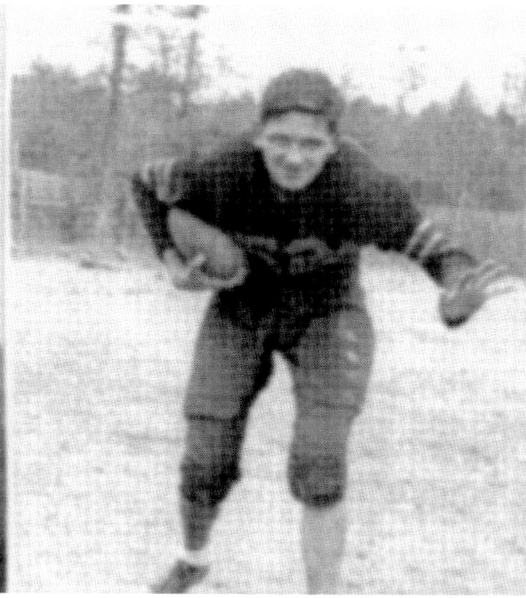

GEORGE SMITH LINDSEY, 1945–1946. Jasper's favorite son, George Lindsey (best known as "Goober"), lettered in both football and basketball at Walker and then played on the only football team that Walker College ever fielded. The team was undefeated at 6-0. After leaving Walker College, he played football for Florence State. He has been a dramatic actor and comedy actor, is in the Alabama Sports Hall of Fame, and has a doctorate degree.

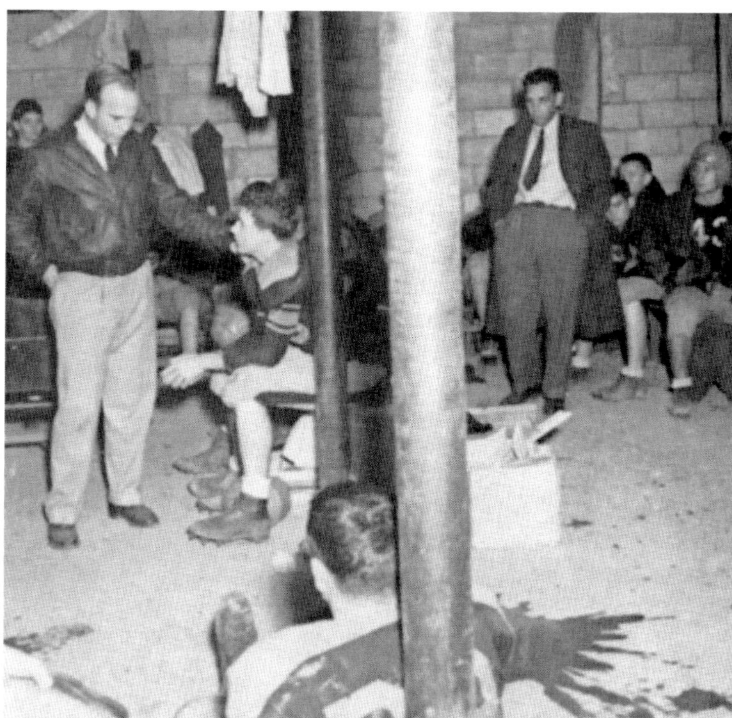

HALFTIME IN THE DRESSING ROOM, 1948. This unusual photograph shows the interior of the dressing room at halftime of a Walker football game. Coach H. M. Smalley (left) discusses strategy with Billy Baird at the intermission of the Leeds-Walker game. The strategy being discussed must have paid off, because Walker won the game 25-6. Looking on are coach Donald Sanford and guard Paul Elmore (43).

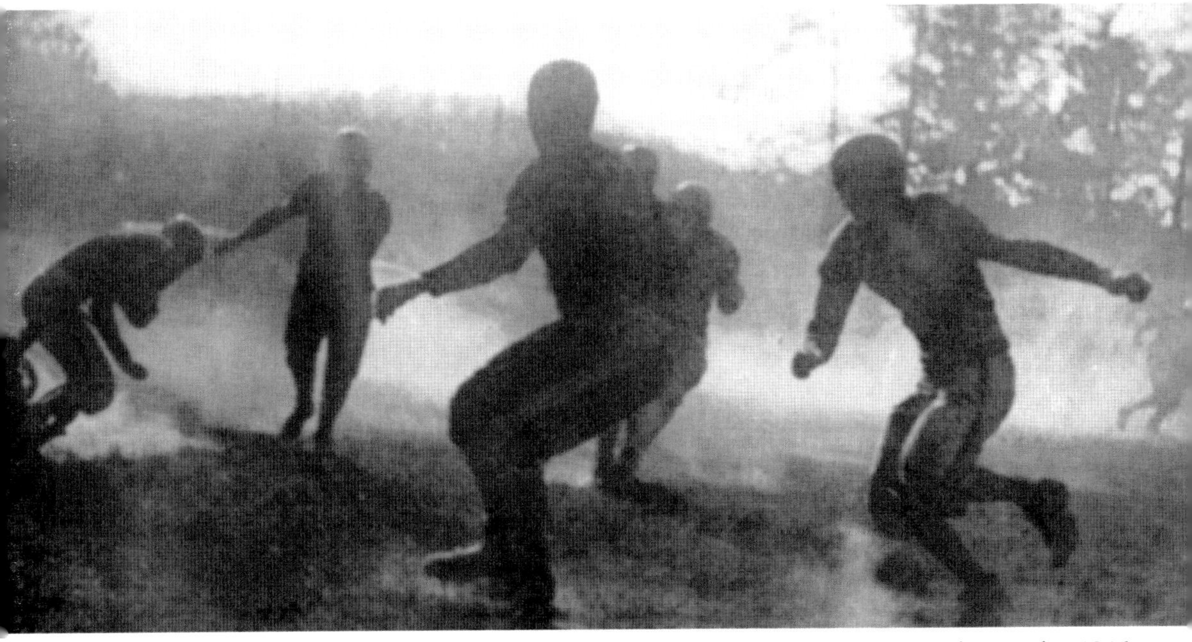

Dust Bowl, 1920–2000. Any young man who has ever played football can relate to this 1946 picture. It is early fall, when everything is dry, the grass has been stomped out of existence, the temperatures are in the 90s and 100s, and there is so much dust in the air that they can barely breath. Coaches are screaming and hollering at them, sweat is in their eyes, they're practicing two or three times a day, they're bruised and sore, and they're starting to question why they are even out here. Then school starts and practice gets a little easier, and they walk the halls with their head high because they are proud that they are Walker Vikings. There is not a man who ever played the game who doesn't look back with fond memories of the good and bad experiences. They are proud of how hard it was, but they survived, and they will always be a member of that brotherhood of football players who will go to their graves with pride knowing that they are Walker Vikings.

2

The Middle Years

1950–1975

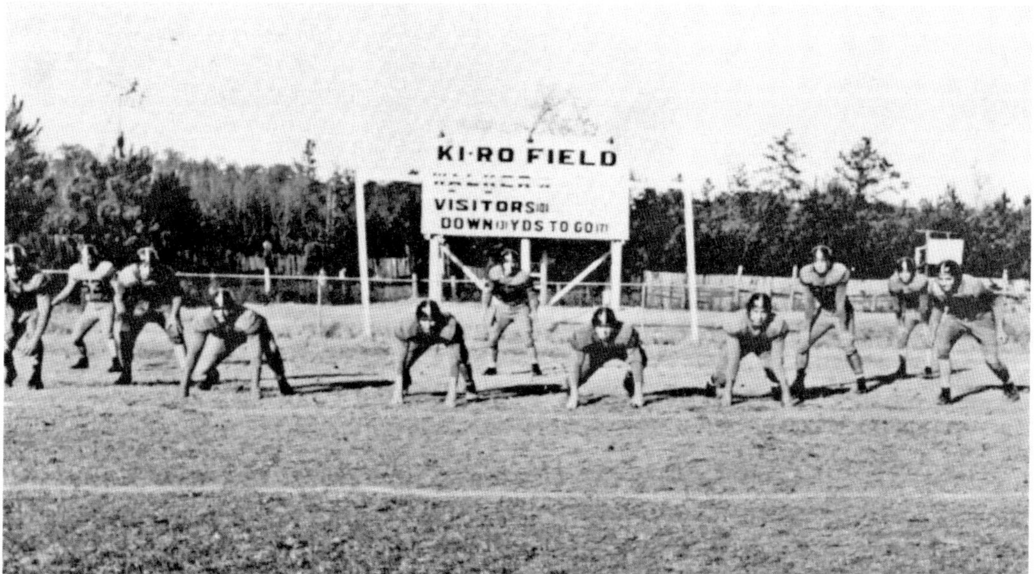

VIKING DEFENSE, 1950. This unusual photograph of an early defense shows the starters in a 6-2 defense lined up by position. From left to right are (end) Lee Swann, (back) Gerald Rogers, (linebacker) Bryant McMillian, (tackle) Orville Starnes, (guard) Gerald Maxwell, (safety) Amon Haygood, (guard) Ed Bates, (tackle) Gerald Kennedy, (linebacker) Harold Owen, (halfback) Howard Haygood, and (end) Howard Cook. Notice the scoreboard in the background.

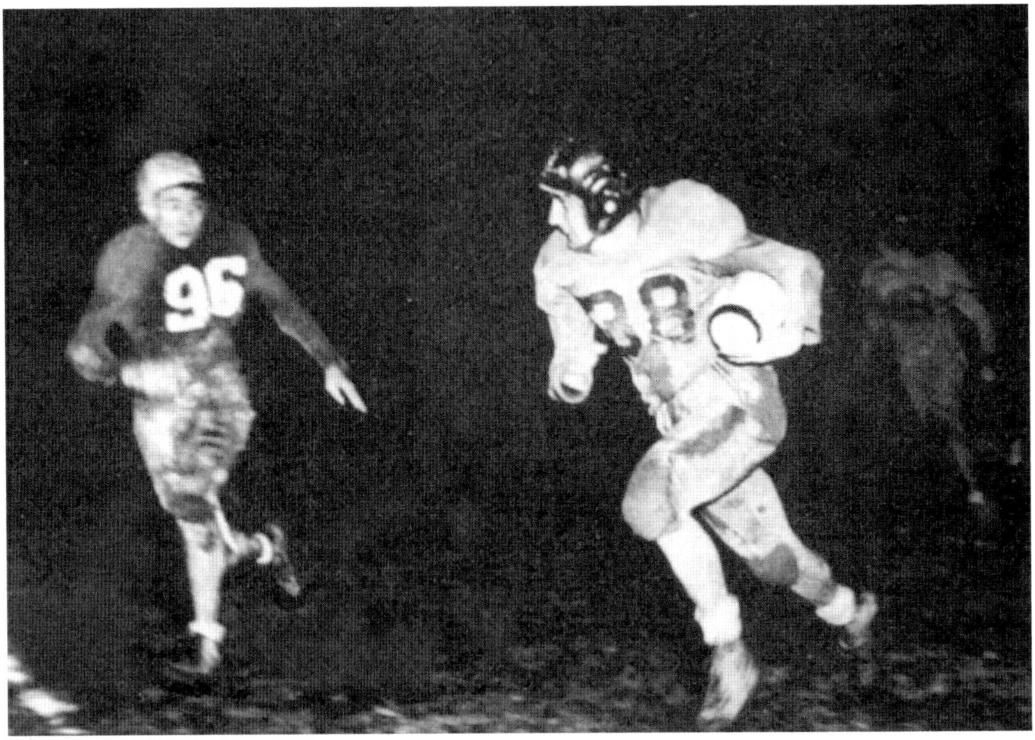

HAROLD OWEN CARRIES, 1951. Harold Owen (38) puts on a burst of speed as he turns the corner to score one of his two touchdowns against the Parrish Tornados. Notice the innovative color of the football being carried by Harold. Sam Cain coached the Vikings for only one year before pursuing a career as a special agent with the Federal Bureau of Investigation under J. Edgar Hoover. The Vikings collected six wins and three losses in 1951.

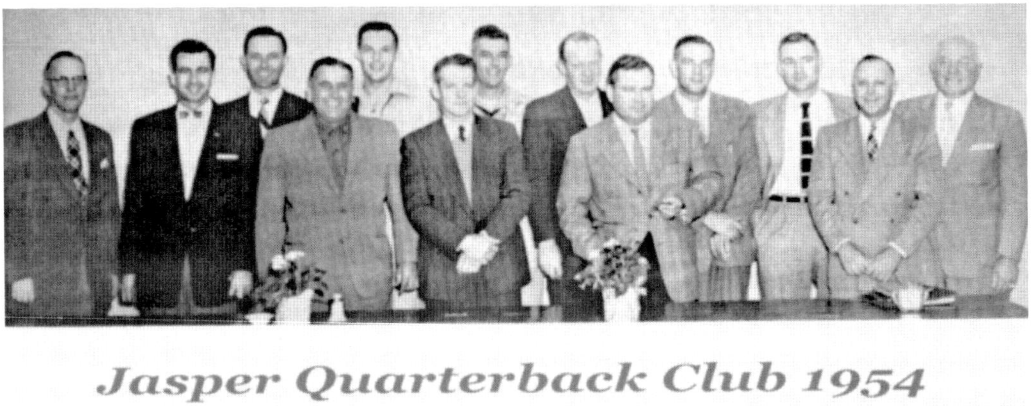

QUARTERBACK CLUB, 1953. Walker has always been blessed with a strong quarterback club composed of local businessmen that care about their football program. Above is an example of the leadership of that club. From left to right are Al Blanton, Bill Cunningham, Bill Edgemon, Harry Sherer, T. D. Norris, Charlie Hoobler, Fred Norris, Red Wright, Bob McKissack, Lacy Kirkpatrick, Caine O'Rear, Jake Waller, and Geddes Self.

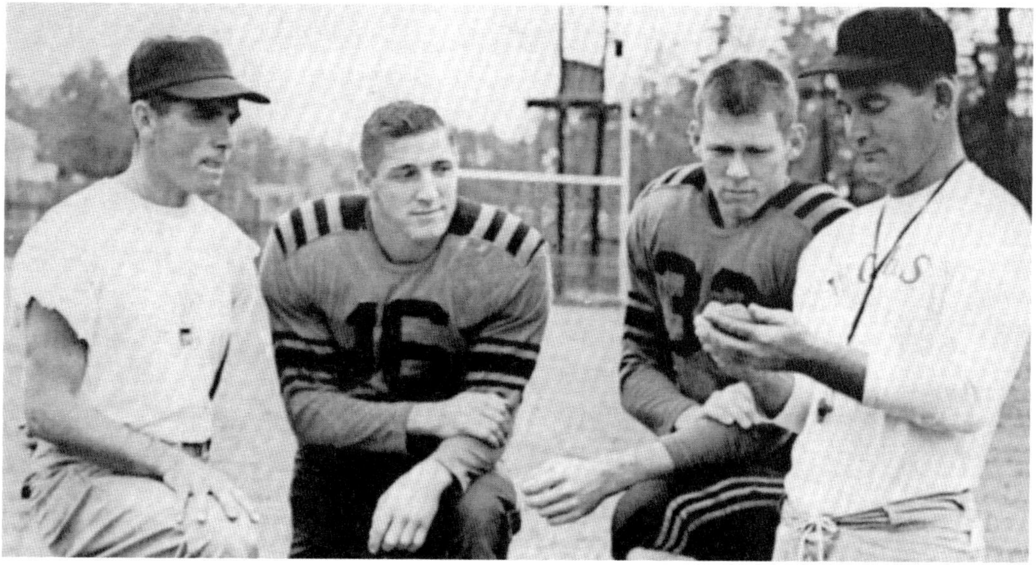

COACHES AND CAPTAINS, 1954. The leaders of the 1954 team were, from left to right, assistant Jack Caldwell, captain Joe Ben Cagle, cocaptain Dodd Holt, and head coach D. Joe Gambrell. Jack Caldwell was a great addition to the Walker staff. He possessed a marvelous defensive mind and was a great basketball coach who always had the best interests of the boys in mind. His basketball record from 1952 to 1960 was 155 wins and 106 losses.

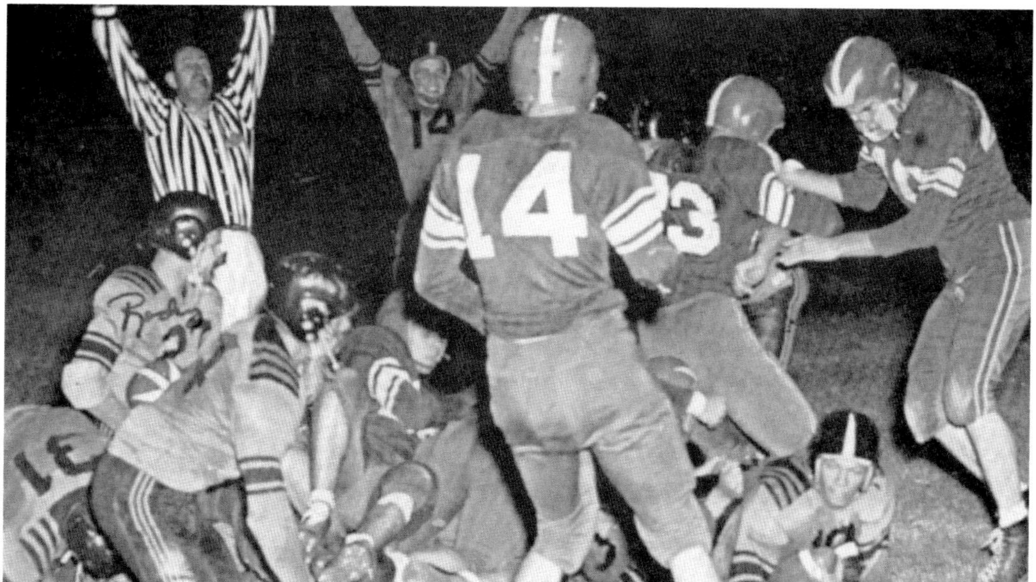

GRADY NOLAN SPARKS SCORES, 1955. Shown sneaking over for a touchdown against Tuscaloosa County is quarterback Grady Nolan Sparks. Garry Neil Drummond (14) excitedly helps the official signal the touchdown. Looking on are Tommy Stonecypher (27), Elton Banks (31), and Bruce Mullins (34). Geddes Self is under the pile. Walker won the game by a score of 27-6 on the way to a 7-1-1 season.

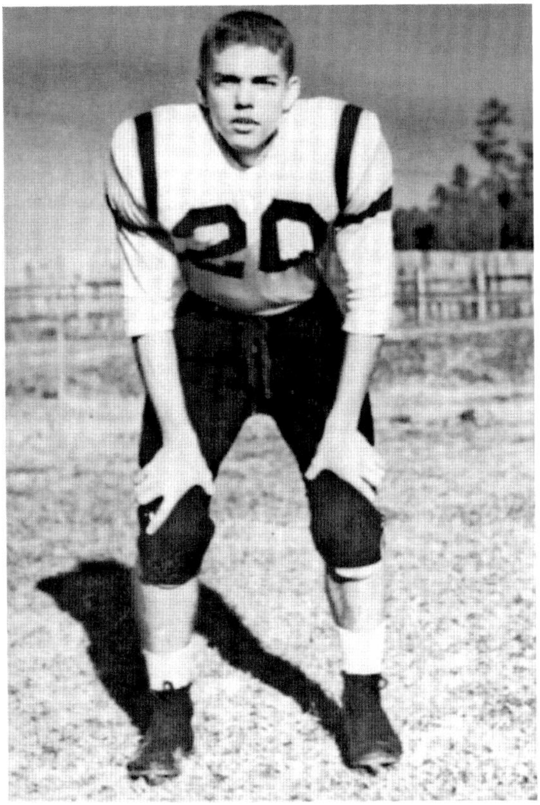

ALL-SOUTHERN BACK BILLY RICHARDSON, 1957. One of the three best-known players in Walker football history is Billy Richardson, the running back on the 1957 state championship team. He was All-State, All-Southern, and honorable mention All-American. He is thought to be the first player recruited by Alabama's Paul "Bear" Bryant. Billy was to lead the Crimson Tide to an undefeated national championship.

CHAMPIONSHIP LEADERS, 1957. Pictured below are the leaders of the 1957 season, the best in 27 years. From left to right are coach Jack Caldwell, captains Charles Sparks and Billy Richardson, and head coach D. Joe Gambrell. Like the 1921 and 1930 teams, the 1957 Vikings were undefeated state champions. This team scored 226 points while giving up only 20. Walker now had its third Alabama state championship.

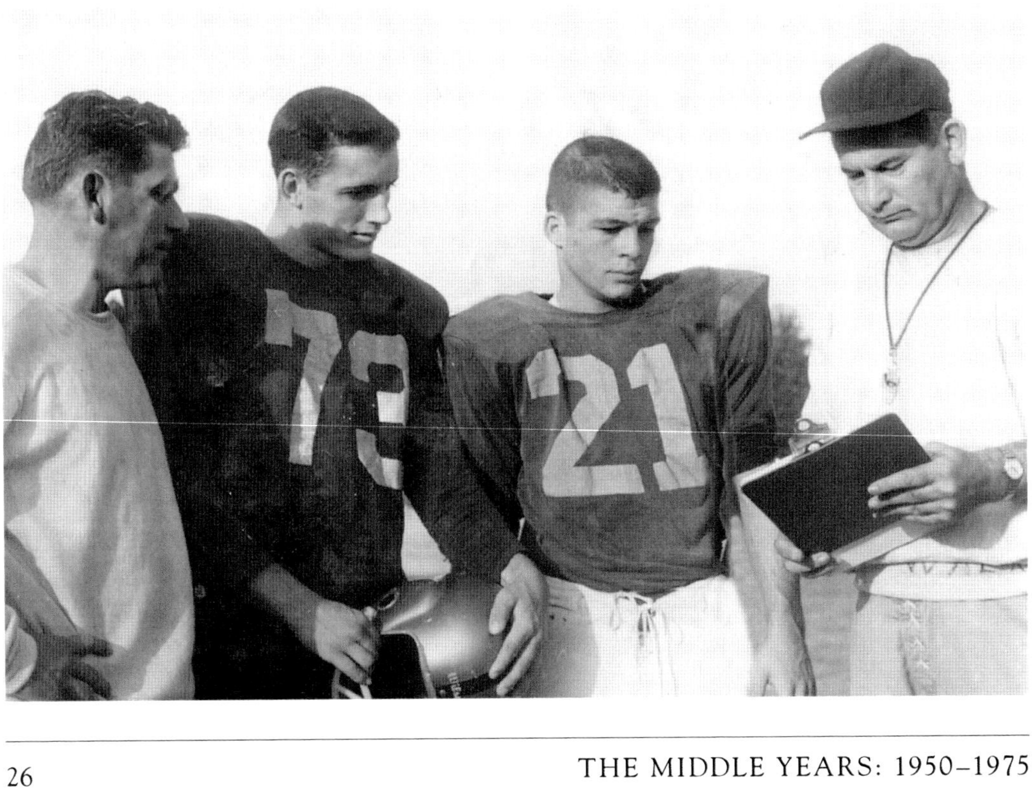

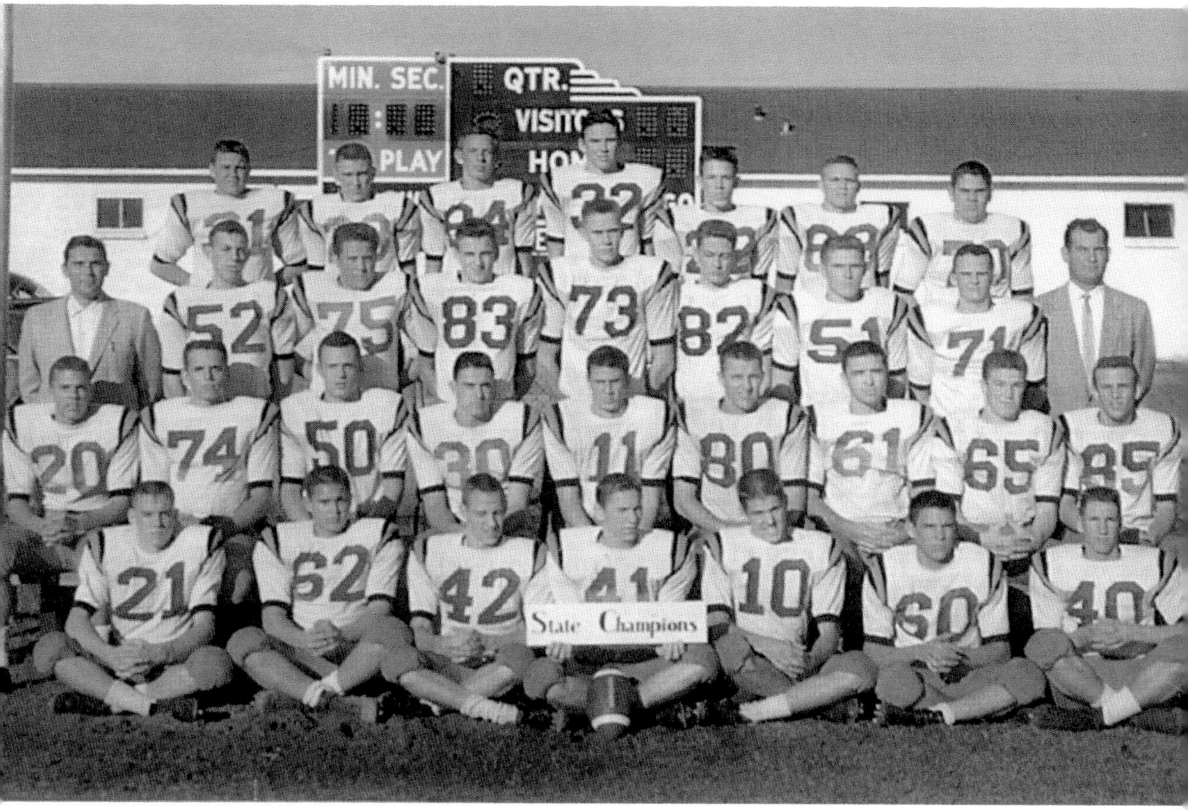

ALABAMA STATE FOOTBALL CHAMPIONS, 1957. They were now the official state champions of Alabama after defeating 10 straight opponents. They shut out seven of those teams and gave up only three touchdowns the entire season. Jack Caldwell and D. Joe Gambrell were the coaches, Geddes Self was the principal, and Charles Sparks and Billy Richardson were the captains. This was to be Walker's last state championship in the 20th century. From left to right are (first row) Clyde O'Rear, Johnny Bagley, Joe Stonecypher, Chesley Barnett, James Morris, Jimmy Turnbow, and Kelly Wright; (second row) Billy Richardson, Newman Bush, Johnny Long, Jimmy Cunningham, Steve Garrard, Charles Sparks, Richard Waller, Jon Sanford, and Tom Sanford; (third row) coach Jack Caldwell, Bill Massey, Carl Elliott, Donny Taylor, Phillip Roth, Howard Lockhart, George James, Buddy Driver, and coach D. Joe Gambrell; (fourth row) Wilson Maddox, Jimmy Hoobler, Travis Lovett, Mike Hudson, Bobby Reid, Jerry Daily, and Talmadge Key. Members of the team not pictured are Buddy Drummond, Tommy Carter, Kelly Wright, Gerry Lynes, Jimmy Pearson, Tommy Simmons, and Donald Blaylock.

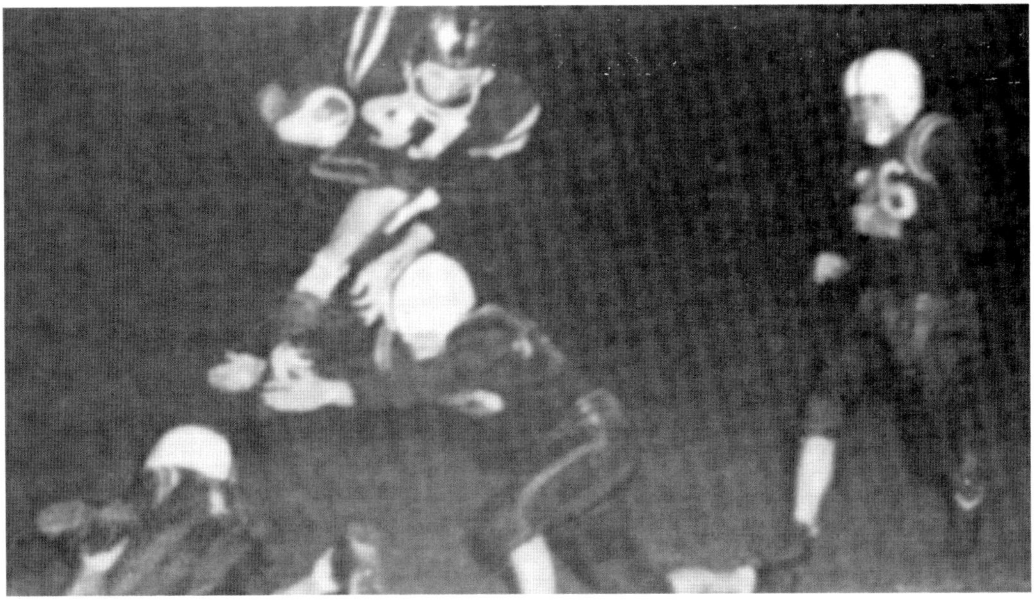

CHESLEY BARNETT LEAPS A DEFENDER, 1958. Chesley Barnett ran with reckless abandon, as shown above. This picture is thought to be of the Vikings-Russellville game that Walker won 13-6. After losing many players from the 1957 championship team, coaches Gambrell, Caldwell, and John Crump did a great rebuilding job to post a 6-1-2 record, and Chesley went on to play at Florence State College.

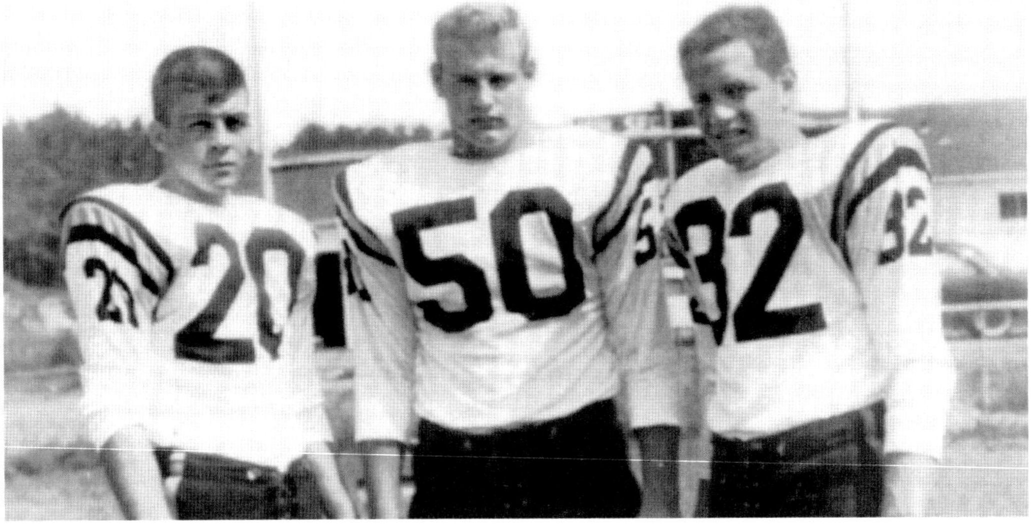

TRI-CAPTAINS, 1960. The Vikings were led by this trio of outstanding captains: from left to right are Billy Edge—the All-State and Auburn star became president of the medical staff at Carraway Hospital; Bud Long—the All-State player became vice president, general counsel, and director of Drummond Company; Garry Neil Drummond—the captain of the football team and president of the student body is now chief executive officer of Drummond Company, a member of the prestigious Forbes 500.

BILLY EDGE, 1961. Billy Edge, pictured at Auburn, was All-State and academic All-State at Walker. Shug Jordan, Auburn's legendary coach, said of Billy, "He was the hardest hitting little man I ever coached." He won the Bill Striet Award (the highest academic award) and the Cliff Hare Award (the top honor given at Auburn). Billy was on the SEC All-Academic Team and played in the Orange Bowl.

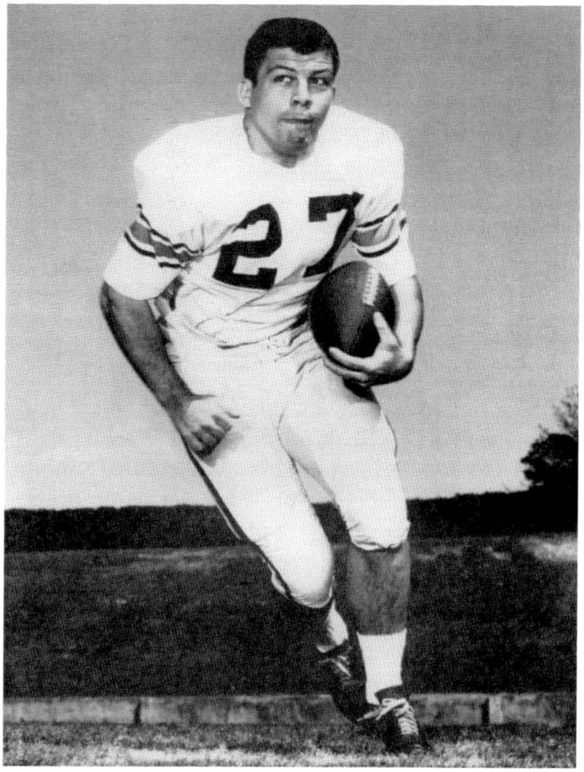

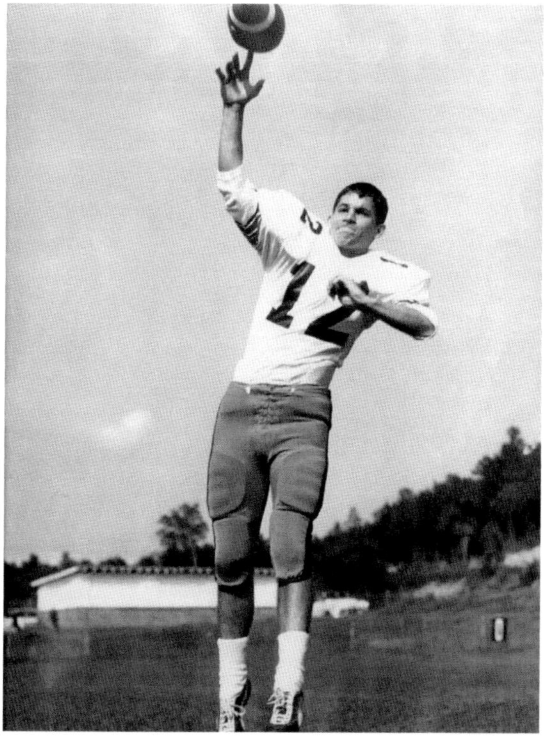

DANNY GAMBRELL, 1952–2000. Danny Gambrell has been involved in athletics at Walker since managing under his father, D. Joe Gambrell. He was later an All-State high school player then a college player; he came back to his alma mater as assistant coach, head coach, assistant principal, and finally principal. If there is a single individual who symbolizes Walker High School, its tradition, its spirit, and its future, it would be Danny. (Courtesy Nancy Gambrell.)

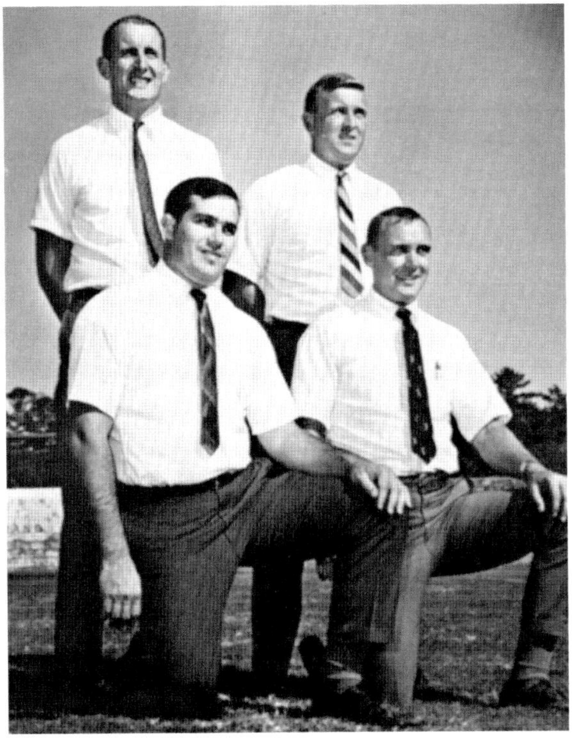

New Coaching Staff, 1968. Felix Smallwood was hired as the principal, and he brought Vic Karabasz (top left) as head coach, David Petty (top right) as defensive coach, and Pat Morrison (bottom right) as offensive coach. Herbert Green (bottom left) was the head basketball coach and worked with the receivers. Herbert was destined to become the winningest basketball coach in the history of Columbus College in Columbus, Georgia.

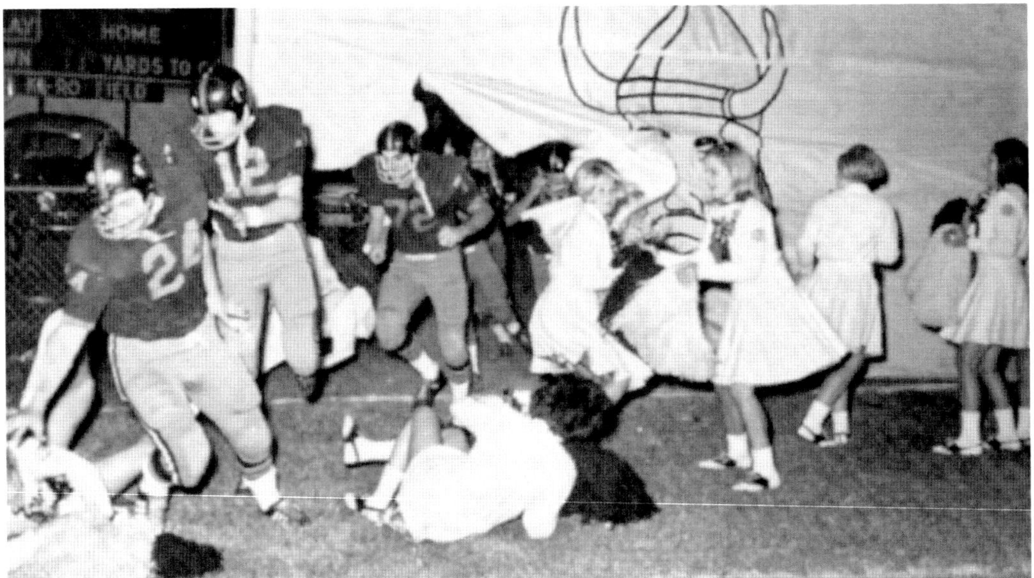

Brom Stiff-arms Cheerleader, 1968. As the Vikings bust through the "run through," it appears that Larry Brom (24) stiff-arms one of the cheerleaders as he leads Allen Trotter (12) and Charles Kimbrell (72) on a zigzag course through the remaining cheerleaders. Two of the cheerleaders are down and Ann Rutledge runs for her life as Millie Wallace looks on. Nobody ever said cheerleading was going to be easy.

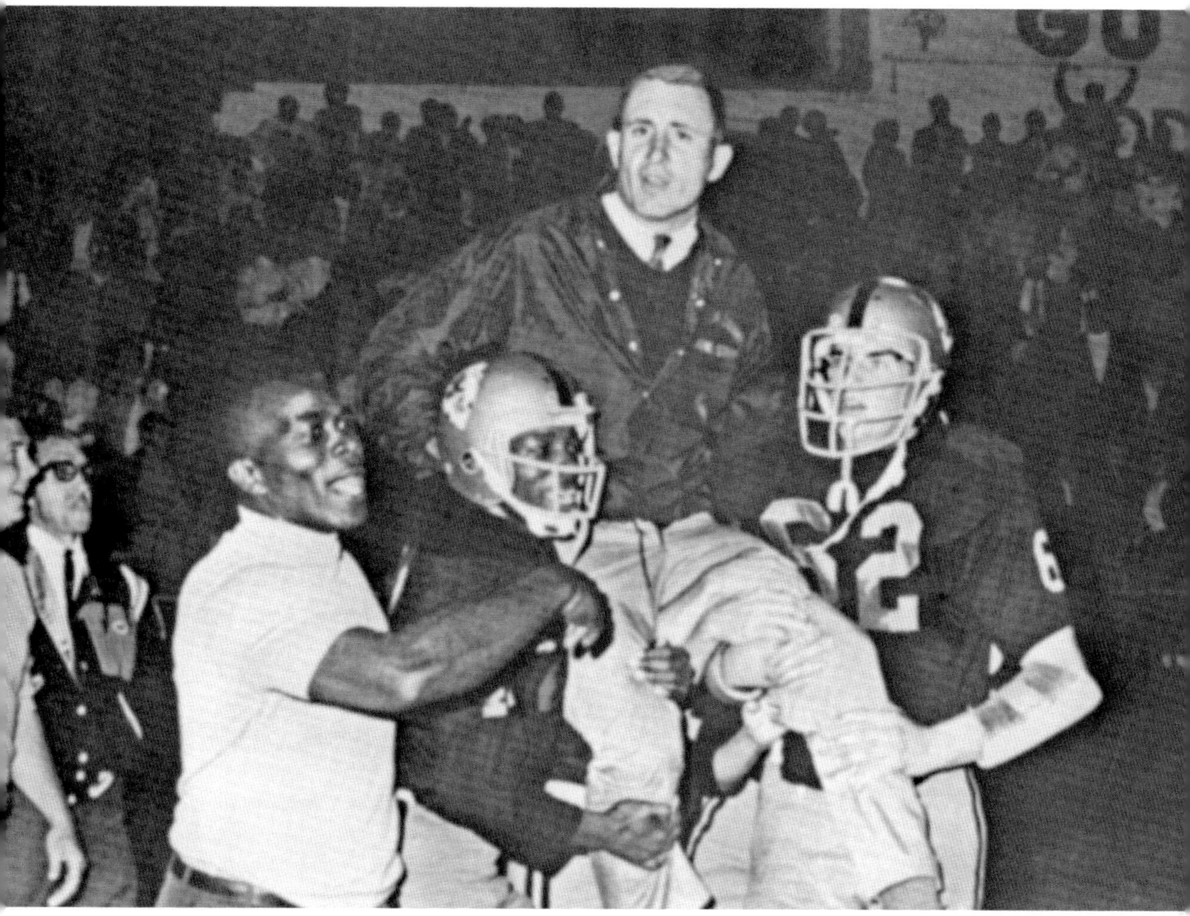

KARABASZ BREAKS THE STREAK, 1969. Coach Vic Karabasz seems to be saying his favorite expression, "Got the blues," as he is carried off the field on the shoulders of Henry Williams (on left) and Rick Tirey. Coach Herman Davis is shown in the foreground getting very excited about Walker's first victory in over three years. In the background, coach Pat Morrison (far left) and team chaplain Fred Lackey can't believe they've finally won after 32 straight losses. The victory came over Phillips High School of Birmingham, the same school Walker defeated to win their first state championship in 1921. During those three years without a victory, Walker's fans never gave up support of their Vikings, and they continued to have larger crowds than their victorious opponents. After this win, the Vikings started their rise back to prominence in Alabama football. Coach Karabasz later developed the first wrestling team at Walker and won the first state championship in that sport.

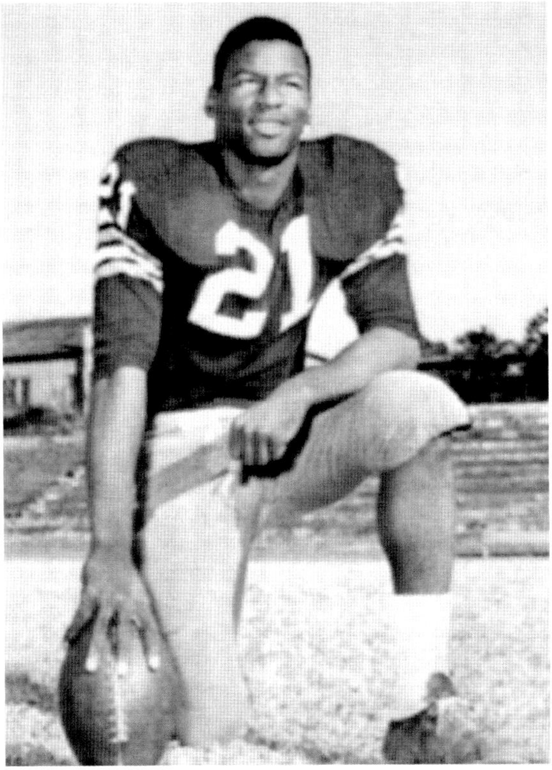

Hezzie Morgan, 1969. In 1968, Hezzie Morgan became the first black athlete to ever play at Walker County High School. He was an outstanding athlete who starred in football, wrestling, and track, and he was captain of the 1970 Viking football team. Hezzie played football at Florence State College, entered the army and rose to the rank of captain, and later returned to his alma mater as a teacher and football and wrestling coach.

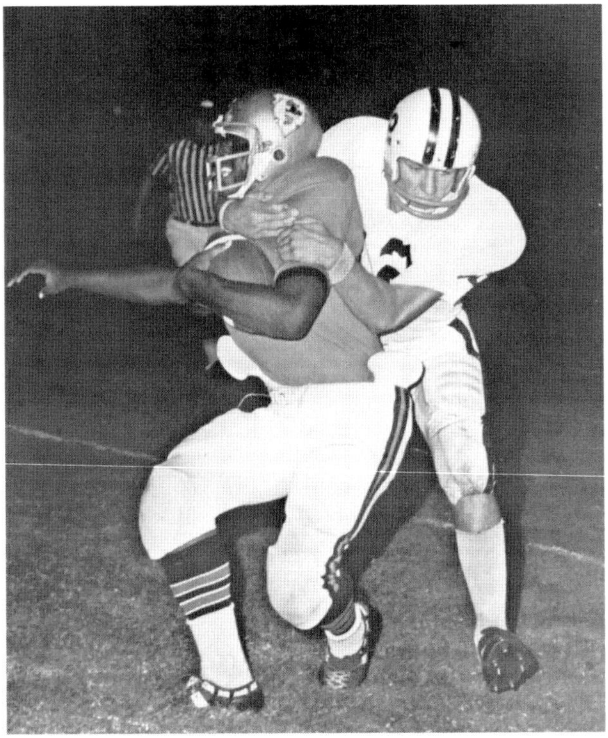

Jimmy Spates Gains Yardage, 1971. Jimmy Spates, a senior on the 1971 Viking football team, struggles for yardage in the Walker-Decatur game. Walker, with a record of two wins and eight losses, was defeated by the Decatur Red Raiders. The Vikings were to have sweet revenge in 1972 when they knocked Decatur from the state playoffs, thus establishing themselves again as a legitimate program.

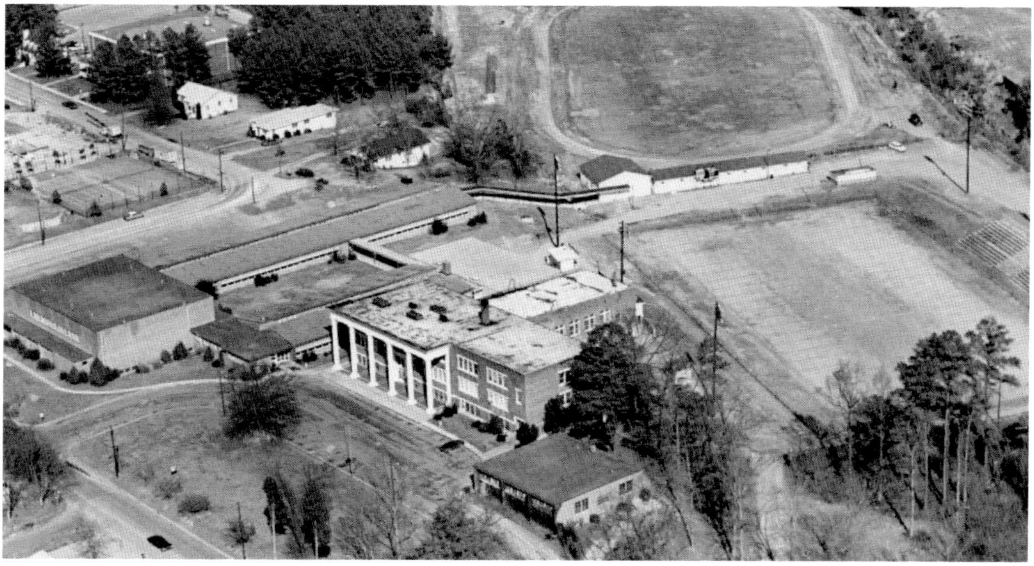

Aerial View of Walker High School, 1972. This 1972 aerial photograph shows the high school with many additions, including the gymnasium, the cinder track with practice field, the field house, and the W-Club concession. The house nearest the high school was occupied by coach Herbert Green and was later called Herbie's Hash House. Coach Vic Karabasz lived in the next one. Both residences were torn down to build Songer Gymnasium.

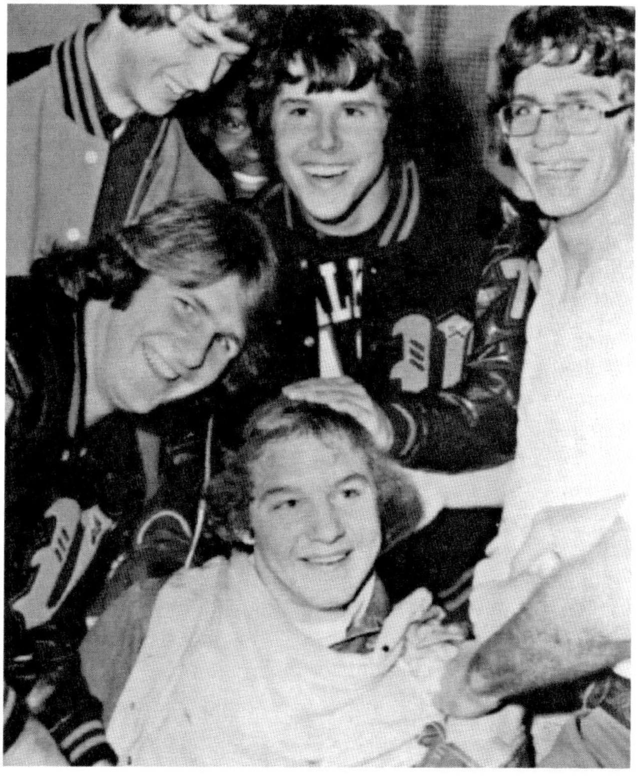

W-Club Initiation, 1974. W-Club initiation was always an exciting and scary time for all new lettermen. One of the rituals in the 1960s and 1970s was the shaving of the heads of the young men who had won honor into this prestigious organization. Linebacker Roland Starnes is about to have his beautiful locks removed. Assisting are his upper-class teammates, clockwise from bottom left, Joe Jenkins, Jackie Odom, Nolan Sparks, and Phil Ingle.

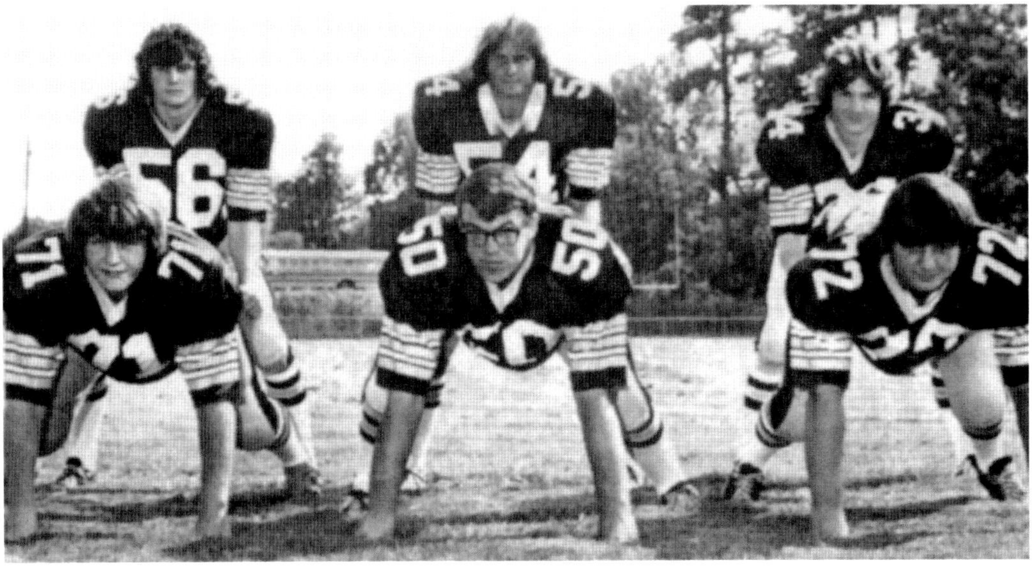

HEART OF THE DEFENSE, 1974. Pictured above are six of the main reasons that Walker had a 7-4 record and secured their first trip to the Alabama High School State Football Play-offs. From left to right are (first row) tackles Mark Marlowe, Julius "Scooter" Lightsey, and Britt Barnett; (second row) linebackers Bobby Gibson, Joe Jenkins, and Roland Starnes. These Vikings anchored an aggressive, hard-hitting, tough-minded defense.

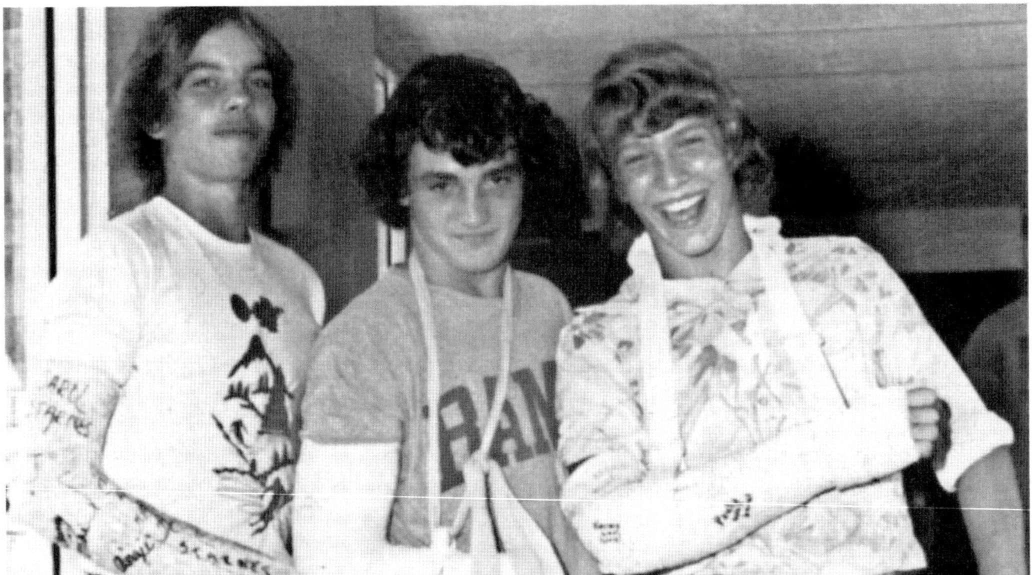

FOOTBALL INJURIES, 1975. One part of the game nobody likes is the very real possibility of injury. It is an inevitable part of any contact sport like football. These three Vikings seem to be making the best out of a bad situation. Injury to key players like the trio above—Mike Jett (left), Brian Drummond (center), and Scott Seals—can mean the difference between victory and defeat. Luckily most well-conditioned young men heal very quickly.

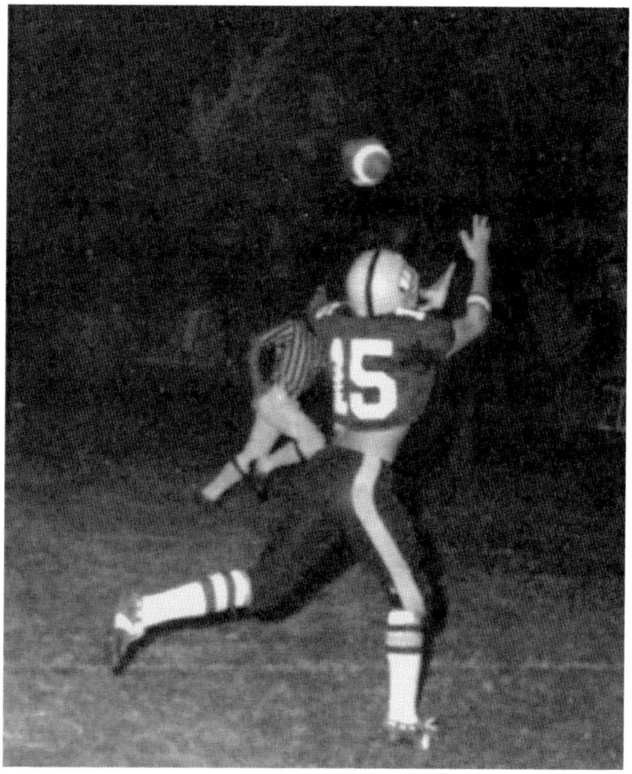

Receiver Mike Adkins, 1975. Mike Adkins (15), going deep for a touchdown, is one of the many sure-handed receivers to have played for Walker over the years. Mike was an outstanding athlete who could run pass patterns all day long without getting tired. He was also a gifted distance runner on the Vikings track team who was legendary for eating huge amounts of food before races.

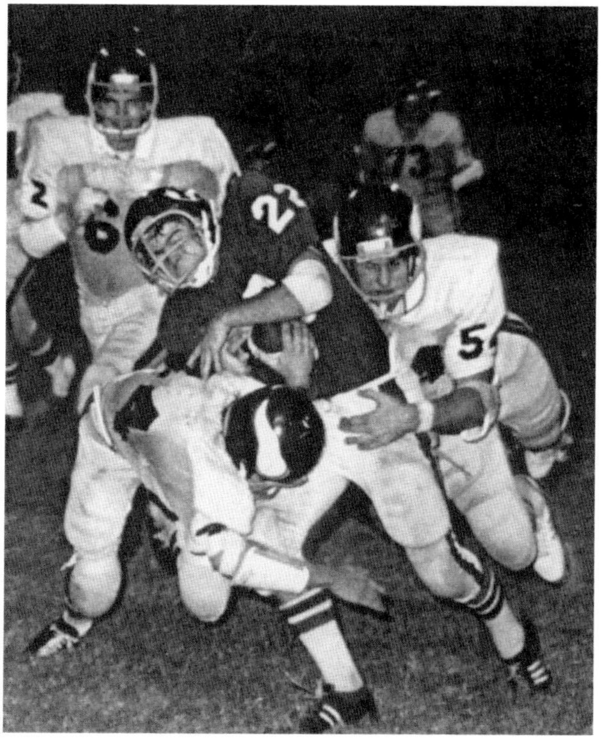

Aggressive Defense, 1975. Walker, known for its hard-hitting, aggressive defenses, is shown gang tackling. Defensive back Steve Hudson (44) is shown getting his head across the Holt runner, and All-State linebacker Joe Jenkins (54) grabs on. Gary Pilling (62) pursues hoping to get a lick on the runner. In the background, tackle Jim Gordon (73) takes a good pursuit angle. Walker won the game 36-13.

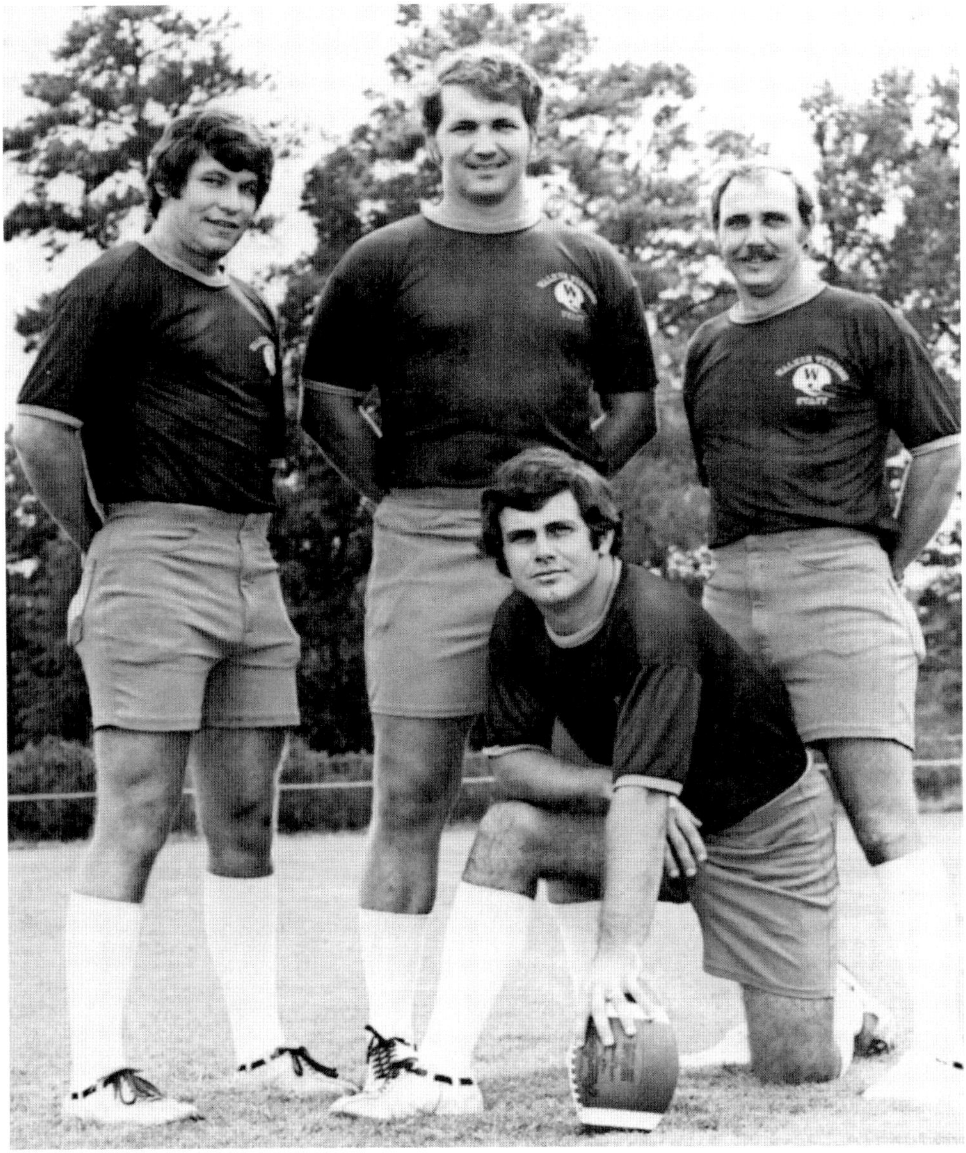

FOOTBALL COACHES, 1974–1975. These coaches ended the middle era of Walker football. Each of these coaches helped to fill the role of athletic director at Walker for almost 30 years. In front, head coach and athletic director Larry Blakeney later became the coach at Vestavia High School, then Auburn University, before becoming the head coach at Troy State University and successfully bringing that program to Division I, where he has the most wins in Troy's history. From left to right behind him are Danny Gambrell, who later became the head coach and athletic director, assistant principal, and then principal of Walker; David Campbell, an All-American at Auburn University and head coach and athletic director at Walker, who made them perhaps the most successful and feared team in Alabama football for 13 years in the 1970s and 1980s; and Pat Morrison, author of this book, who coached football, baseball, basketball, track, cross-country, and intramurals before becoming the athletic director at Walker.

3

THE LATER YEARS

1976–2000

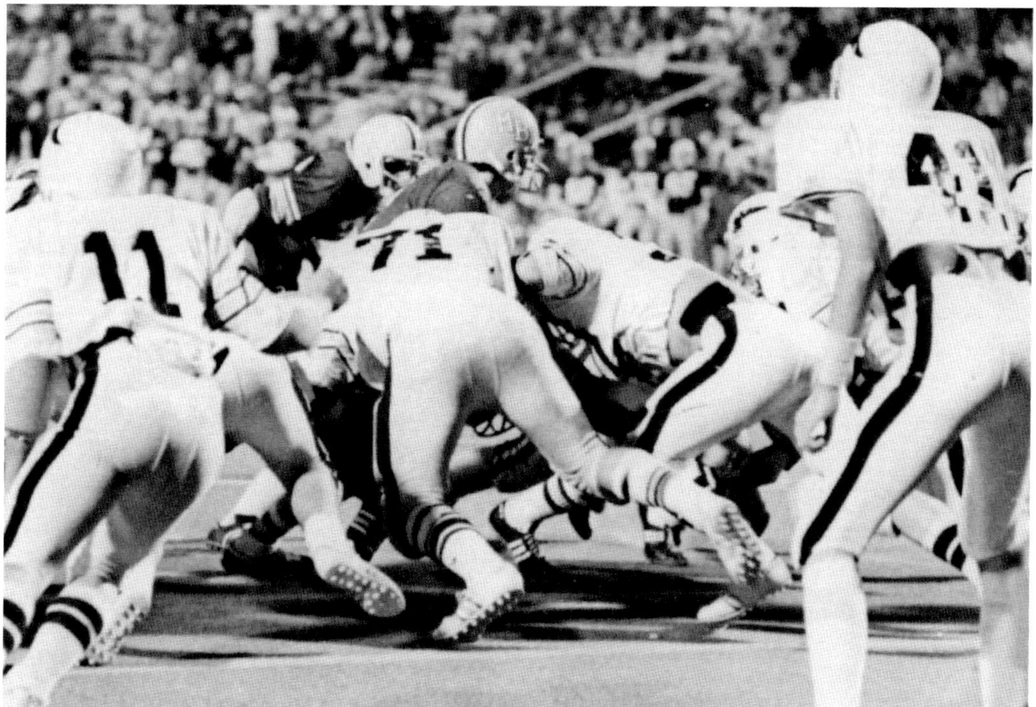

DEFENSIVE CHARGE, 1976. The defense is shown in this photograph charging off the ball against Mountain Brook in the first round of the state playoffs. Pictured from left to right are linebacker J. D. Williams (11), tackle Mark Marlowe (71), and defensive back Johnny Christian (41). Mark is the son of Alabama great Bobby Marlowe, and J. D. became an outstanding high school coach and principal. Johnny is a successful businessman.

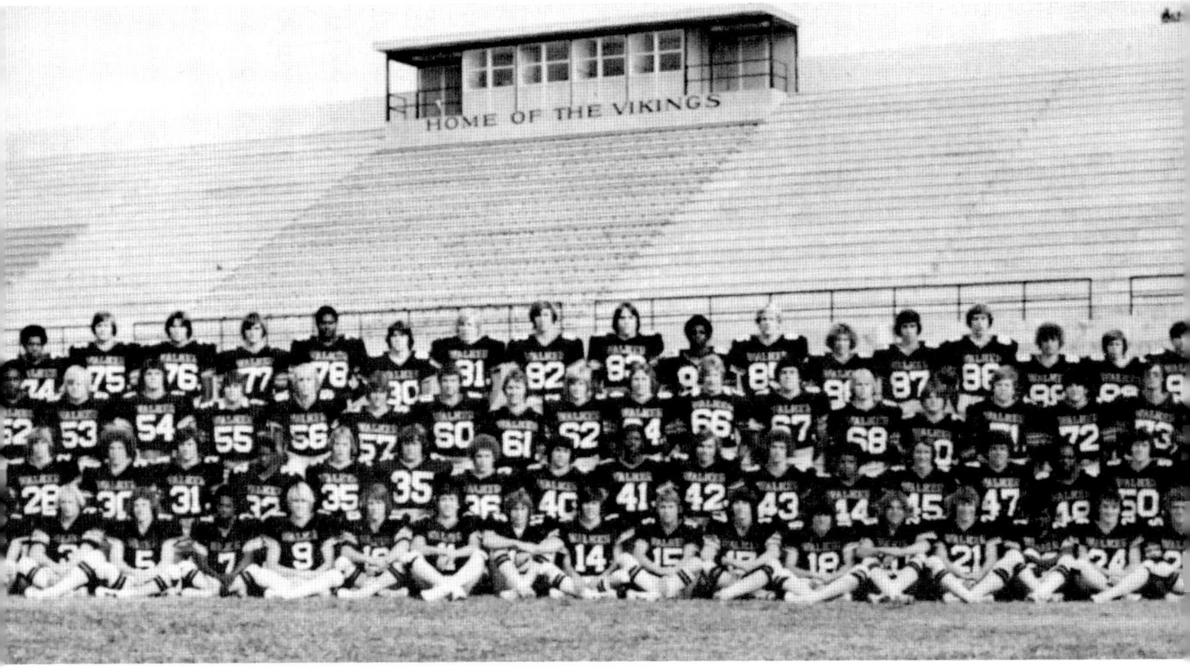

NORTH ALABAMA CHAMPIONS, 1977. This Dave Campbell–coached team goes down as one of the best in Walker history. They were 12-2 and the only team to ever play in the Alabama State Championship game. They were the North Alabama champions, had two shutouts in the playoffs, and were the best team since 1957, with the most wins of any team in Walker history. They were involved in the only playoff overtime at Walker. From left to right are (first row) Scott Ogle, Greg Hendon, Bobby Songer, James Clopton, Darrell Roberts, Wade Hall, Randy Robinson, Larry Harris, Joe Justice, Jerry Nix, Skip Roberts, David Fields, Goober Williams, Scott Seales, Garlin Farris, Brian Drummond, and Ronald Bolen; (second row) Scott Myers, Chris Birdsong, Jeff Best, Linnie Patrick, Tim Smith, Wesley Jones, Gary Norris, Terry Rucker, Isadore McGee, Mike Jett, Kyle Ingle, Alfred Austin, Stan Karabasz, J. D. Williams, Mike McDonald, Nolan Sparks, and Coach Campbell; (third row) Bubba McLemore, Phillip Gilmore, Bobby Gibson, Butch Wallace, Ricky Ingram, Todd Ferguson, Rocky Rogers, Greg Starnes, Joey Gilmore, David Banks, Jeff Love, Floyd Kimbrell, Jeff Hudson, Steve Reeves, Jeff Pate, Jeff Allred, and Russell Smothers; (fourth row) Larry Gouli, Earl Stafford, Jimmy Walton, Eddie Young, Charles Curry, Chris Meacham, Jeff Harbin, Bobby Nix, Paul Hale, Bay Bay Harris, Mark Batson, Jeff Butler, Tim Bradford, Randy Harris, Randy Dill, Keith Houk, and Ricky Pitts.

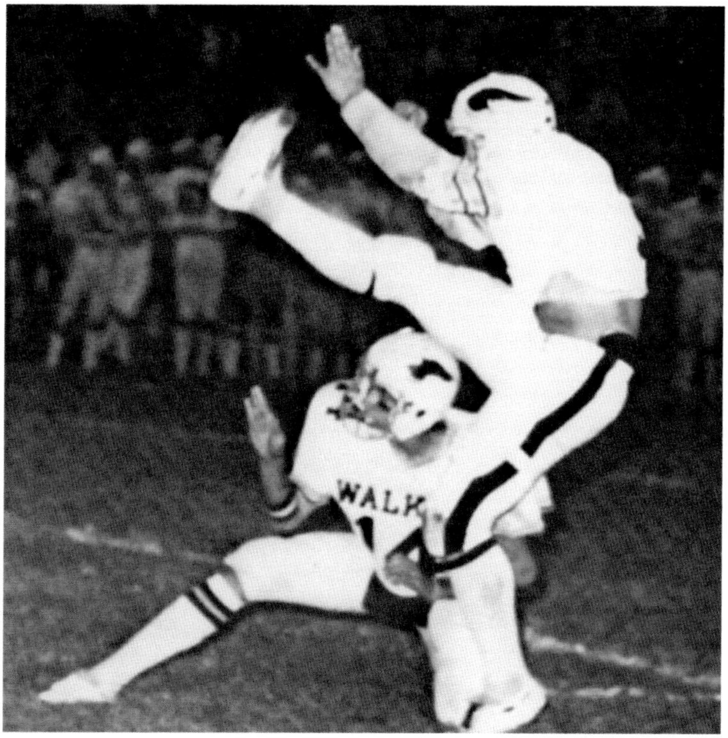

GREG HENDON'S KICK IS GOOD, 1977. Perhaps the most important extra point in Walker High football history was kicked by linebacker Greg Hendon and held by Joe Justice against Decatur High School in the 1977 semifinal of the playoffs. He split the uprights to break a 27-27 double-overtime tie and put Campbell's Vikings in the finals of the state playoffs. Greg played most of the playoff games with a broken hand.

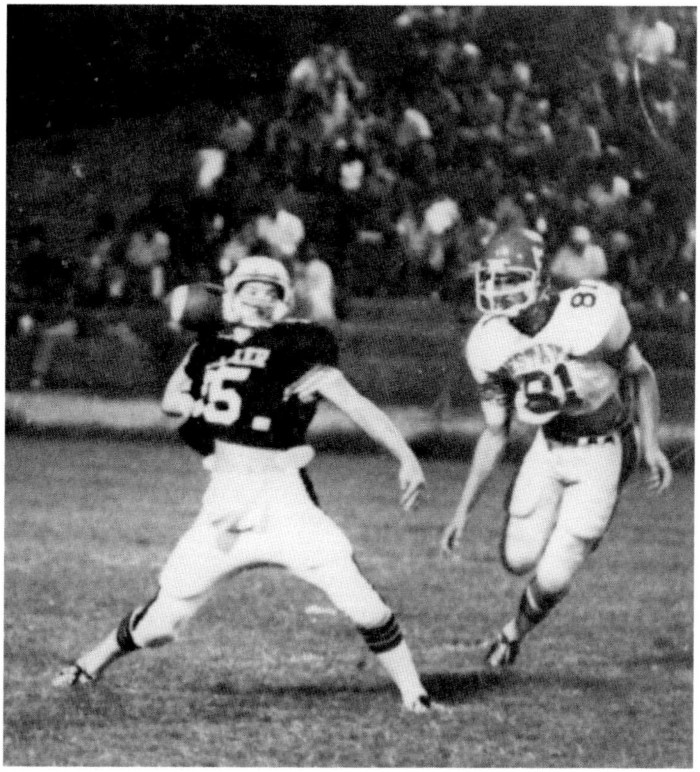

JERRY NIX THROWS DEEP, 1978. Jerry Nix was the quarterback of the 1977 and the 1978 Viking teams and led them to a record of 21 wins and only 3 losses. He was a master field general who seemed to be one step ahead of the opposing defenses. Jerry played on scholarship for the University of Tennessee at Chattanooga, enjoying a successful career with the Moccasins. He became a very successful high school coach.

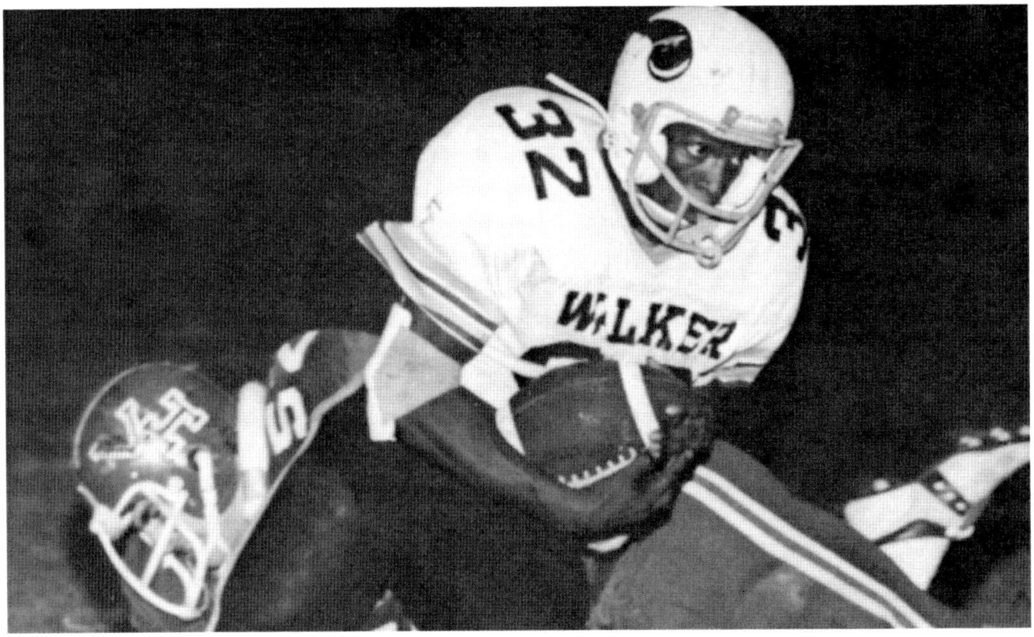

LINNIE PATRICK, 1978. Linnie had a phenomenal high school career, rushing for over a mile in two different seasons. He was a two-time All-State, All-Southern, and possibly the only Parade All-American in Walker High School history. He was the second-ranked player in America behind Hershel Walker. He played at Alabama and then with the Michigan Panthers, where he scored four touchdowns in one game, a Michigan record.

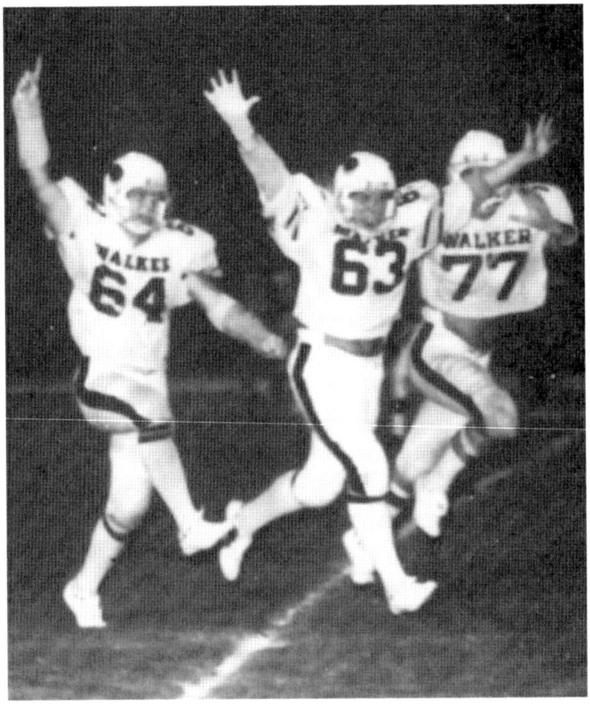

LINEMEN CELEBRATE VICTORY, 1979. The unsung heroes of every football team are the linemen who work in the trenches with very little, if any, recognition. But all good running backs realize that without these guys, life on a football field would be tough. Shown are linemen Scott Posey (64), Harry Wolfe (63), and Eddie Young (77) celebrating a Walker score against Tuscaloosa County High School.

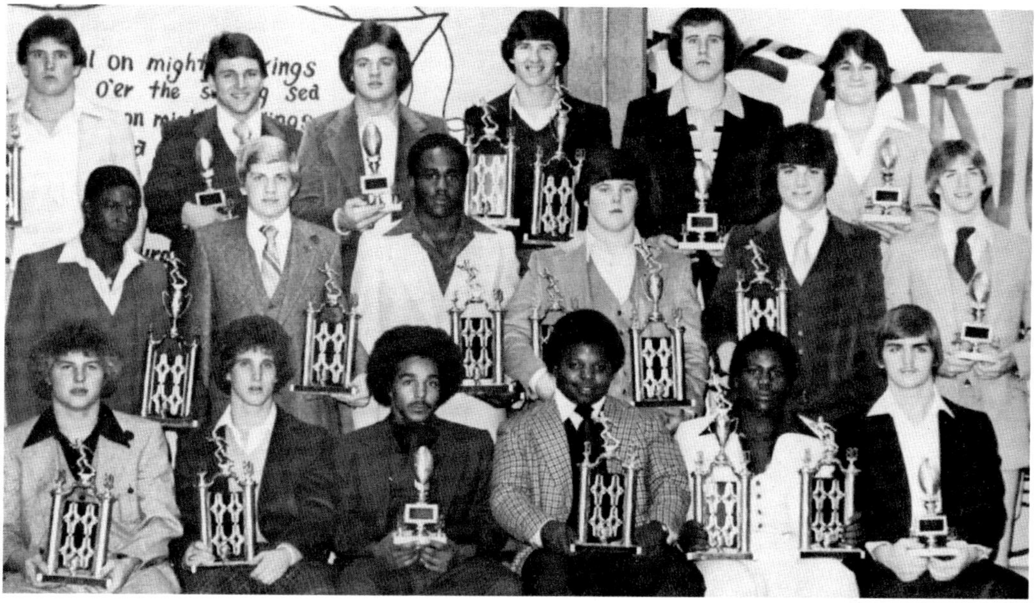

BEST OF THE BEST, 1979. Winners at the 1979 football awards banquet are, from left to right, (first row) Goober Williams, Kyle Ingle, Alfred Austin, Mike McDonald, Willie Scott, and Eddie Young; (second row) Linnie Patrick, Joey Gilmore, Bubba McLemore, G. A. Sherer, Chris Barton, and Scott Myers; (third row) Dean Carr, Todd Ferguson, Bobby Songer, Skip Roberts, Randy Harris, and Tim Meacham.

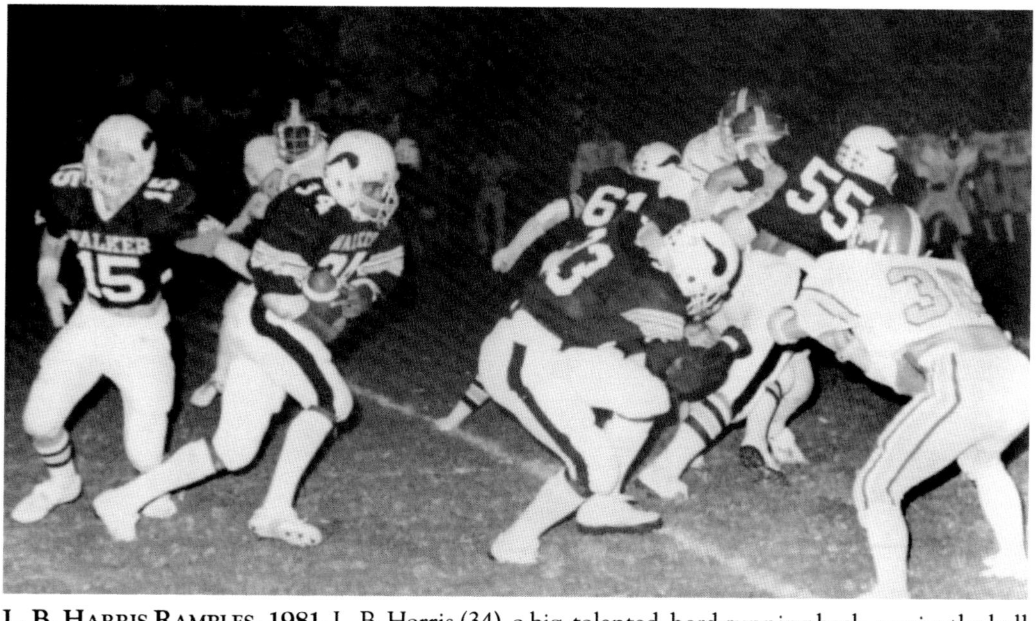

L. B. HARRIS RAMBLES, 1981. L. B. Harris (34), a big, talented, hard-running back, carries the ball against Banks High School of Birmingham. Quarterback Hugh Smith (15) hands the ball off to L. B. as guard Tim Duncan (61) and center Joey Hyche (55) lead the blocking, while fullback Walter Phillips (33) prepares to kick the end out on this play, allowing L. B. to make a nice gain.

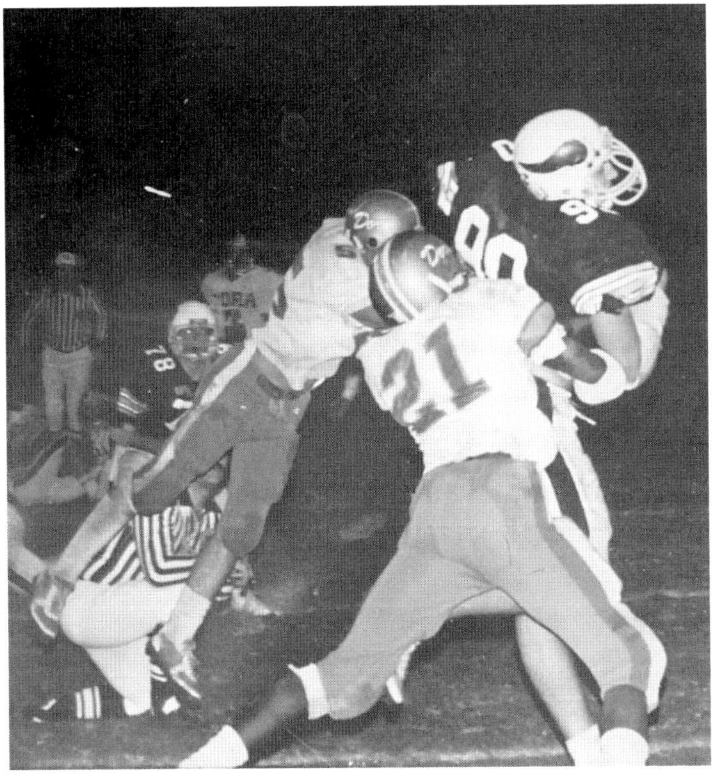

LAST-SECOND VICTORY VERSUS DORA, 1982. Walker's biggest rival in the county in the modern era would undoubtedly be Dora High. David Banks catches a crucial pass and carries two Dora defenders into the end zone in the last seconds of the ball game to give Walker the victory. David signed a scholarship to play football with the University of Tennessee at Chattanooga, where he had an outstanding career with the Moccasins.

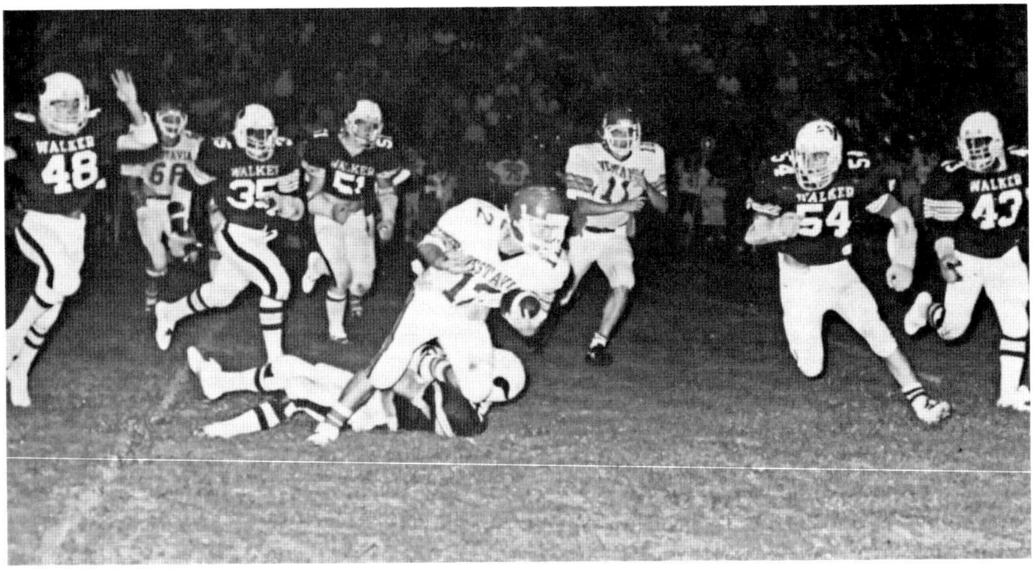

DEFENSIVE PURSUIT, 1982. Members of the 1982 defensive squad close in on the Vestavia runner. One of Walker's chief rivals in 6-A classification was the Vestavia Rebels. From left to right are David Nichols (48), Gary McCray (35), Tommy Cole (51), Greg Hyche (22) making the tackle, Brad Drummond (54), and Earnest McLemore (43). The Vikings won this game by a score of 13-10.

TOMMY COLE, 1983. Tommy Cole was one of the best defensive tackles to ever play at Walker. He was All-County and All-State and attended the University of Alabama, where he lettered three years. Tommy was one of the quickest big men ever at Walker, and he had a knack for collapsing his body to get through small spaces to make a tackle. Tommy is shown signing autographs for some of his fans on picture day at Tuscaloosa.

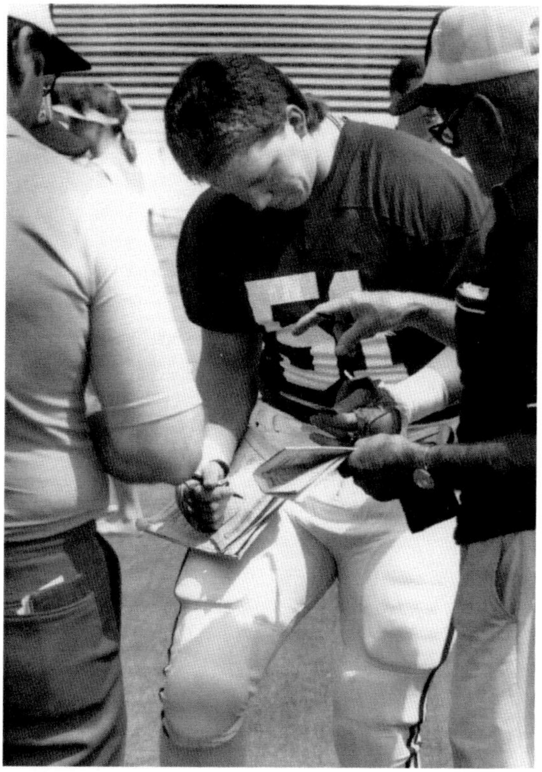

EARL ALLEN, 1984. Every coach needs to be able to tape ankles, especially in the heat of the action. Earl Allen, shown during a lull in the game against the Berry Buccaneers, is being taken care of by coach Donnie Morgan. Earl was a tough defensive end who never let little aches and pains keep him out of the action. Coach Morgan was a player in the 1970s and a coach in the 1980s at Walker.

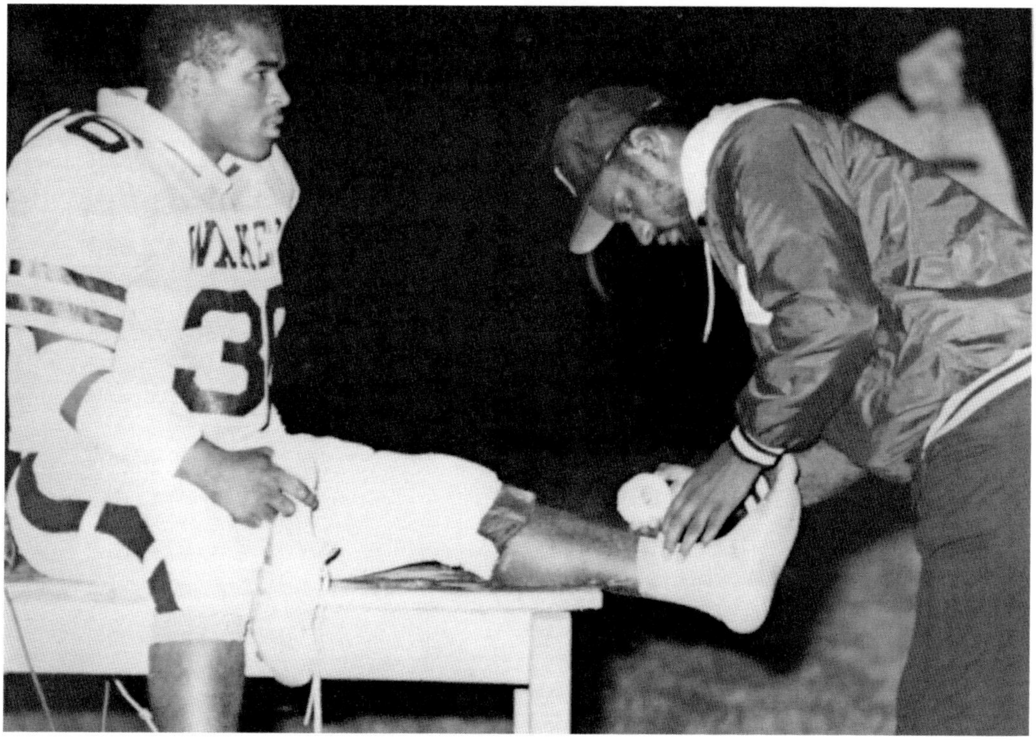

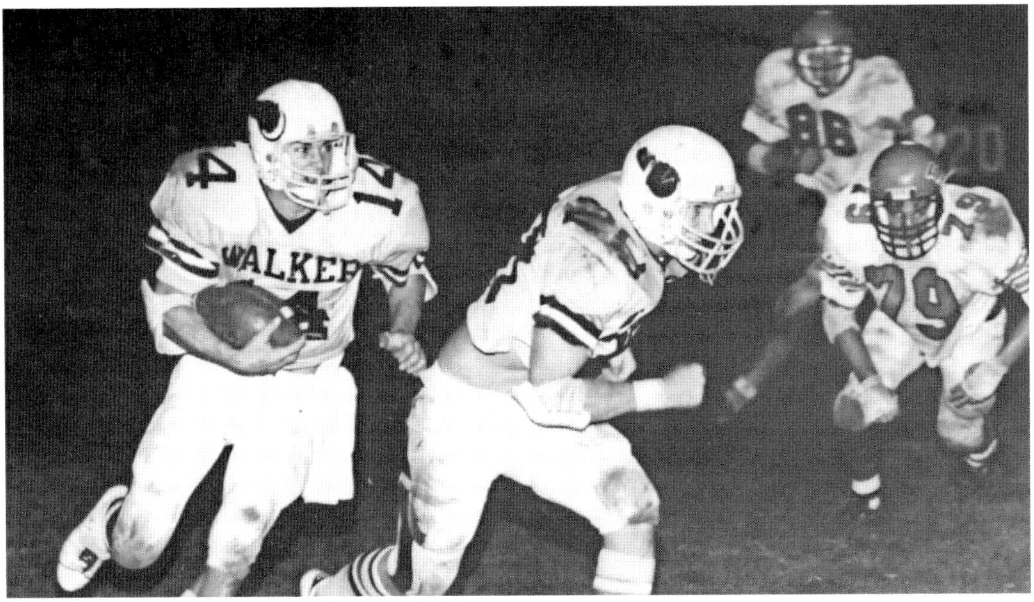

Phillip Drummond Follows the Block, 1984. Lee Smith (28) looks for someone to block as he leads Phillip Drummond (14) up field against the Berry Buccaneers, who are coached by one-time Walker assistant Bob Finley. Phillip was a quarterback–running back combination who gained 1,026 yards on his way to a great senior year. He signed a scholarship and played football for the University of North Alabama in Florence.

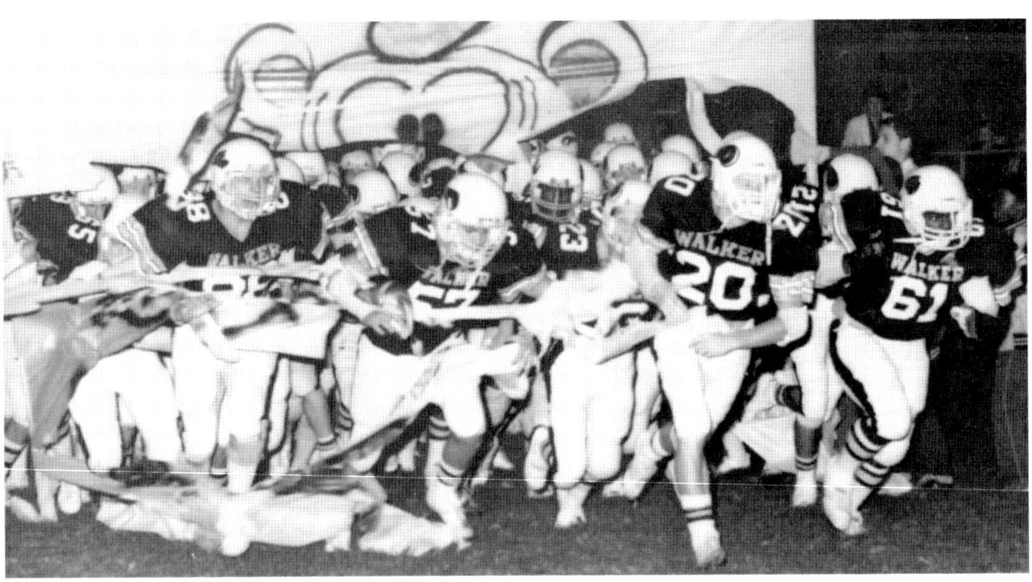

Run Through, 1985. One of the most anticipated moments for the fans (especially young ones), as well as the players, is the moment the team bursts through the banner. Leading the pack are linebacker Spencer Powell (65), running back Lee Smith (28), linebacker Keith Nix (57), running back Jeff Cushen (23), defensive back Bubba Crump (20), and defensive tackle Randy Harris (61).

SCOTT BROWN, 1985. The first Walker County–wide decathlon was held May 1985 at Walker High School, and Scott Brown (shown at right) was the junior winner. The participants had to compete in bench press and dead lift, 40-yard dash, 100-yard dash, mile run, punt-pass-kick, softball throw, and free throws. Scott was an outstanding linebacker for the Commodores at Vanderbilt University. The decathlon was the brainchild of David Campbell.

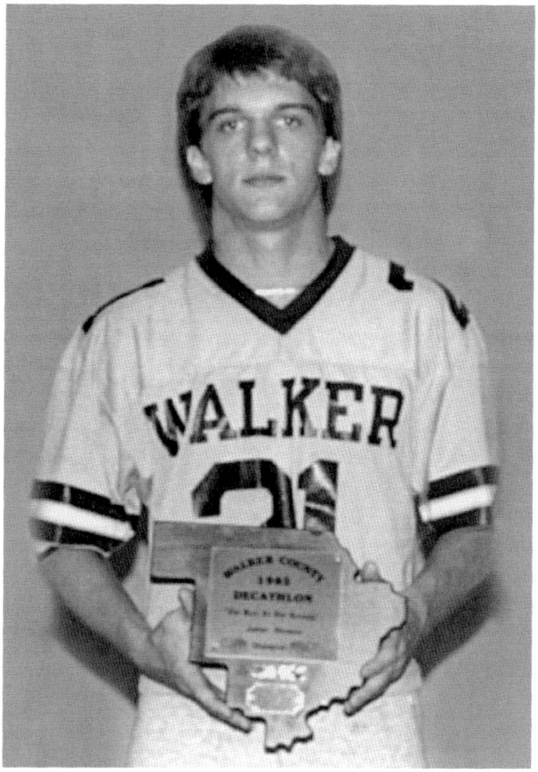

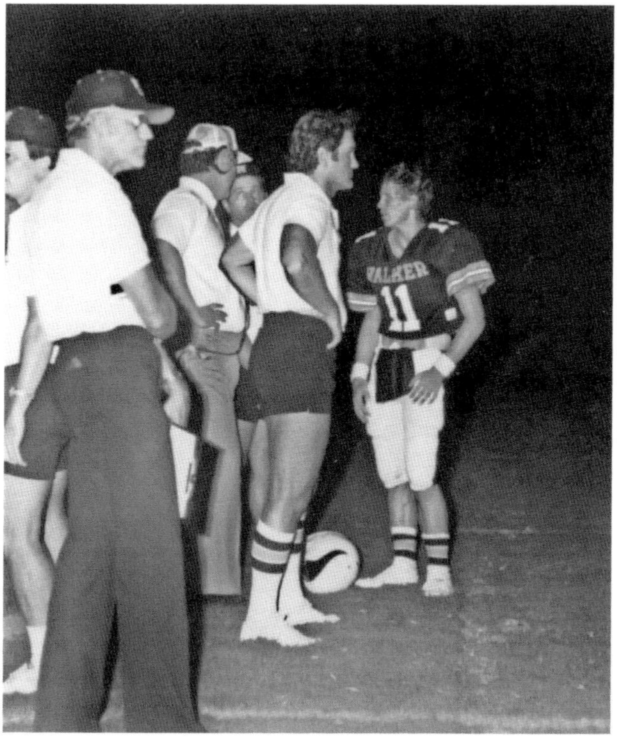

SIDELINE STRATEGY, 1985. Coaches on the sidelines discuss what their next move will be with quarterback Michael Abner. The "brain trust" is, from left to right, receiver coach Gary Pilling, longtime statistician Bob Woods, head coach David Campbell, later head coach at various Alabama high schools Rick Brown, and offensive coordinator Gary Borden, arguably the best offensive line coach ever at Walker.

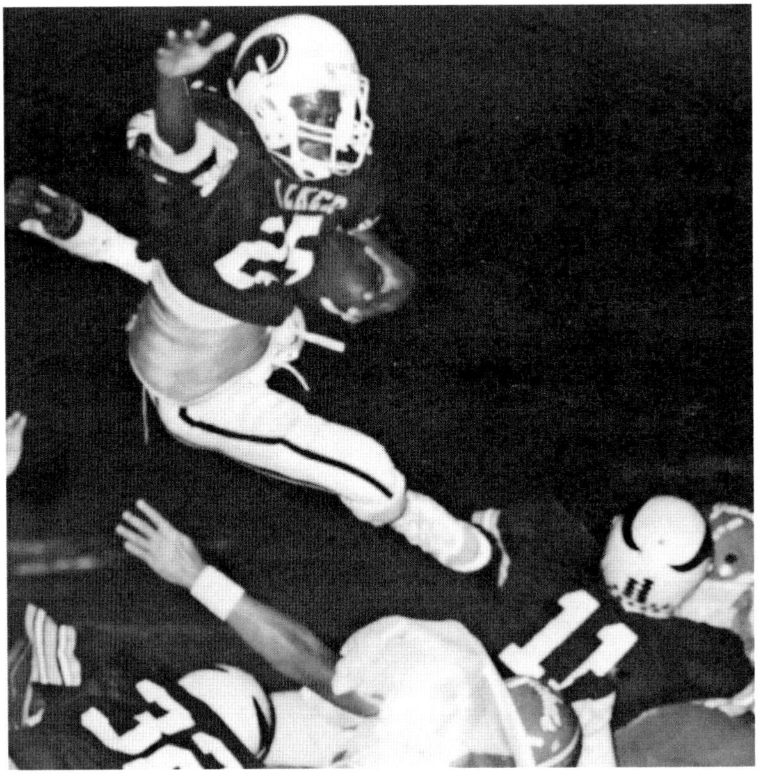

MARK WALDROP HURDLES, 1986. This picture shows the determination and agility that made Mark Waldrop (25) a top running back for the Vikings. Mark was a small player by any standard but made up for that by the size of his heart and the reckless abandon with which he ran the ball. Blocking their men to the ground are his fellow backs Michael Abner (11) and Joey Housley (32). All three were outstanding sprinters in track.

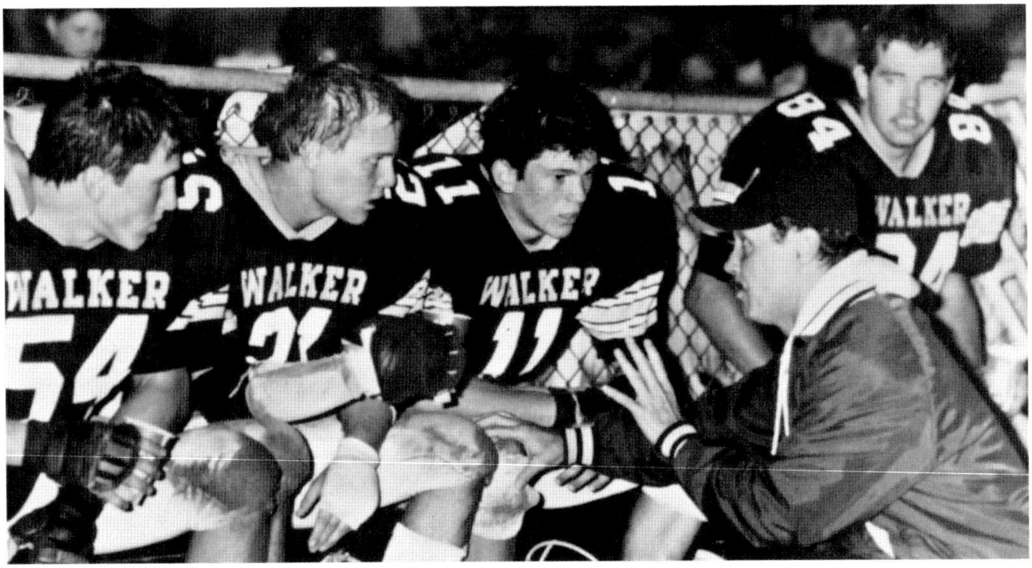

SIDELINE ADJUSTMENTS, 1988. When players come off the field, they gather with their coach to discuss possible problems or situations. Coach Pat Morrison gathers his linebackers to explain adjustments. From left to right are Jason Ferguson (54), Chris Morrison (21), and Phil Hill (11); defensive tackle Shannon Pate (84) listens in. Shannon was the best lineman prospect in 30 years at Walker.

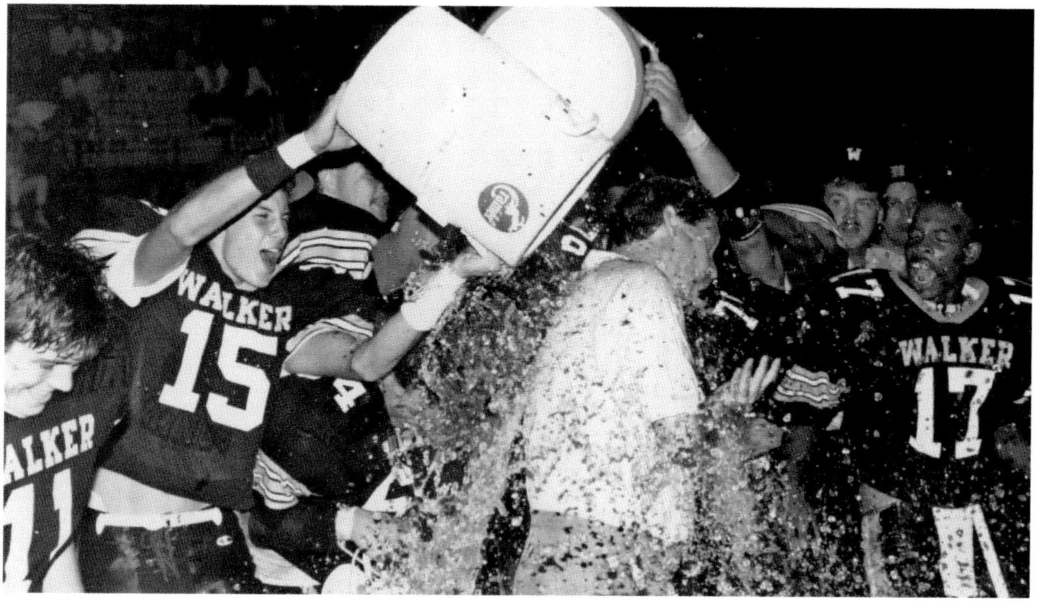

COACH GAMBRELL GETS A COLD SHOWER, 1989. Quarterback Chad Key (15) gives head coach Danny Gambrell a cold shower of Gatorade after the Vikings beat the eventual state champions Jess Lanier by a score of 17-16. Looking on and enjoying the celebration are linebacker Phil Hill (11) and defensive back Cedric Wilder (17). This could well have been the biggest victory at Walker High School in the 1980s.

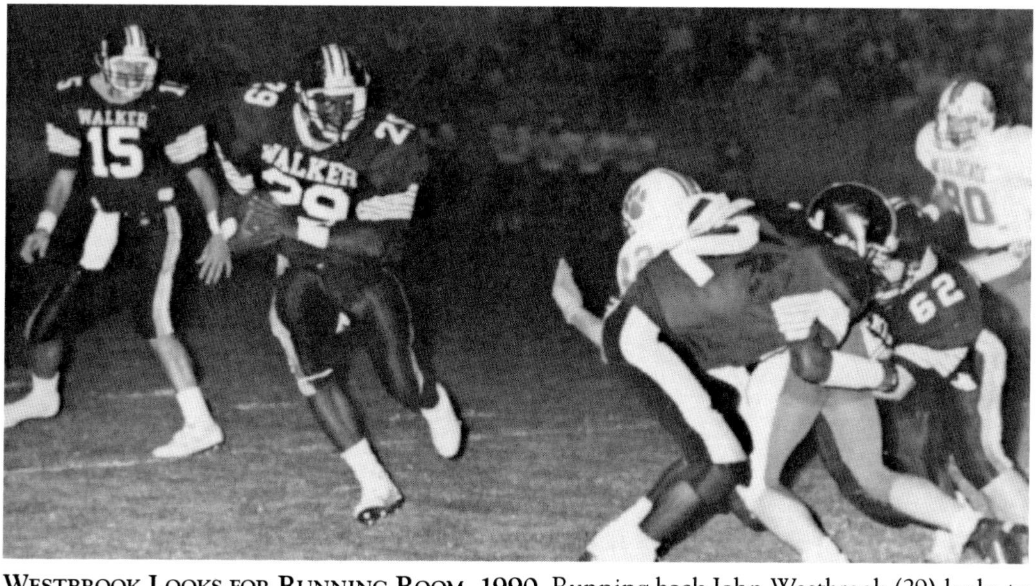

WESTBROOK LOOKS FOR RUNNING ROOM, 1990. Running back John Westbrook (29) looks to follow the block of slot back Andrea Housley (2) and guard Eric Ingram (62) against a tough Tuscaloosa County team as quarterback Chad Key (15) watches the play develop. John Westbrook continued his football career at the University of the South in Sewanee, Tennessee, and Chad Key played at the University of Alabama.

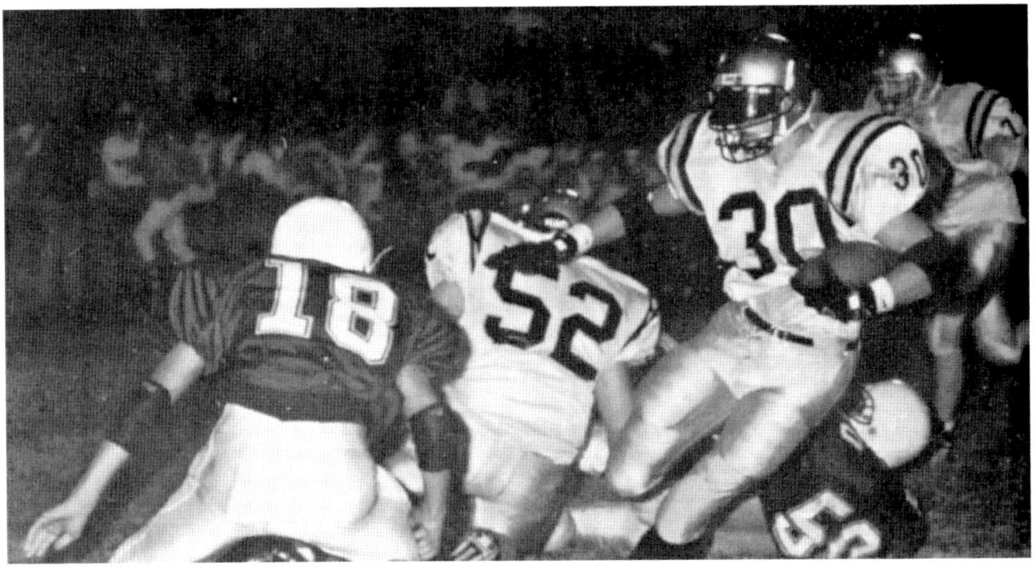

Adam Cox Carries the Ball, 1995. Adam Cox, another exceptional back at Walker, carries the ball for yardage against Curry. Adam had two 1,000-yard seasons for the Vikings before going to the University of Alabama, where he played running back and linebacker. Blocking for Adam are the Myhand brothers, Dustin (52) and Brandon (77). Brandon was an outstanding lineman at Samford University.

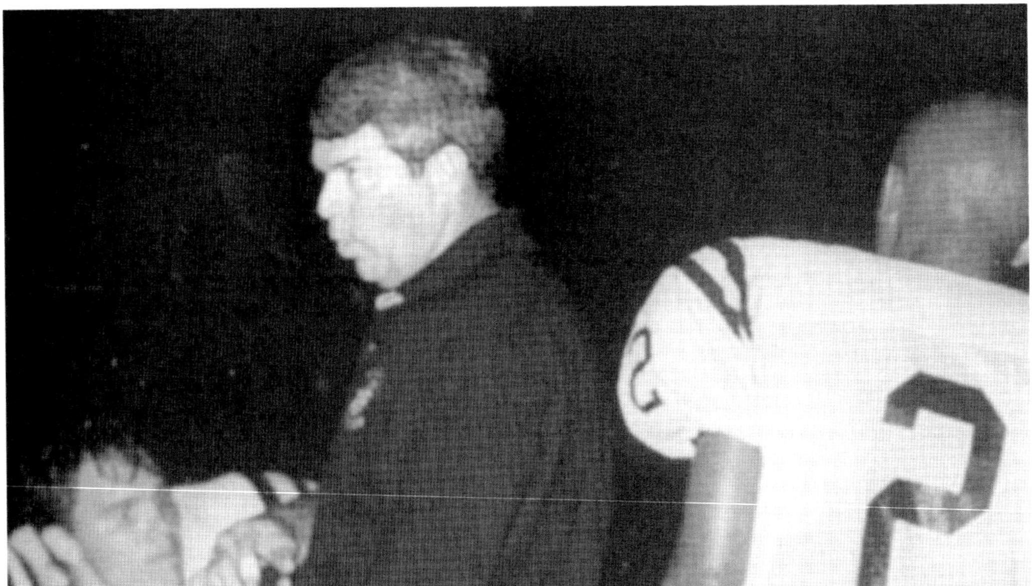

Coach Bubba Davis, 1996. Bubba Davis came to Walker in 1993 from Mississippi, where he had a career reaching almost legendary status. His first year, he led a floundering Walker High School program back to prominence, registering a 7-4 season and making the state playoffs. Coach Davis was to have two undefeated seasons during his tenure at Walker, something no other Viking coach had ever done.

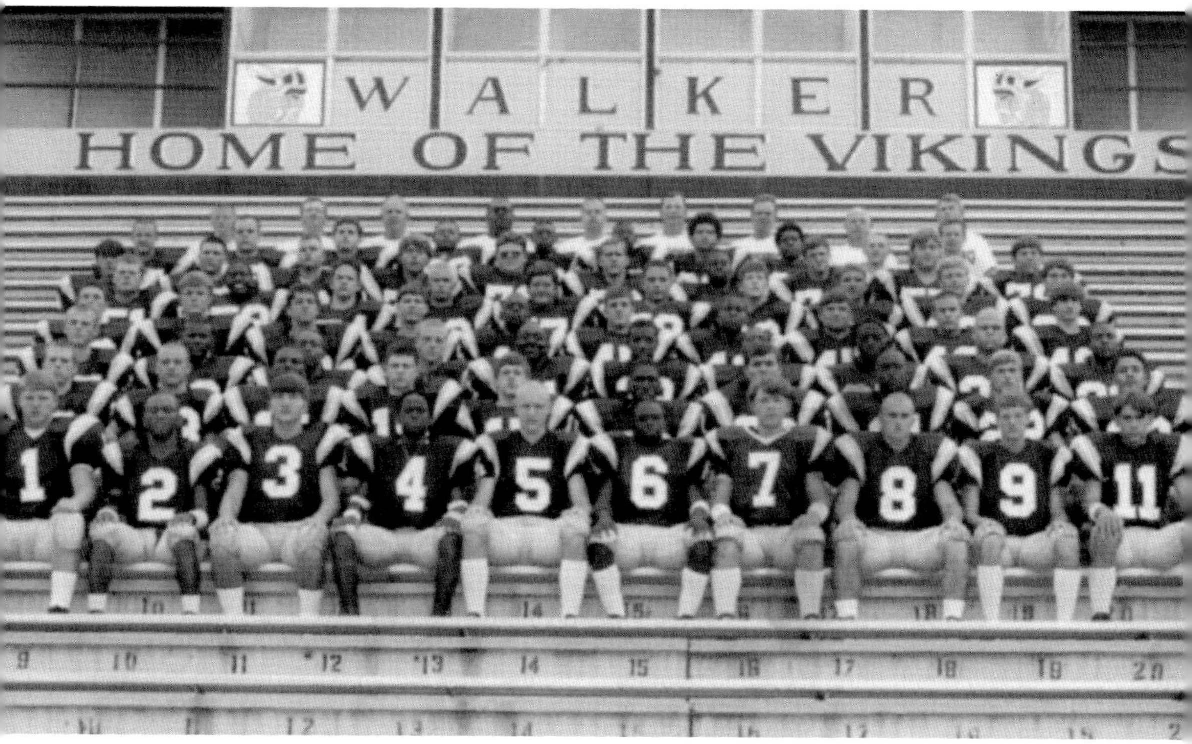

UNDEFEATED 10-0 VIKINGS, 1997. The first undefeated regular season team since 1957 is, from left to right, (first row) Scott Gilchrist, Shaun Mercer, Wayne Gross, Lionel Cook, Zac Johnson, A.P. Evans, Kevin Farley, Drew Thornley, Donald Baker, and Charles Waldrop; (second row) Sam Watts, Taylor Mosley, Marcus Shanklin, John Hataway, Jacob Cox, Lucus Hughes, Daniel Smith, Terance Shamburger, Josh Trotter, and Ty Theus; (third row) Brandon Garrett, Lee McElrath, Ricky Rogers, Nick Hendrickson, Ken Holiday, Marlon Hudson, Tariko Satterfield, Demetrius Farris, Jonathon McCollum, and Brian Hankins; (fourth row) Jason Romine, Landon Howell, Chris Deason, Thad Myrick, Andre Breeding, Brad Nix, Terry Abrom, Henry Swindle, Will Herzig, and Dale Johnson; (fifth row) Matt Adams, Jay Holston, Keith Goodson, Chris Pittman, Adam Light, Cliff Bolinger, Sam Evans, Jared Daniel, Michael Schwab, and Brad Baker; (sixth row) Jesse Brown, David Mize, Craig Price, Patrick Redmill, Carthell Williams, Delly Richardson, Donald Davis, David Smith, Ric Gilliland, and Justin Winfree; (seventh row) Jason Terry, Paul Nichols, Nathan Woodley, Anthony Flemming, Kelly Hudson, Ronnie Cummings, Kalee McCollum, Jay Pierce, and two unidentified managers; (eighth row) Jeff Tempest, coaches Roger Satcher, Gary Borden, Mike Montgomery, Mark Kell, Mike King, Grady McCluskey, and David Norwood, and head coach Bubba Davis.

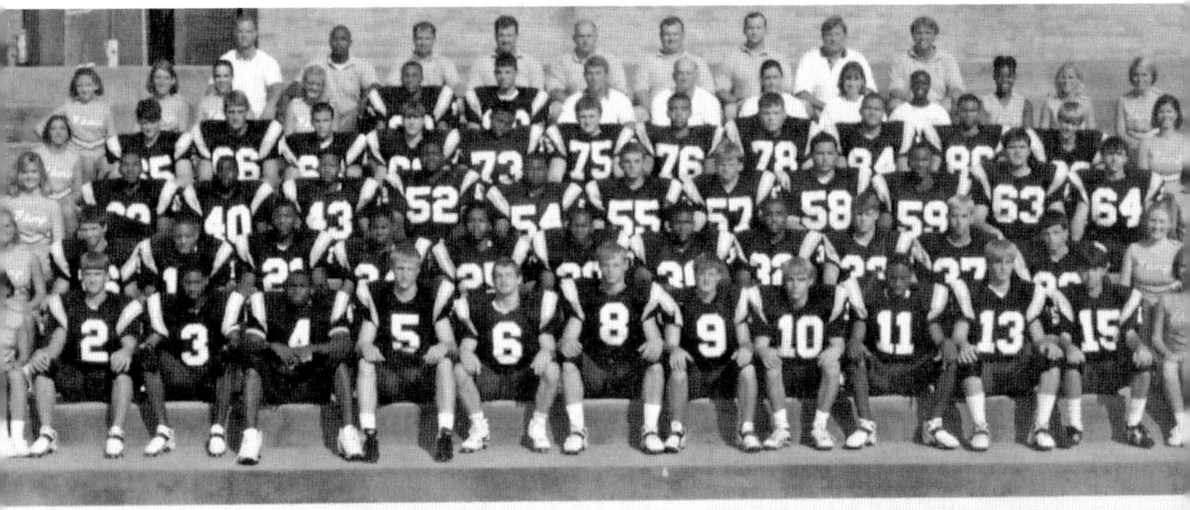

1999 Undefeated Regular Season 10-0 Head Coach Bubba Davis

UNDEFEATED TEAM, 1999. This is the second undefeated team, shown with cheerleaders, for coach Bubba Davis. From left to right are (first row) Caroline Thornley, Patrick Wilson, Lee Medlock, Bobby Hankins, Zac Johnson, Jacob Cox, Chad Borden, Donlad Baker, Wayne Matthews, Antwon Courington, Todd Laye, Brian Zorbini, and Ashley Garrett; (second row) Anna Kate Laskoski, Zach Norris, Mitch Henderson, Eric Oliver, Blake Farris, Terry Abrom, Jonathan Hardie, Levern Johnson, Marlon Hudson, Nolan Williams, Daniel King, Michael Taylor, and Laurel Price; (third row) Lisa Gilchrist, Brian Hankins, Ryan Stewart, Darnell Clay, Jay Holston, Anthony Archie, Chris Prince, Pierce Wiederecht, Cliff Bolinger, Daniel Crutchfield, Brad Baker, Jesse Brown, and Jennifer Boshell; (fourth row) Erica Vance, Mickey O'Rear, Peyton Sides, Will Herzig, Bubba Ellenburg, Donald Davis, Zach Woods, Justin McCollum, Cameron Sanders, Kalee McCollum, Paul Terrell, Brett Sparks, and Laura Balcar; (fifth row) Jennie Grice, Kristy Beall, Brittany Woodby, Allison Taylor, Ahmad Flemming, Colby Grelle, coach Bubba Davis, trainer Jack Lamon, Jana White, Holly Jaye, Lashirl Wilder, Lindsey McWhorter, Lauren Peters, and Casey Morrow; (sixth row) coaches Chad Shannon, Kerry Williams, Grady McCluskey, Brian VanDevender, Gary Borden, Roger Satcher, Mike King, John Sasser, and Thad Burgess.

4

THE EARLY YEARS

1920–1970

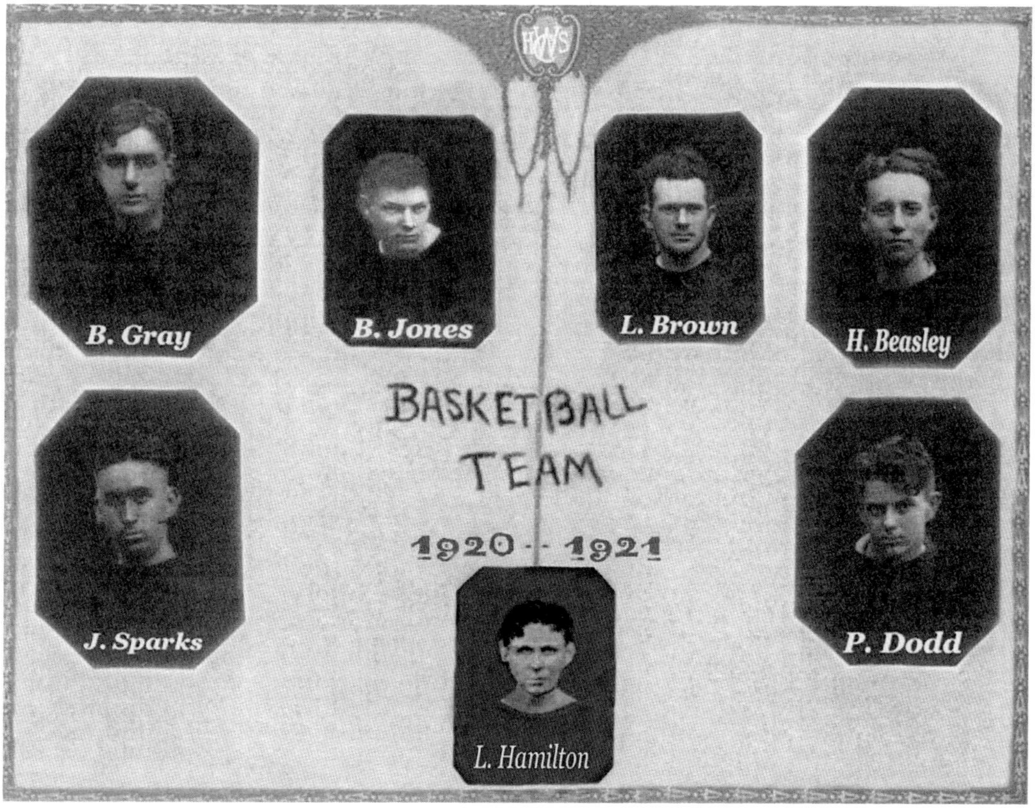

BASKETBALL TEAM, 1920–1921. This composite photograph of the 1920–1921 basketball team at Walker shows, clockwise from top left, Bill Grey, Bruce Jones, Lawrence "Moxie" Brown, Hansel Beasley, Pervy Dodd, Lee Hamilton, and James Sparks. This talented group of players finished second in the Alabama State Basketball Tournament and third in the Cotton States Tournament (consisting of teams from Alabama, Georgia, and Mississippi), making it the biggest high school tournament in the South at that time.

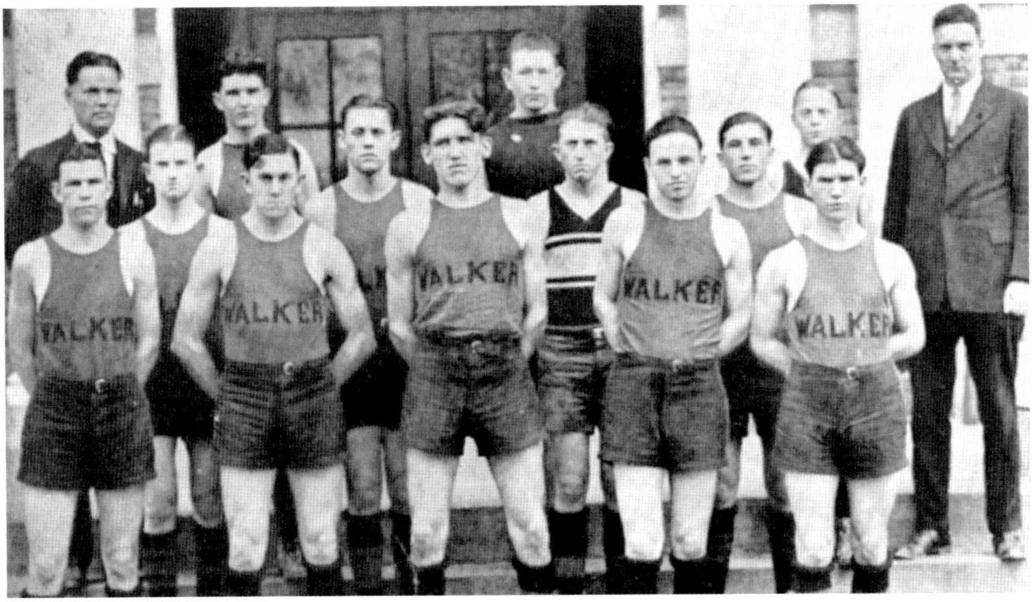

Basketball Team, 1924–1925. This team beat University High School in the Birmingham Tournament. From left to right are (first row) Clint Elliott, Jess Hudson, Silas Key, Claude Shubert, and Earnest Cain; (second row) Erskin Brakefield, Lowell Nichols, Dewey Hudson, and Luke Lancaster; (third row) coach John C. Goodwin, James "Treetop" McKeever, unidentified, Al Blanton, and Principal F. D. Dowdy. (Courtesy of WCHS.)

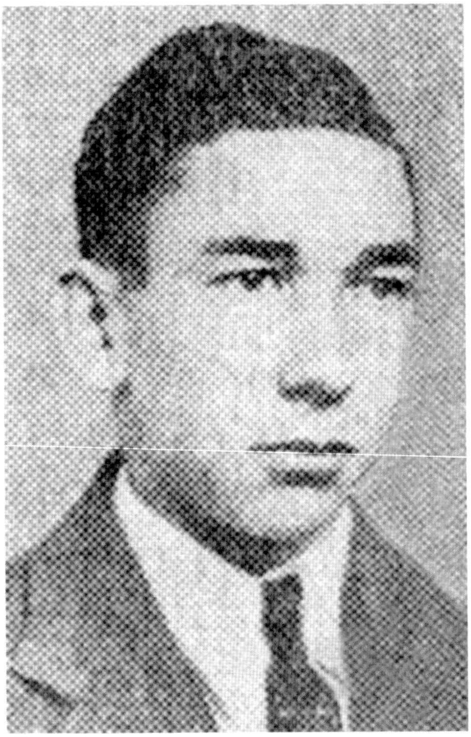

William "Wick" Hudson, 1935. Wick Hudson was captain of both the basketball and football teams and pole vaulted on the track team. In basketball, he set a school record of 34 points against Carbon Hill and broke his own record with a 39-point performance against Dora (a record that would stand for over 25 years). This was in an era when most teams would only score 15 to 20 points. He played college football at Union University.

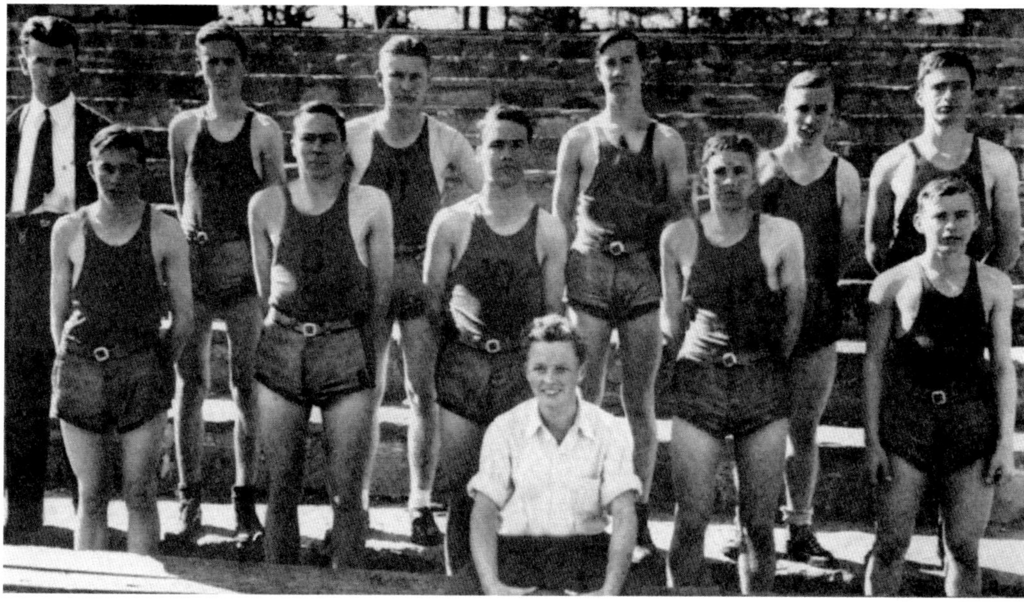

BASKETBALL TEAM, 1940–1941. Manager J. E. Black is in the front middle. From left to right behind him are (first row) Irving Bankston, Hulan Smith, T. E. Segars, Tony Lee, and Hugh Farris; (second row) coach ? Trimm, Ray Price, Ray Sherer, James Harold Chafin, Craig Hudson, and Guy Farris. Cheerleaders for the Vikings (not pictured) were Doris Williams, Mickey Davis, Stanley Maddox, Peggy Bedenbaugh, and Maxine Hamner.

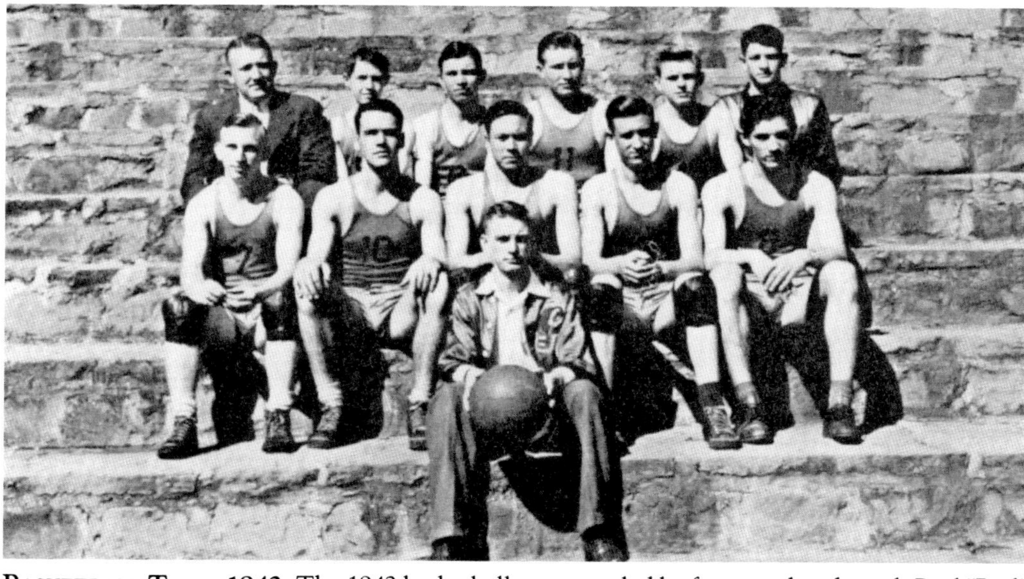

BASKETBALL TEAM, 1942. The 1942 basketball team was led by first-year head coach Paul "Red" Hudson, a previous star in both football and basketball for the Vikings. Pictured above from left to right are (first row) Howard Wilson, manager; (second row) Craig Hudson, T. E. Segars, Hulan Smith, Ray Rice, and Tony Lee; (third row) coach Paul Hudson, J. G. Abbott, Norris Morgan, Ray Sherer, Hugh Farris, and Charles Tucker.

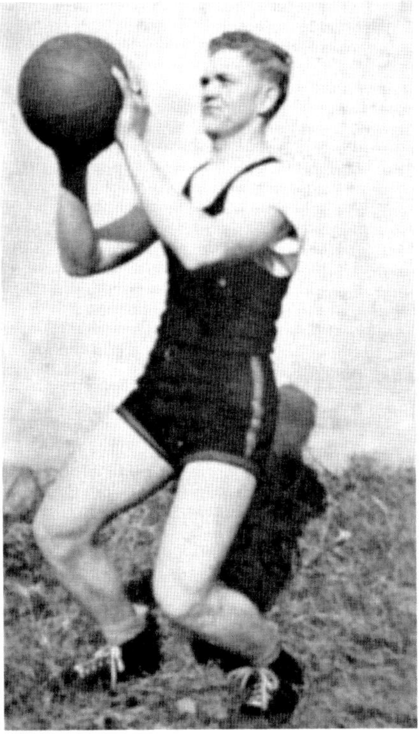

SHERWOOD "WOODY" BROWN, 1946. Woody was a star player on the 1943–1946 football and basketball teams, serving as captain of the 1945–1946 Viking basketball team. He was a four-year starter and All-County player in both sports and played under coaches L. F. Lockridge, Harry Erwin, and Paul Hudson. Other notable members of that team were Ralph Hamner, Walker County's most decorated Vietnam veteran, and actor George "Goober" Lindsey.

WALKER COUNTY CHAMPS, 1948–1949. The 1948–1949 Walker County Championship basketball team, coached by Virgil Ledbetter, was led by All-County players Segal Drummond, Kay Don Salmon, and Joe Johnson. From left to right are (first row) manager Bobby Underwood; Harold Faught, Leslie Black, Jimmy Segars, and Bryant Ashmore; (second row) Segal Drummond, Joe Johnson, Kay Don Salmon, and Bobby Hyche.

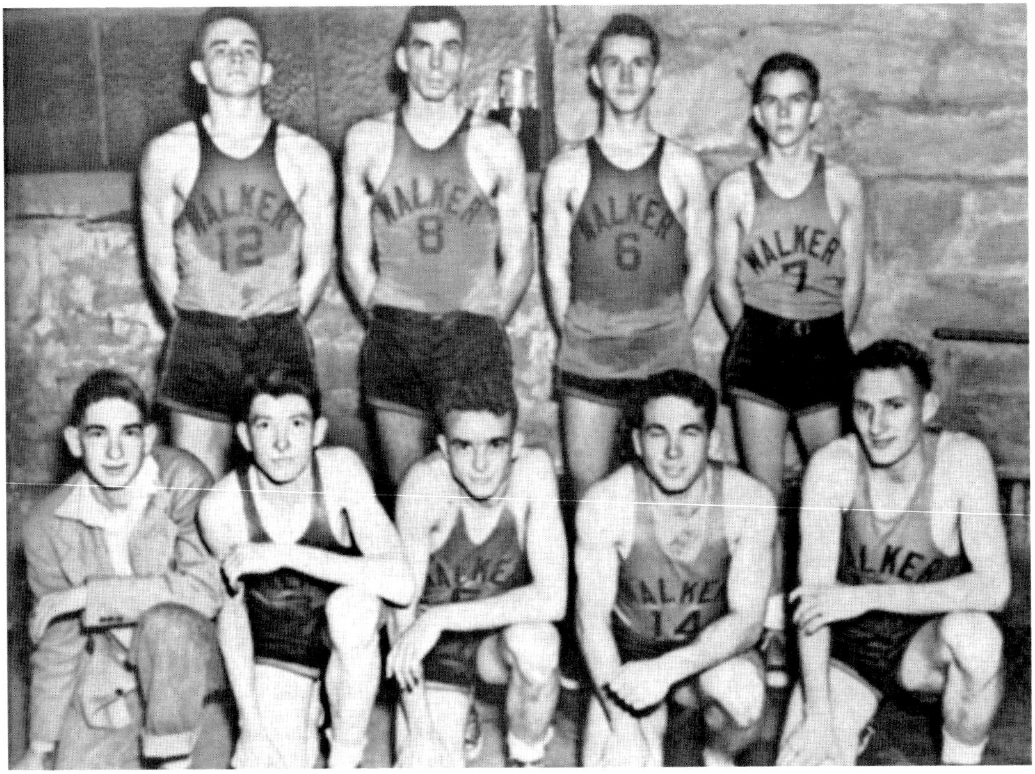

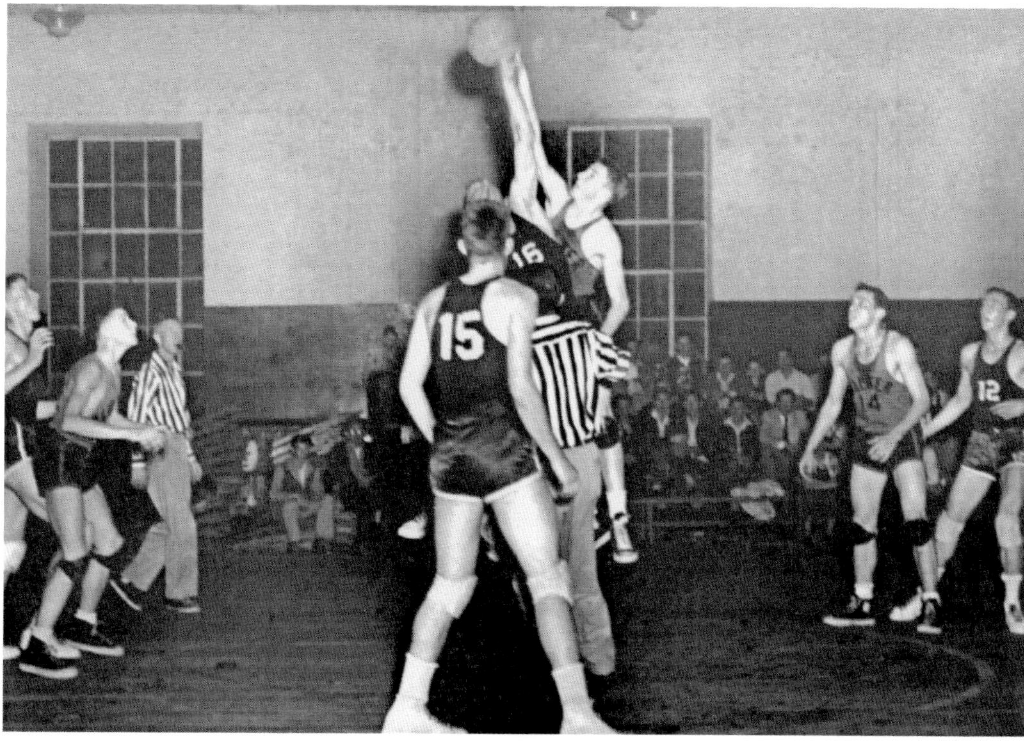

BASKETBALL TEAM, 1949–1950. This action shot of the 1949 Viking basketball team shows William Woodson jumping (center) as guards Joe Johnson (left) and Segal Drummon (right) prepare to get the tipped ball. This team practiced and played in the Walker County High School auditorium. They had to move the chairs each day to provide an area large enough to serve as a basketball court, then move them back in for study hall the next day.

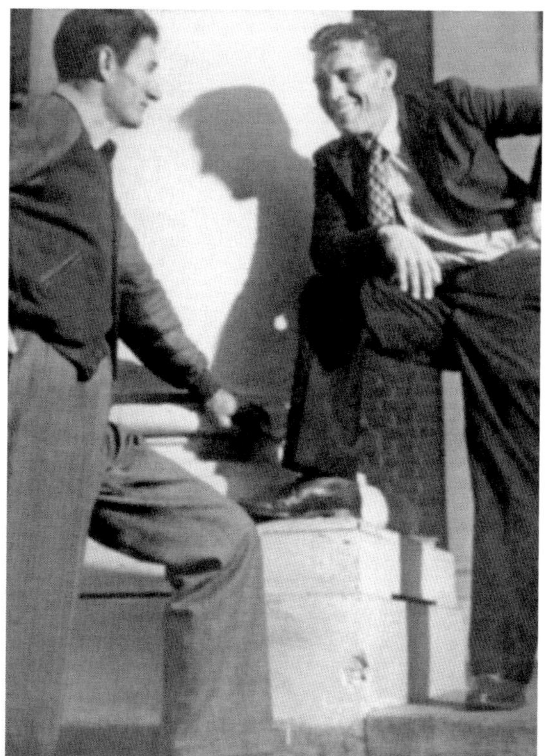

WALKER COACHES, 1946–1951. Pictured here are coach Virgil Ledbetter (left), the head basketball and baseball coach, and coach Donald Sanford, the head football and "B" team basketball coach. Virgil Ledbetter's last two years at Walker were his best. His 1950 record was 17-5, and his 1951 Vikings surpassed that by winning 21 games and losing only 6. Unfortunately they lost in the finals of the Walker County tournament.

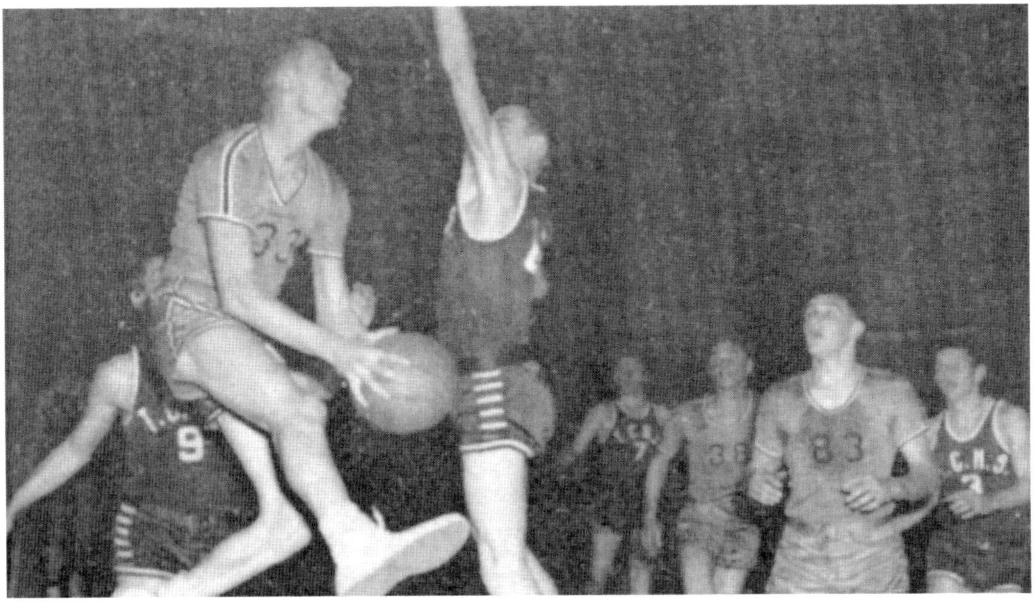

REX MURRAY DRIVES, 1952–1953. Rex Murray, shown driving for two more points against Tuscaloosa County High School, was one of those great Walker athletes who played both major sports. He was All-County and All-District and played in the first Alabama State High School All-Star game. Looking on are Emmett Sanford (83) and Gerald Faught (38). This was coach Jack Caldwell's first year at Walker; his team posted a 20-4 record.

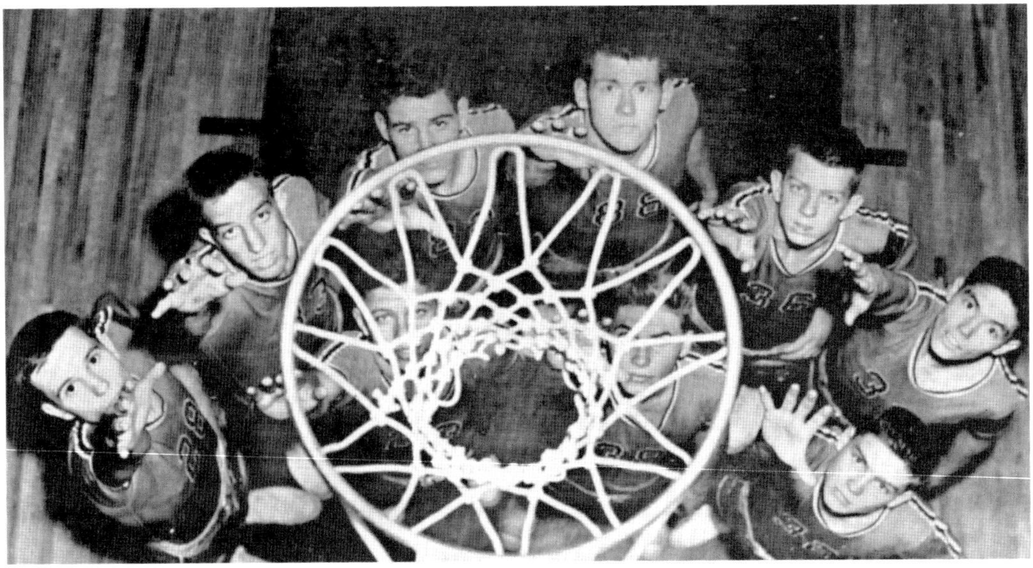

VARSITY SQUAD, 1954–1955. The Vikings were again county champions, runners-up in the Fifth District, and qualified for the state tournament. Junior M. A. Woodley was selected All-County and All-District. From left to right are (outer circle) Gordon Durham, M. A. Woodley, Bruce Mullins, Dodd Holt, Bill Cain, and Walter Will Harris; (inner circle) Grady Sparks, Vernon Holman, and Jimmy Lee. This team played in the first game at Walker's new gymnasium.

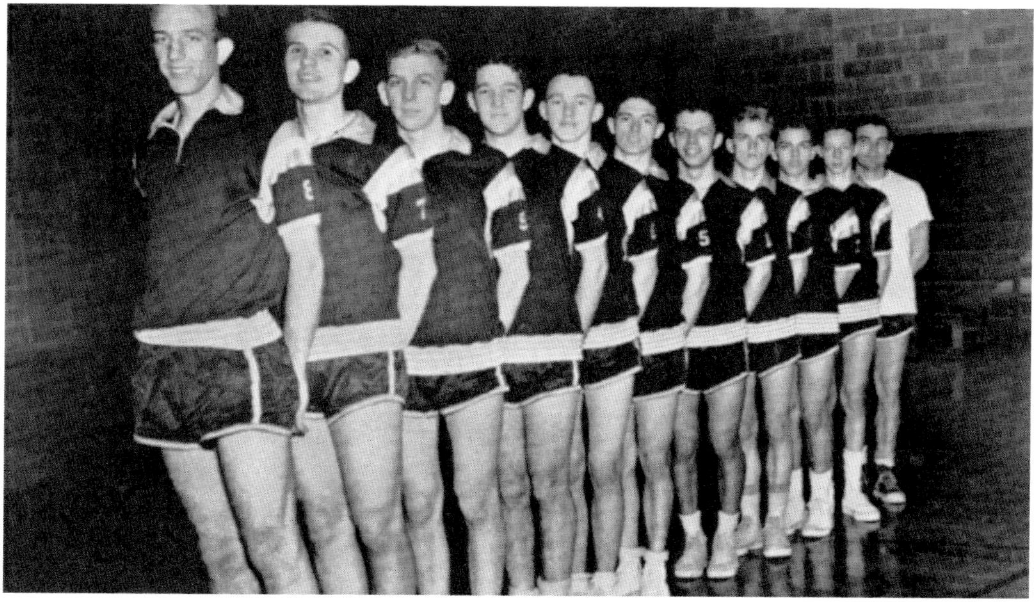

VIKING SQUAD, 1955–1956. The Vikings recorded a 27-4 season and were Walker County champions. From left to right are M. A. Woodley (MVP of the district tournament who played in the state All-Star game), Gordon Durham (MVP of the county tournament), John Parks Grey, Tony West, Woody Odom, Walter Will Harris, Grady Sparks (MVP of the county tournament), Ronald Harris, Billy Richardson, Joe Murray, and coach Jack Caldwell.

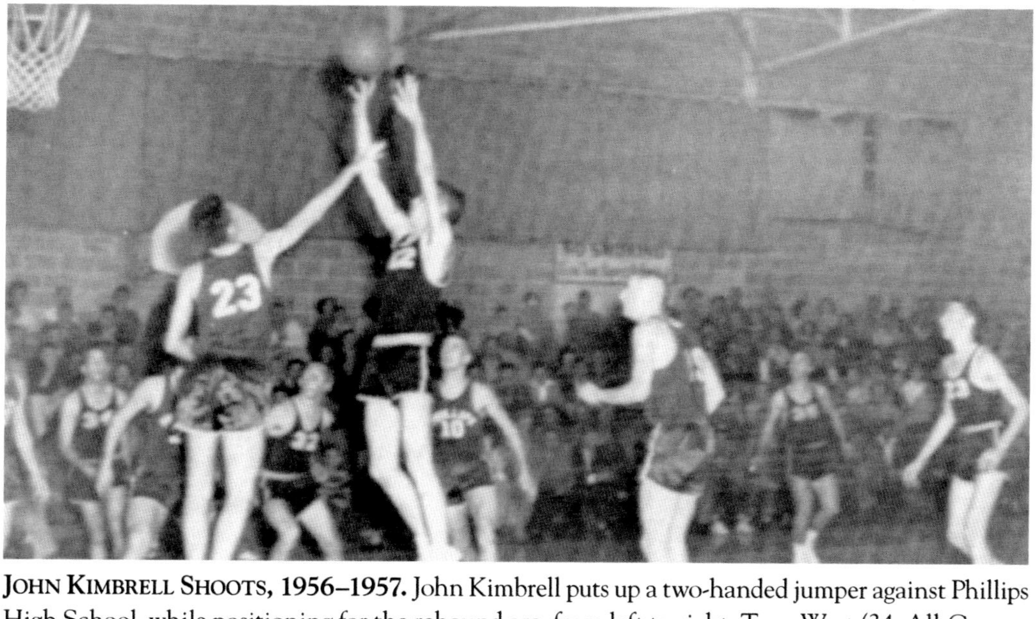

JOHN KIMBRELL SHOOTS, 1956–1957. John Kimbrell puts up a two-handed jumper against Phillips High School, while positioning for the rebound are, from left to right, Tony West (34, All-County and All-TVC [Tennessee Valley Conference]), Woody Odom (32, All-County), John Kimbrell (12), Billy Richardson (35, All-County, All-TVC, and MVP of the TVC tournament), and Joe Murray (23, All-County and All-TVC). Coach Caldwell's Vikings finished the year 21-8.

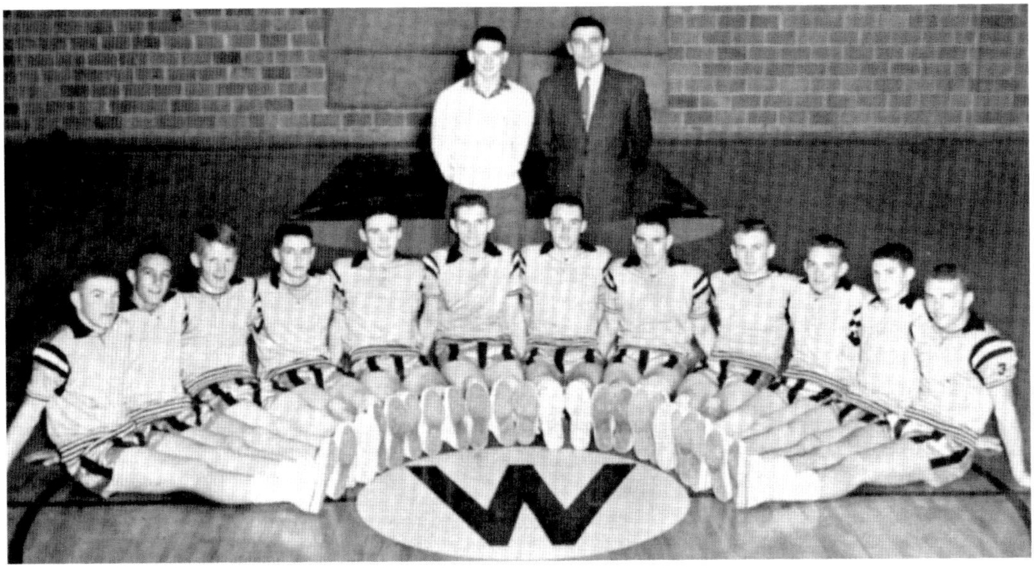

TVC CHAMPS, 1957–1958. The Vikings won the Tennessee Valley Tournament, staying undefeated during the tournament championship. From left to right are (seated) Jon Sanford, Dewayne Woodley, Donald Woodley, Howard Lockhart, Mike Hudson, Gerald Dutton, Woody Odom, Jimmy Cunningham, Donnie Taylor, Doug Richardson, Neil Hyche, and Billy Richardson; (standing) manager Jack Lamon and coach Jack Caldwell.

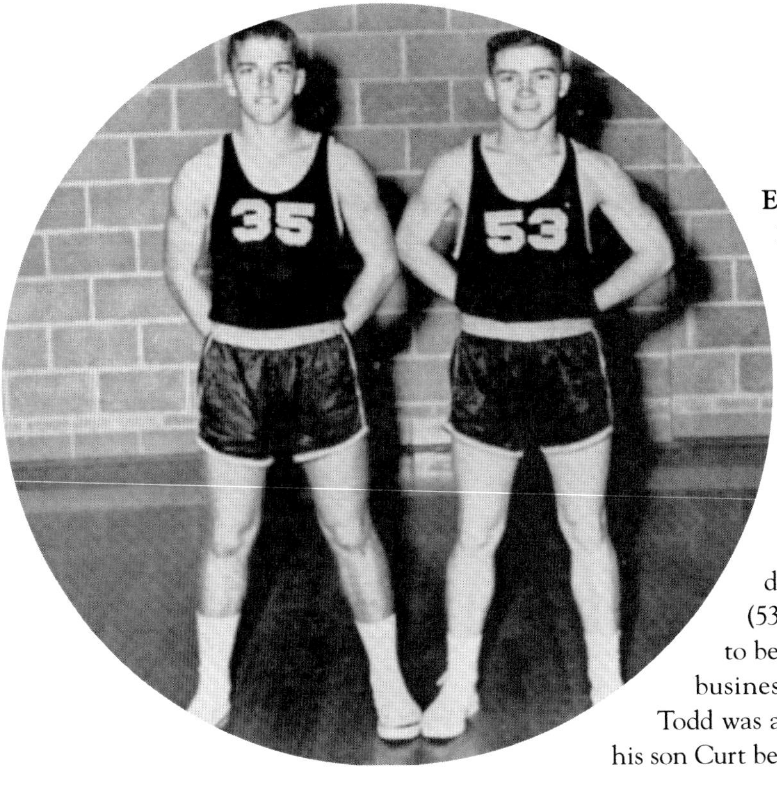

EDGE AND LEE, 1960–1961. Walker has always been known for the quickness of their point guards, and these two were certainly no exception. Billy Edge (35) was a great scholar-athlete at Auburn who became a celebrated medical doctor, while Jimmy Lee (53) was to stay in Jasper to become a successful local business leader. Jimmy's son Todd was an All-State golfer, and his son Curt became a state senator.

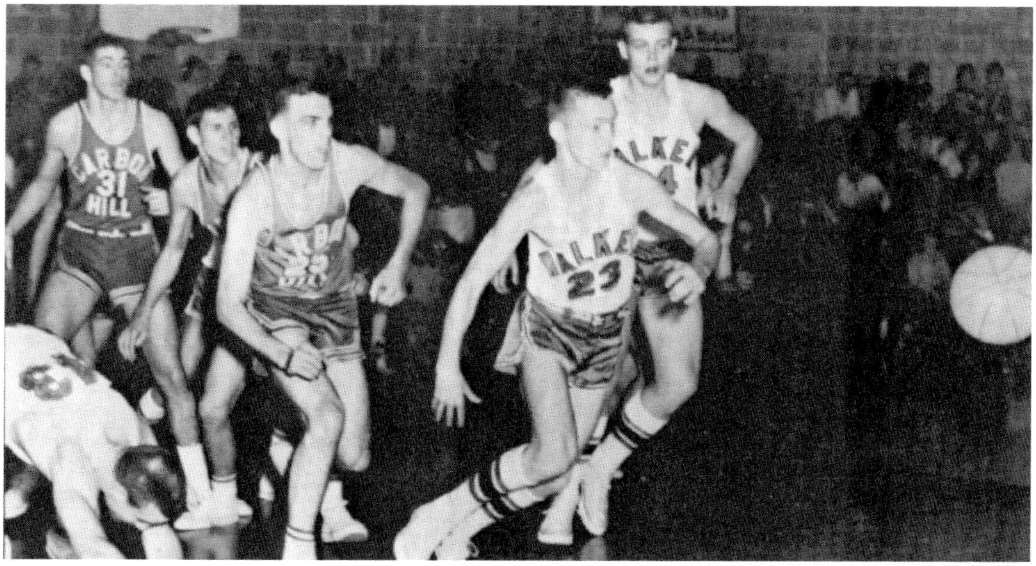

KEN LAKEY, 1962–1963. Shown in action against Carbon Hill is Ken Lakey (23), another small guard from Walker. Ken, possibly the smallest of those to play that position, hustles after a loose ball. Ken was arguably the best junior high basketball coach in all Walker County history. From left to right are George Fitzpatrick (43), Lakey, and James Short (44).

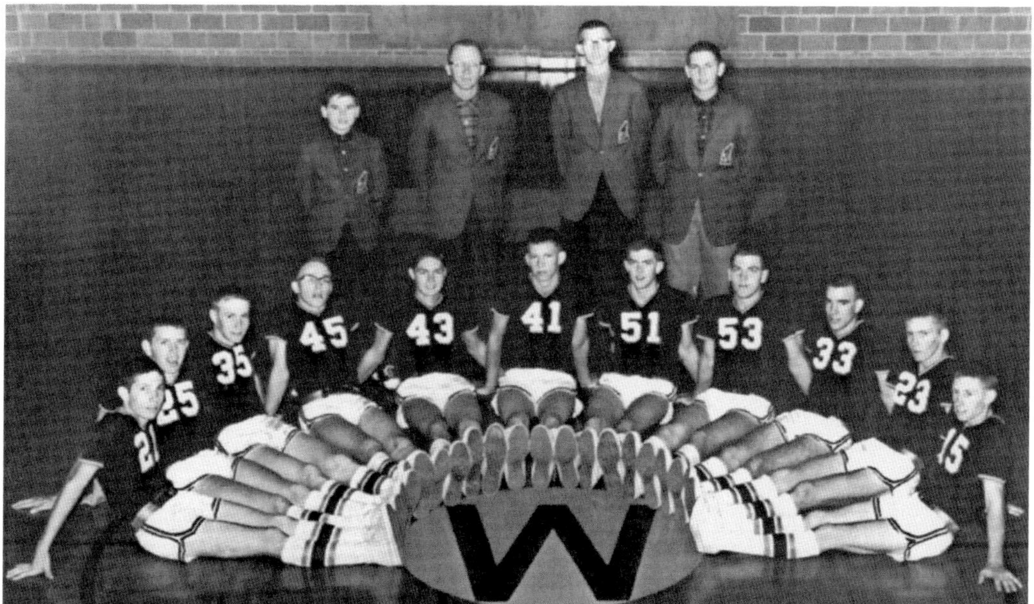

BASKETBALL TEAM, 1963–1964. This team coached by Pat Upton was small but aggressive. From left to right are (seated) guard Mike McReynolds, guard Bobby McCoy, forward Jerry Colvin, forward Nolan Hudson, center Ronald Wilson, center Mike Kilgore, forward Al Simmons, forward Bill James, guard Conrad Smith, guard Milton Lay, and guard Ken Lakey; (standing) John Underwood, coach Pat Upton, Ricky Talley, and Bobby Aldridge.

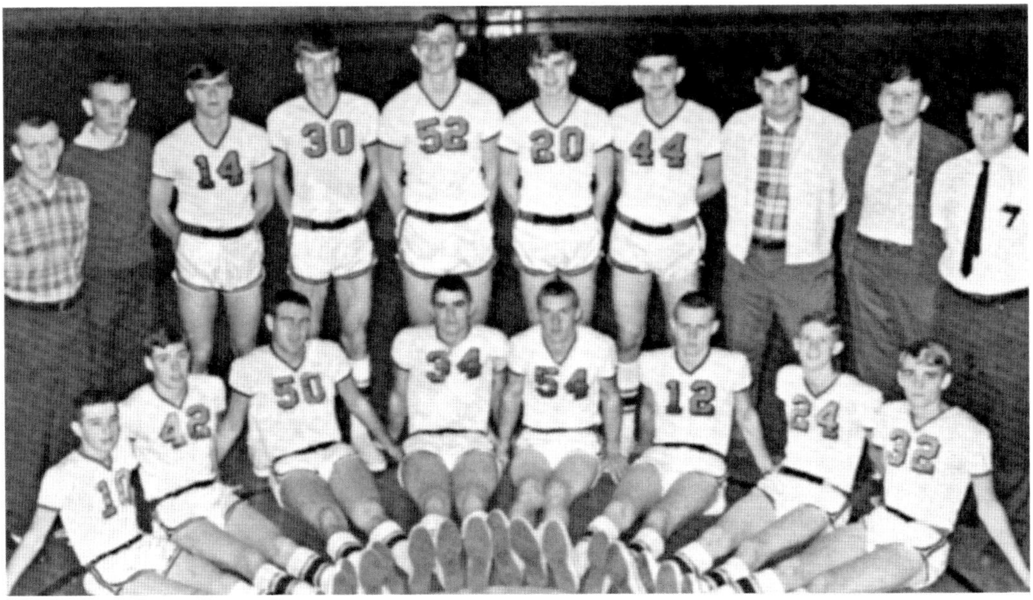

Basketball Team, 1965–1966. The 1965–1966 team is, from left to right, (seated) A. J. McDanal, George Hiller, John Kirkpatrick, Wayne Banks, Mark Myers, unidentified, Larry Cox, and Eddie Bull; (standing) Steve Weddle, Eddie Williams, Al Blanton, Tommy Kilgore, Murray Argo (one of Walker's top-five all-time players), Randy Britton, Eddie Williams, David Baird, Terry Roberts, and coach Jimmy Jones.

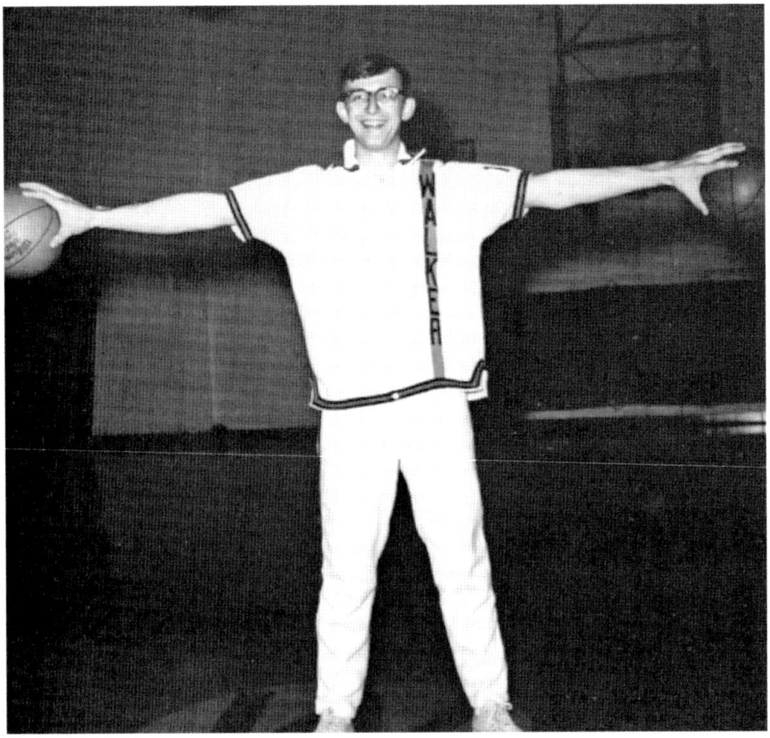

Murray Argo Palms Two Balls, 1967–1968. Murray Argo, a 6-foot-7-inch center, was the first really big man to play at Walker. Coach Herbert Green said he was the first big man he had ever coached that could really move. He used this skill to make the Alabama All-State team his senior year. As a freshman, he led the Walker College Rebel team to the Alabama Junior College Championship.

COACHES GREEN AND MORRISON, 1968–1969. Herbert Green was the only basketball coach to have an undefeated basketball season in Walker's history and holds the highest winning percentage. He was the head coach at the University of Auburn at Montgomery, assistant at Auburn University, and head coach at Columbus College, where he holds the record for number of wins. Pictured on his right is longtime assistant Pat Morrison.

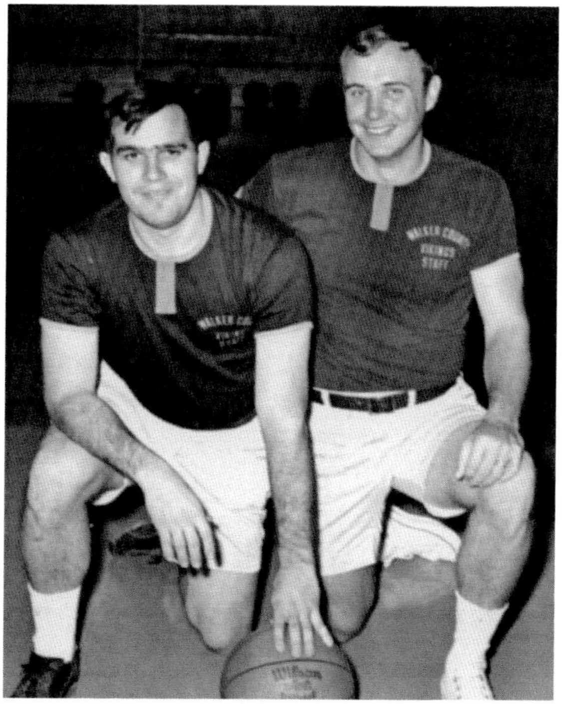

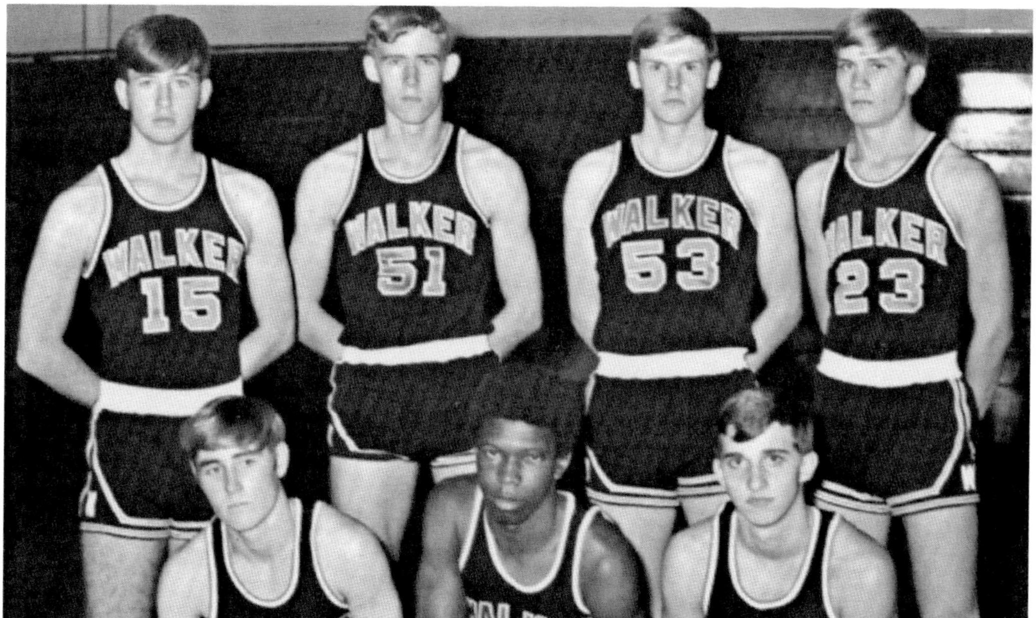

SENIOR BASKETBALL PLAYERS, 1969–1970. Ending the chapter on the early years is this group of seniors from coach Herbert Green's 1970 basketball team. In Coach Green's fourth year at Walker, he had already set expectations for all teams to excel, and this one was no exception. From left to right are (first row) Paul Kilgore, Tommy Powell, and Buddy Cross; (second row) Terry Hudson, Wayne Key, Bertice Kimbrell, and Derrel Kimbrell.

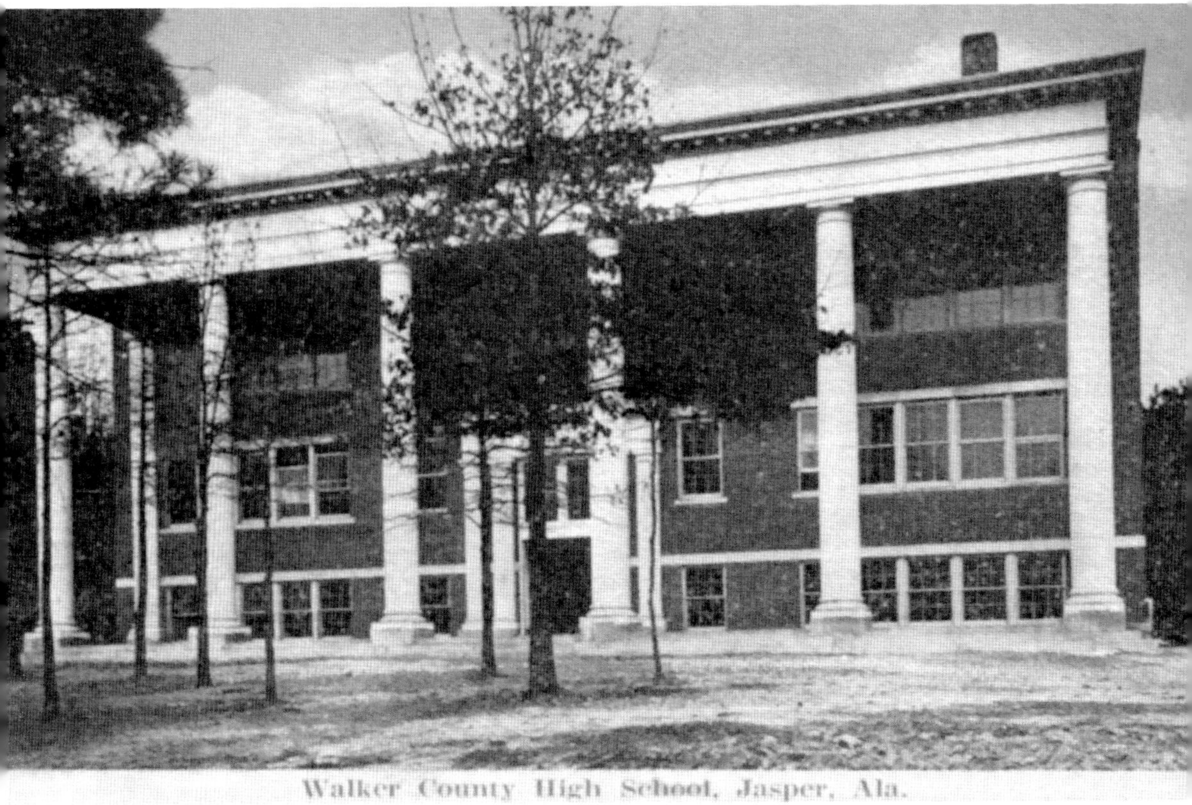

WALKER COUNTY HIGH SCHOOL, 1970. This is how the front of the high school looked from 1916, when it was built, until it was torn down in 1973 to make room for a new and more modern school facility. Many past students from Walker were disappointed to see the historic old brick building with the big columns torn down, bringing an end to a great era and to a monument of those days. It will always live in the hearts of those students and athletes who attended the old school. It was the beginning of a new era in both athletics and academics, as the old Walker County High School became Walker High School, a Jasper city school. It is important to have pride in the new but at the same time remember the past and those who lived it.

5

THE LATER YEARS

1971–2000

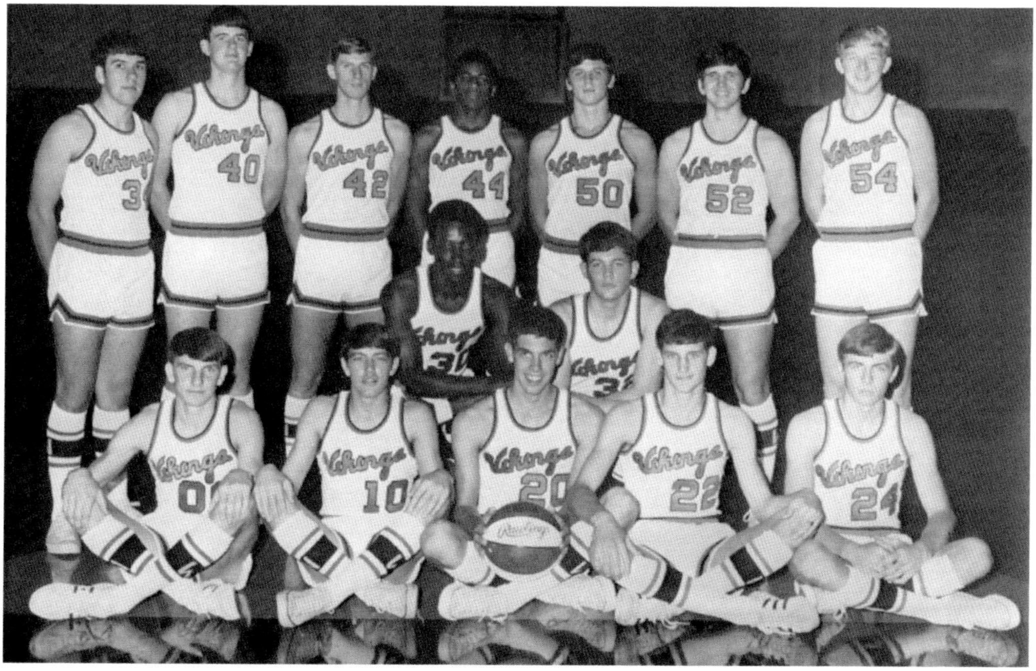

WALKER COUNTY CHAMPS, 1970–1971. This Herbert Greene–coached team was the 1971 Walker County basketball champions. From left to right are (first row) Anthony Benson, John Ed McDanal, Randy Daniels, Stewart Upton, and Greg McDade; (second row) Vincent Medlock and Guy Able; (third row) Tab Hudson, Tommy Kelly, Mike Robinson, Will Fuller, Phillip Simmons, Hal Brakefield, and Mitch McCullers.

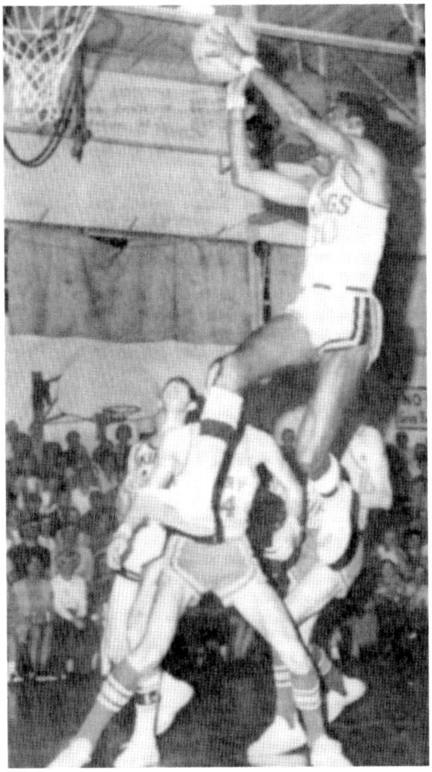

VINCE MEDLOCK SKIES, 1971. Senior forward Vincent Medlock (30) shows off his athletic ability against Curry High School, as junior All-County MVP Mike Robinson looks on. Vince was the first black basketball player at Walker and the first black head basketball coach in the history of Walker High School. Vince was a football and basketball player at Walker and then at Alabama A&M.

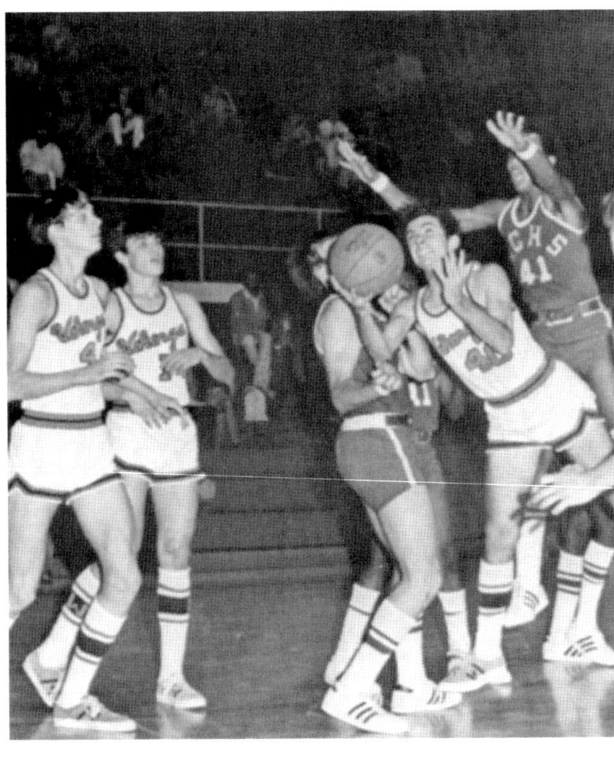

TONY PRICE REBOUNDS, 1971–1972. Junior guard Tony Price (40) battles for a rebound against rival Tuscaloosa County High School. Looking on and ready to enter the action are center Ronnie Shaw (44) and forward Chuck Justice (14). All three of these juniors would play on the only undefeated basketball team Walker ever fielded. Each would also have the opportunity to play college basketball or football.

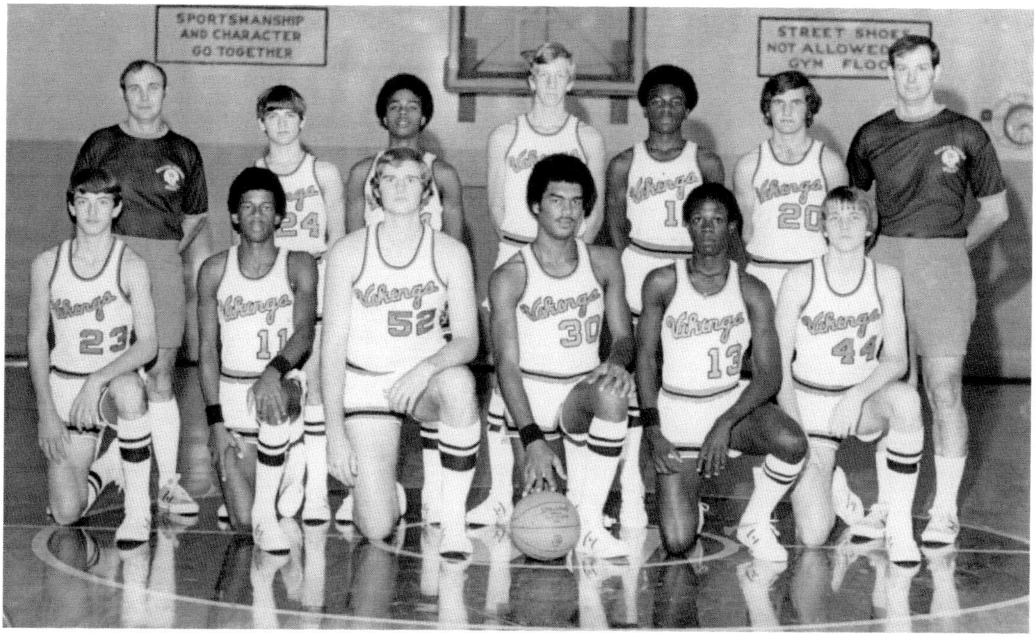

BASKETBALL TEAM, 1973–1974. Phil Schumacher arrived at Walker in 1973; he led the Vikings for the next 23 years. From left to right are (first row) Frankie Ellis, Greg Farris, Scott Jackson, Robert Page, Ronnie Cummings, and Bobby Bull; (second row) coach Pat Morrison, Wayne Tedford, Leon Harton, Buddy Woodley, Willie Lofton, Robin Woods, and Coach Schumacher.

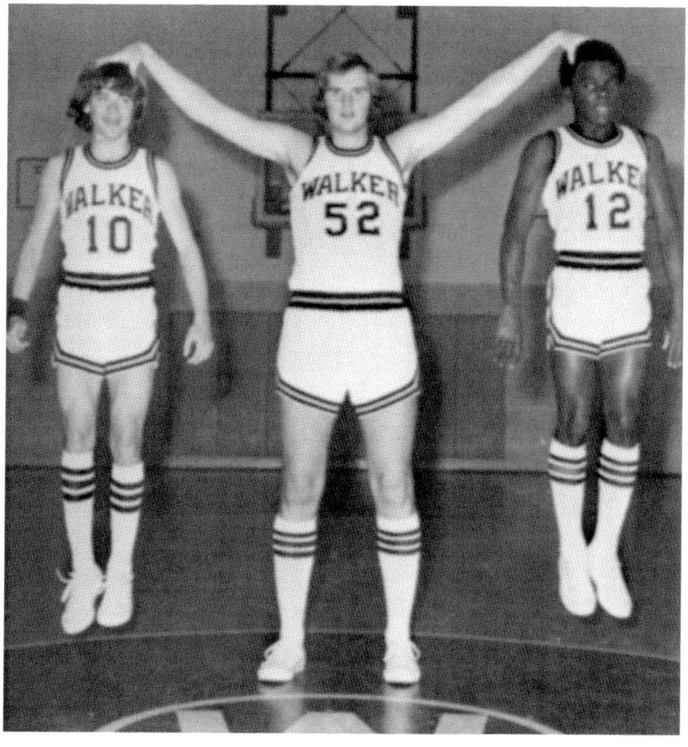

PALMING HIS TEAMMATES, 1974–1975. Wayne Tedford (10), Scott Jackson (52), and Willie Lofton (12) mug for the camera. Scott, at 6 feet, 9 1/2 inches, was one of Walker's tallest players, while Wayne and Willie were two in a long line of small, quick, and aggressive players giving Coach Schumacher's Vikings a reputation for quick defenses, which were extremely difficult to get the ball down the court against.

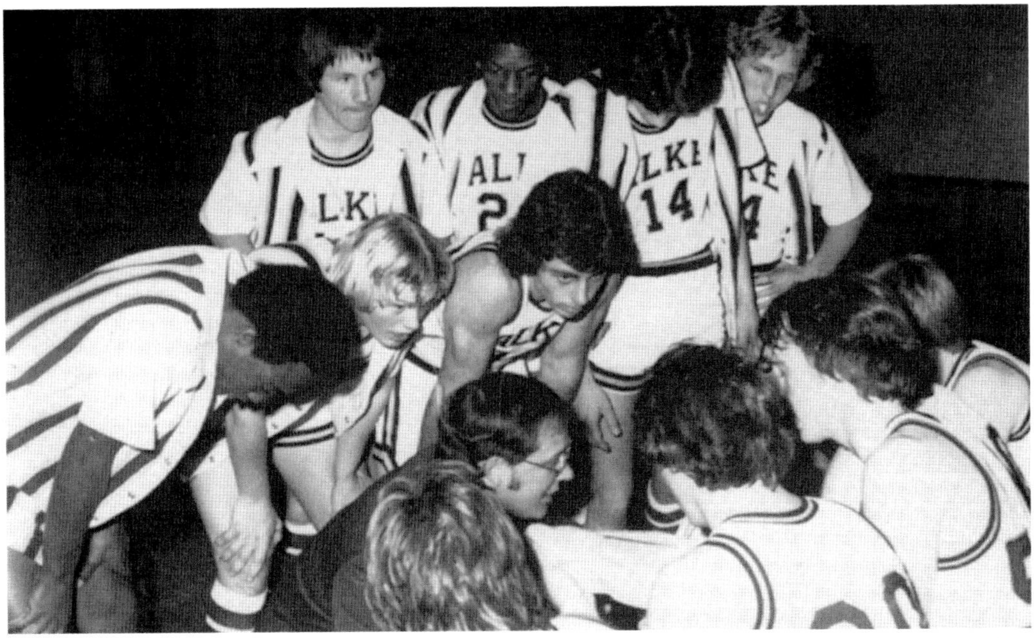

Time-out, 1975. This photograph was taken during a time-out against the Carbon Hill Bulldogs at Songer Gymnasium. Pictured with their backs to the camera are, from left to right, Steve Hudson (44), Frankie Ellis (20), Johnny Whatley (54), and Sanford Hendon. Listening over Coach Schumacher's back are, from left to right, (first row) Willie Moore, Greg Hendon, and Robin Edgil; (second row) Lee Meacham, Derrick Morgan, Ricky Lee, and Ricky Allred.

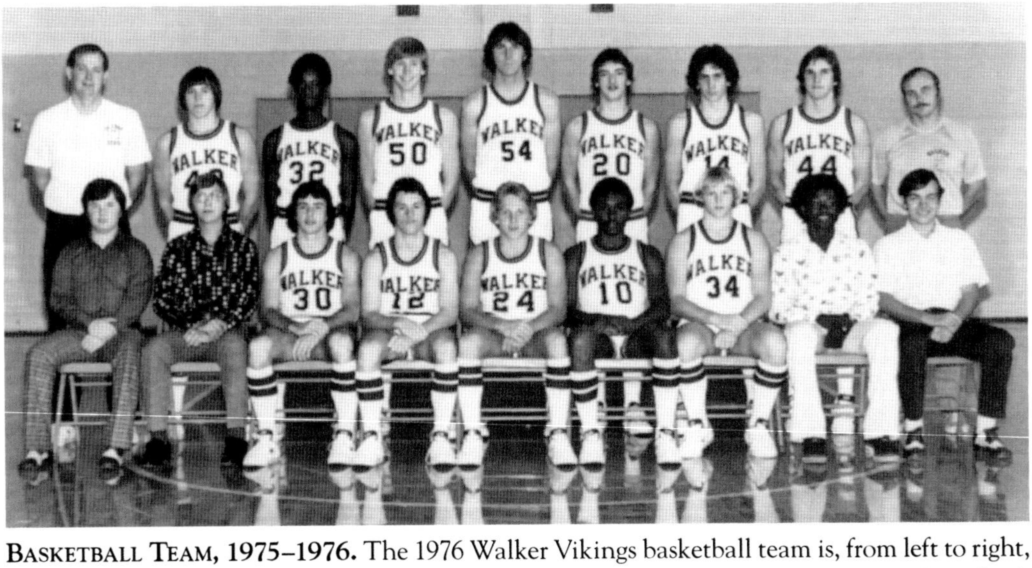

Basketball Team, 1975–1976. The 1976 Walker Vikings basketball team is, from left to right, (first row) managers Randy Lamon and Randy Watts, Robin Edgil, Lee Meacham, Ricky Allred, Willie Moore, Greg Hendon, and managers Eugene Nixon and Steve Gunter; (second row) Coach Schumacher, Sanford Hendon, Derrick Morgan, Jerry Lee, Johnny Whatley, Frankie Ellis, Ricky Lee, Steve Hudson, and Coach Morrison.

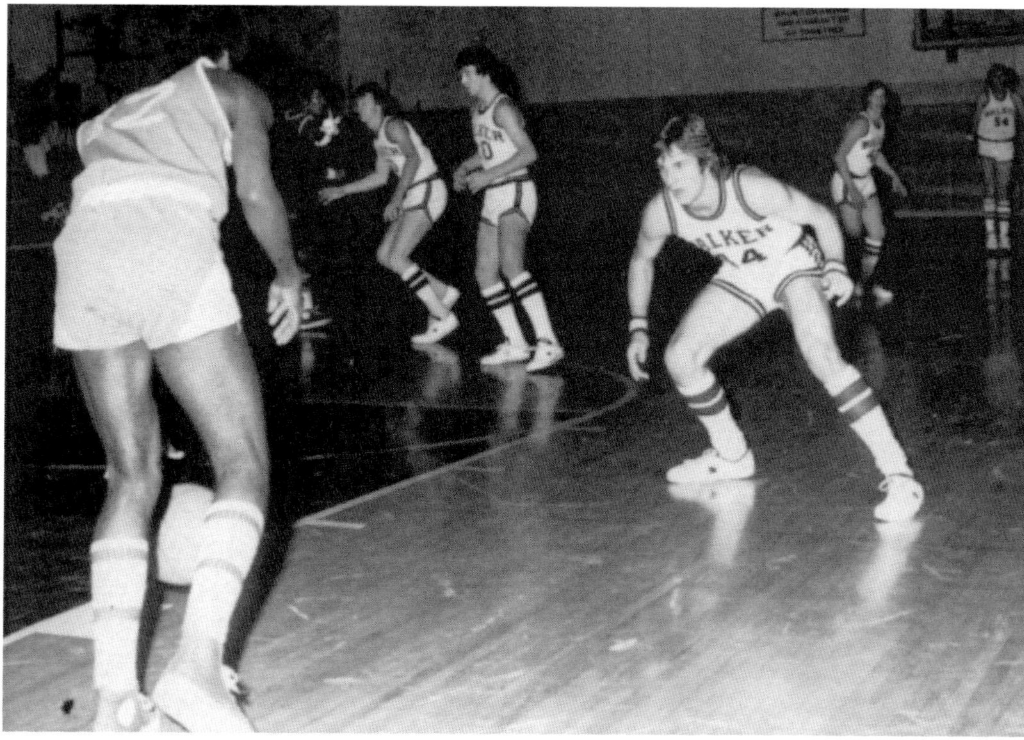

FULL-COURT PRESS, 1976. Here is an example of the full-court press used by Coach Schumacher to intimidate teams attempting to bring the ball down the court. This team was a master at pressure defense. Steve Hudson (44) breaks down with his eye on the ball, as Frankie Ellis (20) and Jerry Lee (50) pick their men up and Samford Hendon (40) and Johnny Whatley (54) attempt to pick off the long pass.

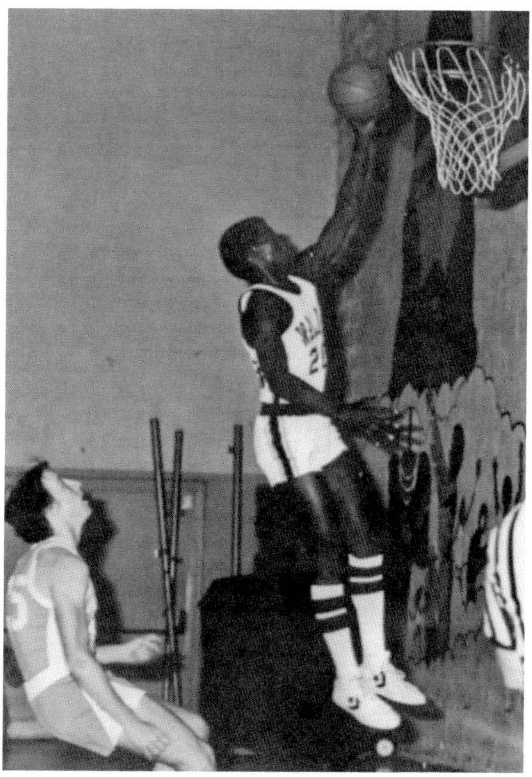

REGGIE CUMMINGS, 1977–1978. Reggie Cummings goes in for a lay-up against Winfield High. A coach's dream is a player who does what he is taught, going in on the left side of the bucket using his left hand. Coaches drill and drill the use of the left hand but most players revert to their right in the game. Reggie was the second of three exceptional Cummings brothers (Ronnie, Reggie, and Chris) to play at Walker.

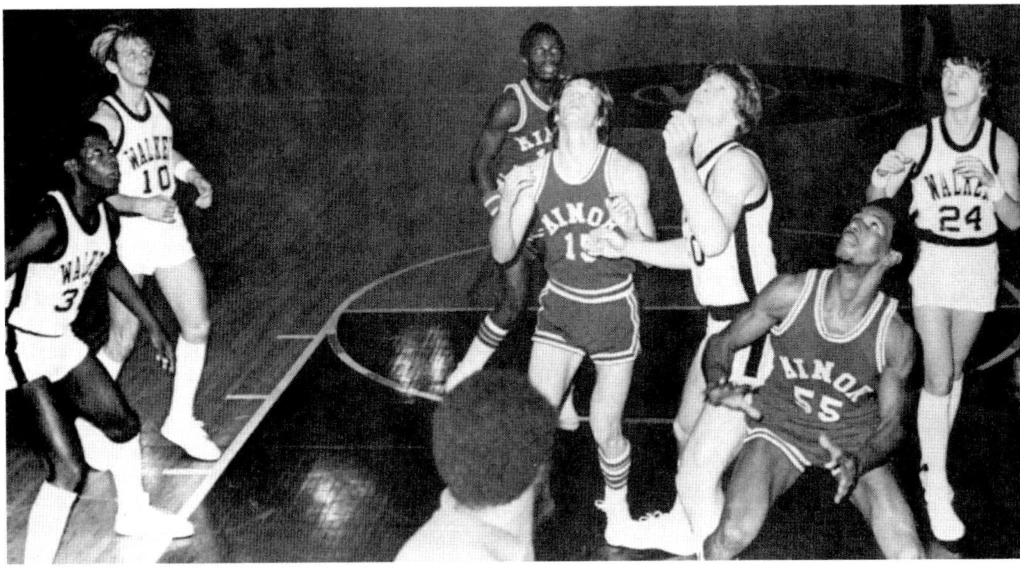

REBOUNDING, 1978–1979. One of the most important parts of the game of basketball is rebounding. Getting into position is just as important as being able to jump high, and players who are able to do both are destined to become great. Looking for the ball to come down after a shot by a Minor High School player are Reggie Cummins (31), Barry Cooner (10), Mark Fowler (50), and Dennis Naramore (24).

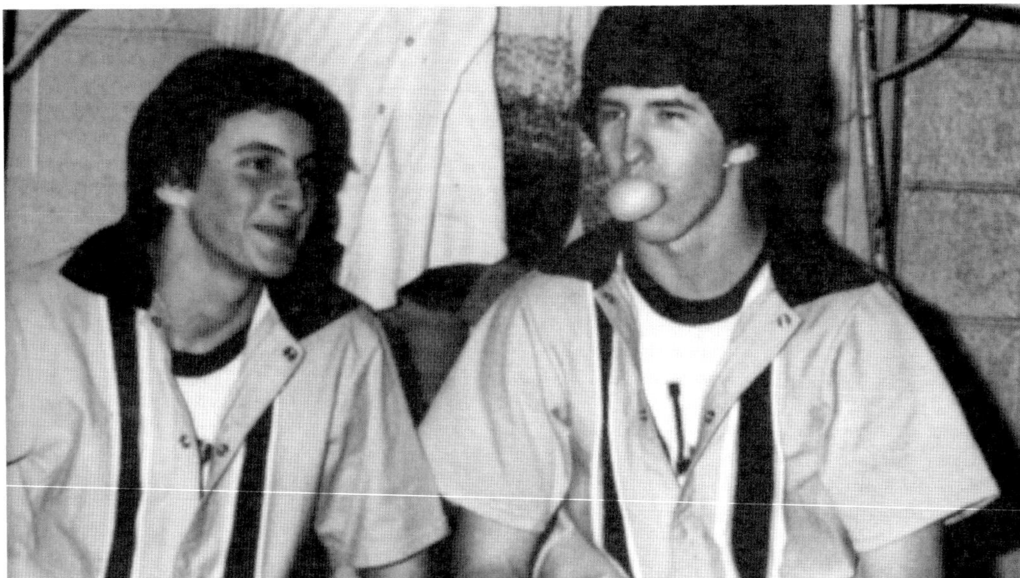

PRE-GAME PREPARATION, 1978–1979. Relaxing before the game is a good way for some players to get emotionally ready to play. At left, Stan Karabasz seems to think that the bubble being blown by Skip Roberts is entertaining. Stan not only played basketball, but he was also an outstanding tennis player for coach Pat Upton. Skip was a starter in basketball and a very successful quarterback and receiver on the football squad.

GLENN CLEM SLAMS, 1981–1982. Glen Clem shows the form he used to win the Alabama State Slam Dunk Contest at the state tournament in Montgomery. Coach Schumacher's team finished with a record of 18-10, winning both the Walker County Invitational and the tournament. Looking on with pleasure are, from left to right, Cafonza Welch (52), Terry Jackson (50), and Jeff Davis (44).

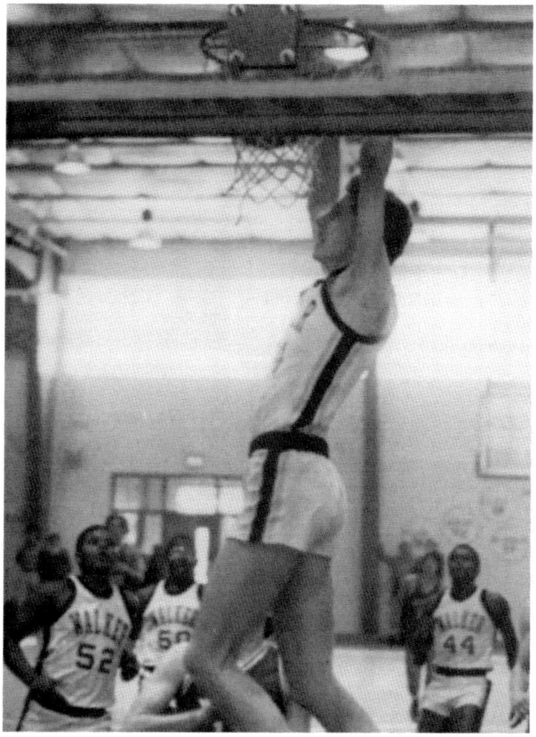

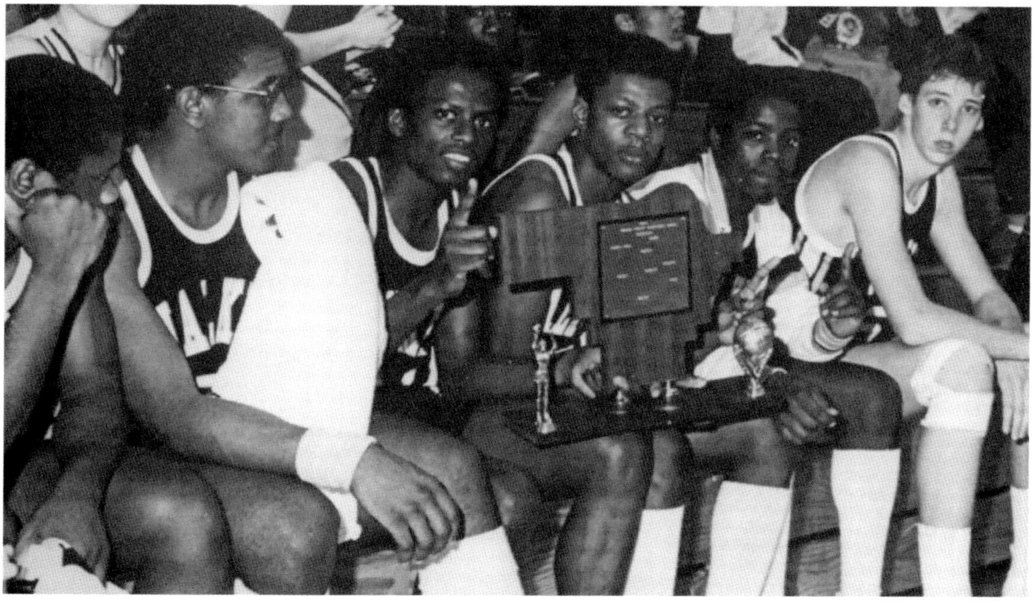

COUNTY CHAMPS, 1982–1983. Coach Schumacher's Vikings had a 19-7 record and are shown holding the championship trophy of the Walker County Tournament. From left to right are Gary McCray, Terry Jackson, Baron Farris (with trophy), Charles Gilmore, Reginald Stewart, and Glenn Clem. Glen played at Vanderbilt University before playing professional basketball. He also played on Walker's 1981 state championship golf team.

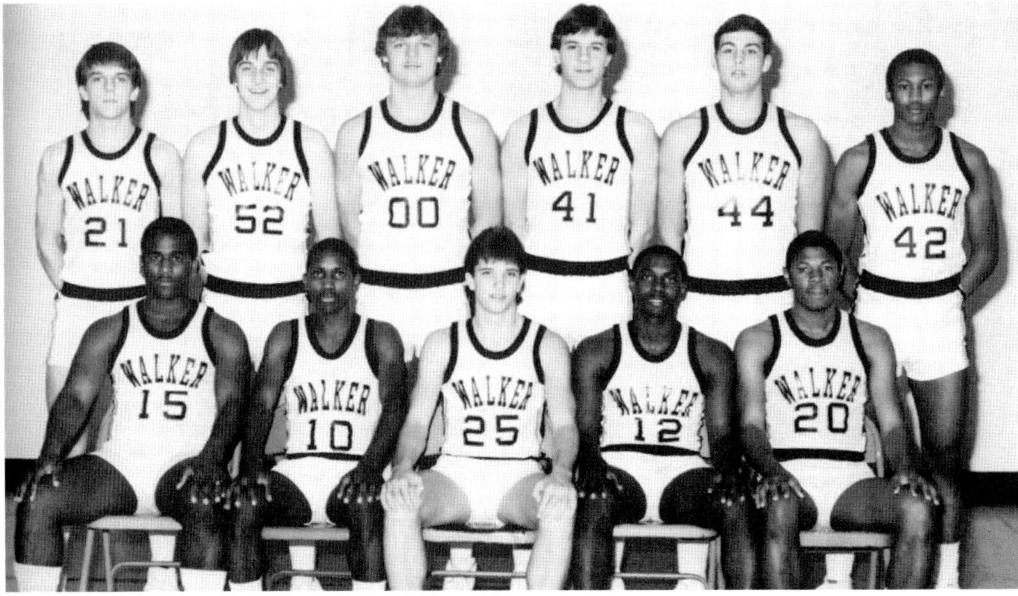

BASKETBALL TEAM, 1984–1985. These Walker County champions shot the highest free-throw percentage in coach Phil Schumacher's 21-year career. From left to right are (first row) Earl Allen, Rodney Harris, Nicky Woods, Jerry Callahan, and Nick Woods; (second row) Scott Brown, Allen Bonner, Robert Holladay, Alan Kirkpatrick, Mark Woodley, and John King. John King was Walker's all-time scoring leader with a record 1,173 points.

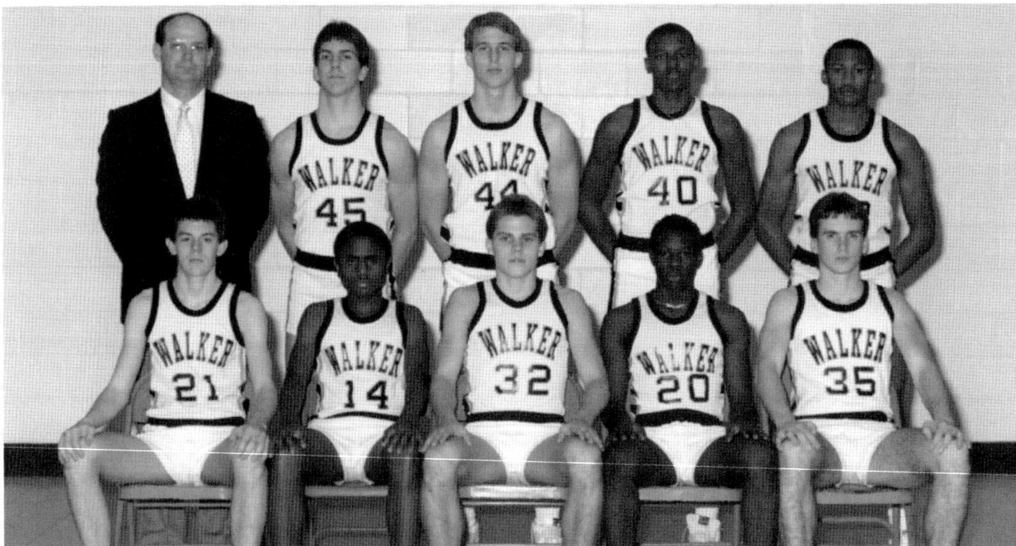

BASKETBALL TEAM, 1986–1987. This was a very good year for the Vikings; they went 18-14 and were Walker County champions. Coach Schumacher added Walker County Coach of the Year to his résumé. From left to right are (first row) Steven Fields, Anthony Harris, Stevie Mosely, Chris Cummings, and Freddie Franks; (second row) Coach Schumacher, Harry Padbury, Brad Reynolds, Tim Austin, and John King.

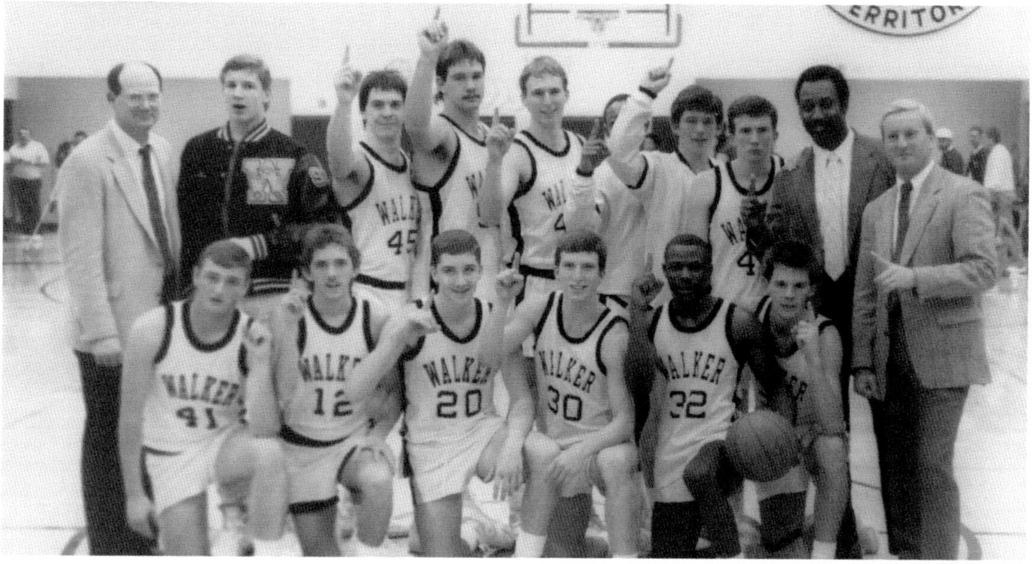

AREA CHAMPS, 1988–1989. This team was area champions and the only Schumacher-coached team to participate in the state playoffs. From left to right are (first row) Shannon Kilgore, Jeff Cooner, Chris Maddox, Phillip Rogers, Chris Cummings, and Steven Fields; (second row) Coach Schumacher, Chad Key, Harry Padbury, Shannon Pate, Brad Reynolds, Tony Chapman, Phil Hill, Paul Rogers, and coaches Vince Medlock and Jim Clark.

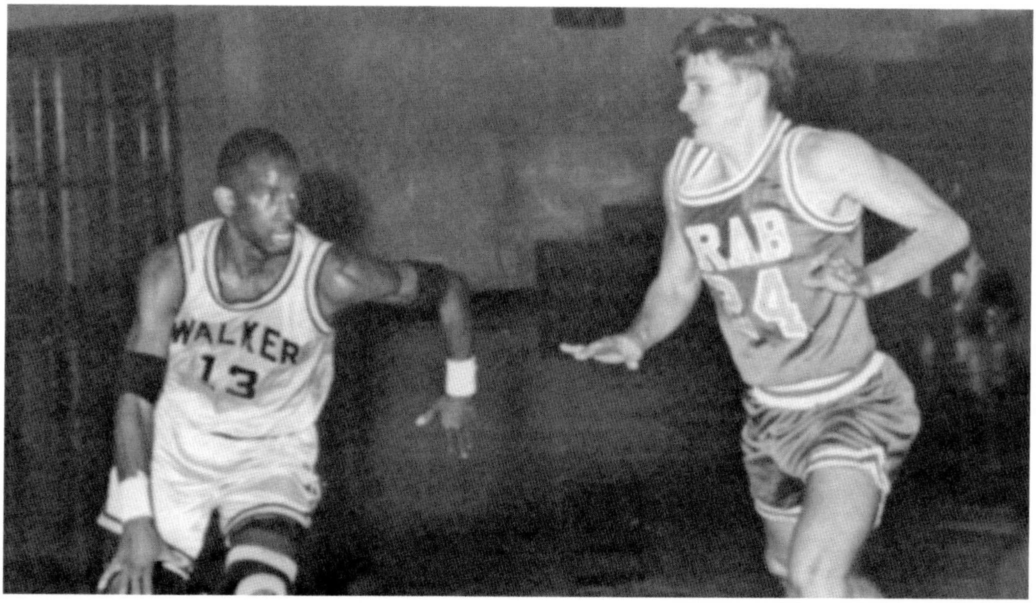

DEMETRIUS "MEAT" SHELTON, 1991–1994. A great player for the Vikings, Demetrius Shelton shows the concentration and quickness that made him a force to contend with in all sports. "Meat" had the opportunity to play football for the University of North Alabama and was an intricate part of their National Championship team as a freshman. He returned to Walker College and played basketball for legendary coach Glen Clem.

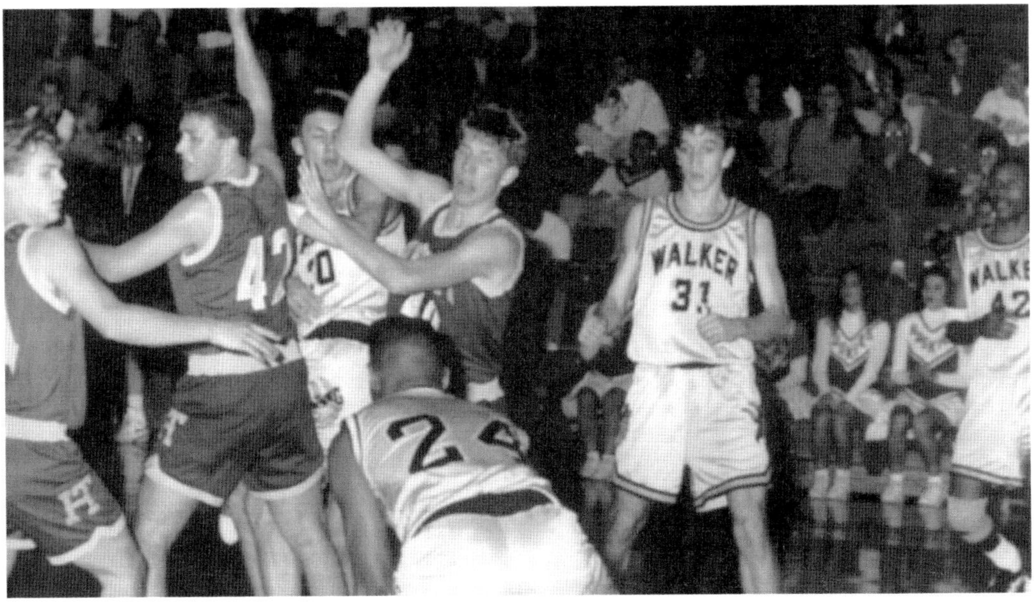

FIGHTING FOR POSITION, 1992–1993. Junior Jimbo Cunningham (30), the MVP of the area tournament, knocks around under the basket for rebounding position against Huett-Trussville as Percy Goode (24) prepares to take a shot from outside. Looking on are Josh Woodley (31) and Brandon Johnson (42). This photograph was taken in the finals of the area tournament, which Coach Schumacher's squad won.

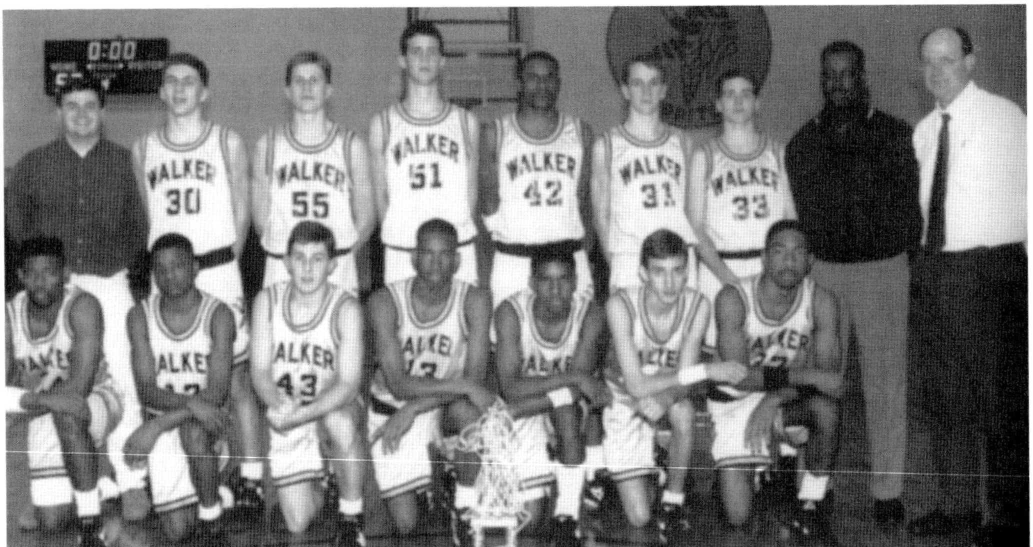

BEST RECORD, 1992–1993. This team was area champions with a 21-6 record, the best in Coach Schumacher's career. From left to right are (first row) Percy Goode, Andrea Webster, Jeremy Windham, Demetrius Shelton, Nick Hammond, Jeremy Barrentine, and Kendrick Evans; (second row) Patrick McCartney, Jimbo Cunningham, Al Blanton, Jeremy Beasley, Brandon Johnson, Josh Woodley, Kenny VanZant, and coaches Vince Medlock and Phil Schumacher.

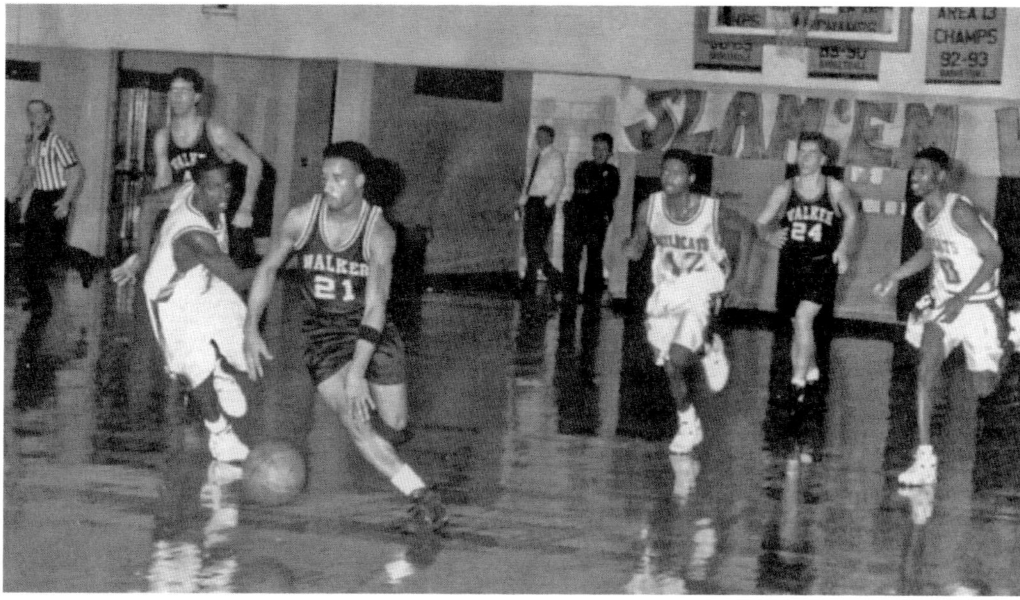

FAST BREAK, 1994–1995. Demonstrating the fast break is Jonathon Page (21) as he takes the ball to the middle of the court. Jeremy Beasley (51, at far left) fills the right outside lane, and Chris Berry (24) trails. This worked well against this Tuscaloosa County High School Wildcat team. Jeremy played at Auburn University, while Chris went to Walker College, where he played on the last team coached by the legendary Glen Clem.

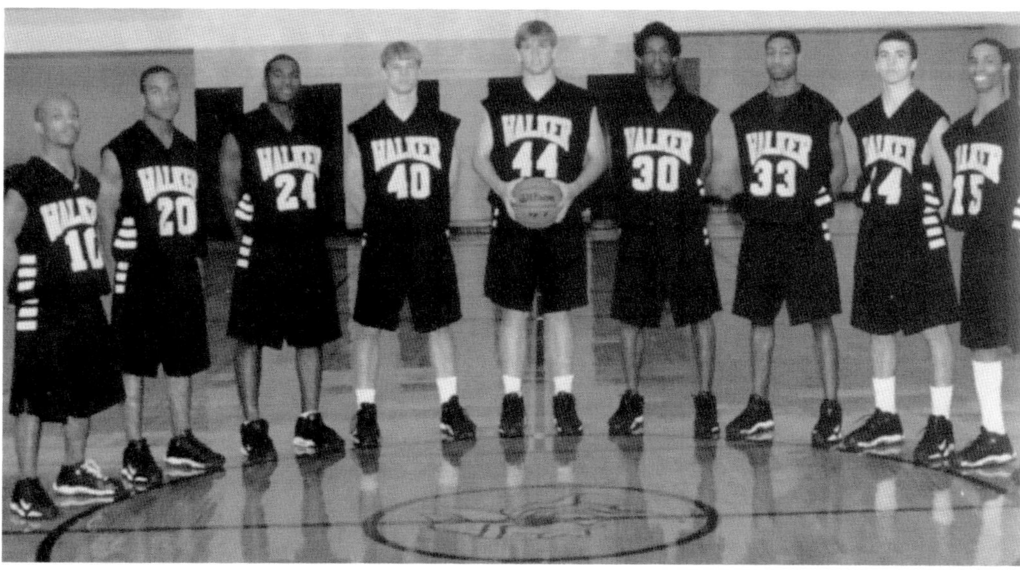

BASKETBALL TEAM, 1998–1999. This Donnie Goodson–coached team was a small team by modern standards, but they made up for their size with aggressive play. From left to right are guard Glenn Jones, guard Brian Hankins, forward Marcus Shanklin, forward Chad Borden, center-forward Jed Allen, center-forward David Cherry, forward Lee Medlock, forward Keith VanZant, and guard Darrell Flemming.

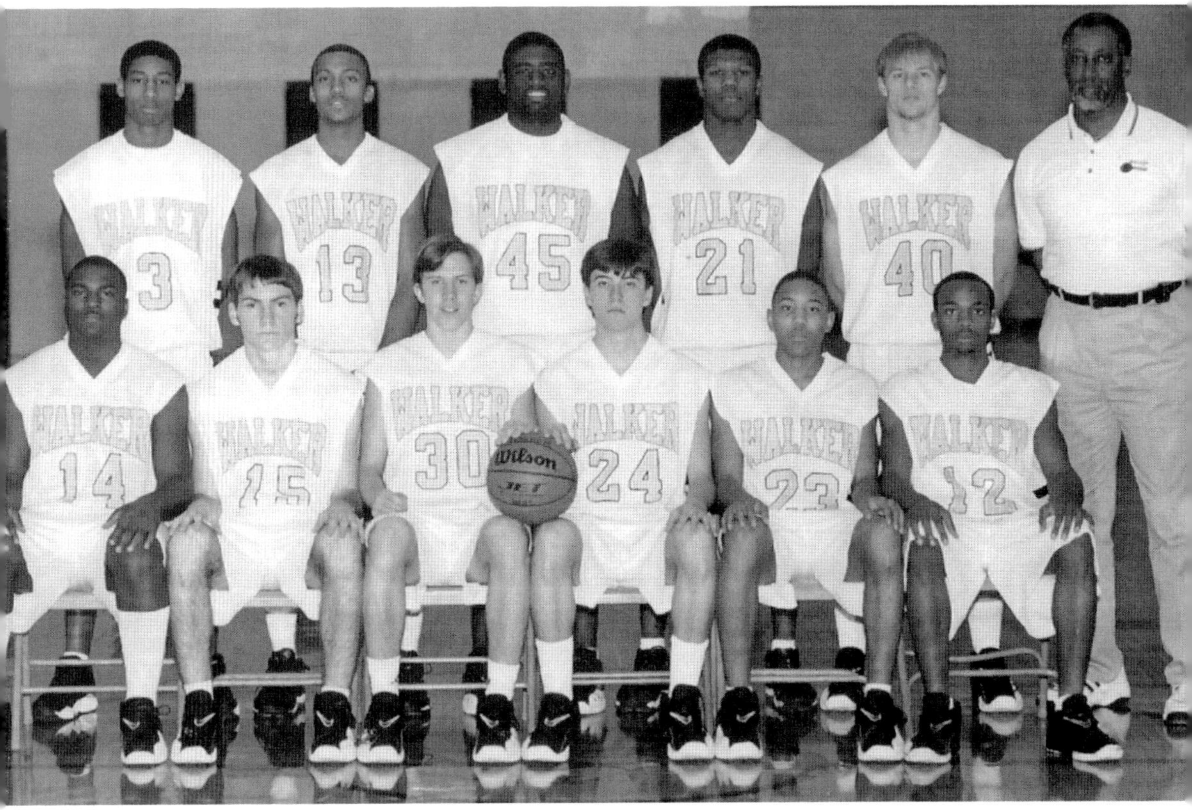

Last Team of the Millennium, 1999–2000. This team had the first African American head basketball coach at Walker. Vincent Medlock played basketball and football and ran track at Walker. He broke the color barrier in basketball when he participated on the junior-varsity squad in 1968, and in his senior year, he was president of the student affairs committee. He played basketball and football at Alabama A&M University. Vince was at various times the boys' "B" team basketball coach, head girls' basketball coach, head track coach, and finally the boys' head coach in 1999. The first team he coached is pictured above; from left to right are (first row) Marcus Shanklin, Kevin Richardson, Ricky Taylor, David Cain, Don Reed, and D. J. Smith; (second row) Lee Medlock, Ahmad Flemming, Spencer Evans, Eric Oliver (who had a great career in football as a defensive back at the University of Mississippi), Chad Borden (who played football at Livingston State University), and Coach Medlock.

6

Walker High School Spirit

1920–2000

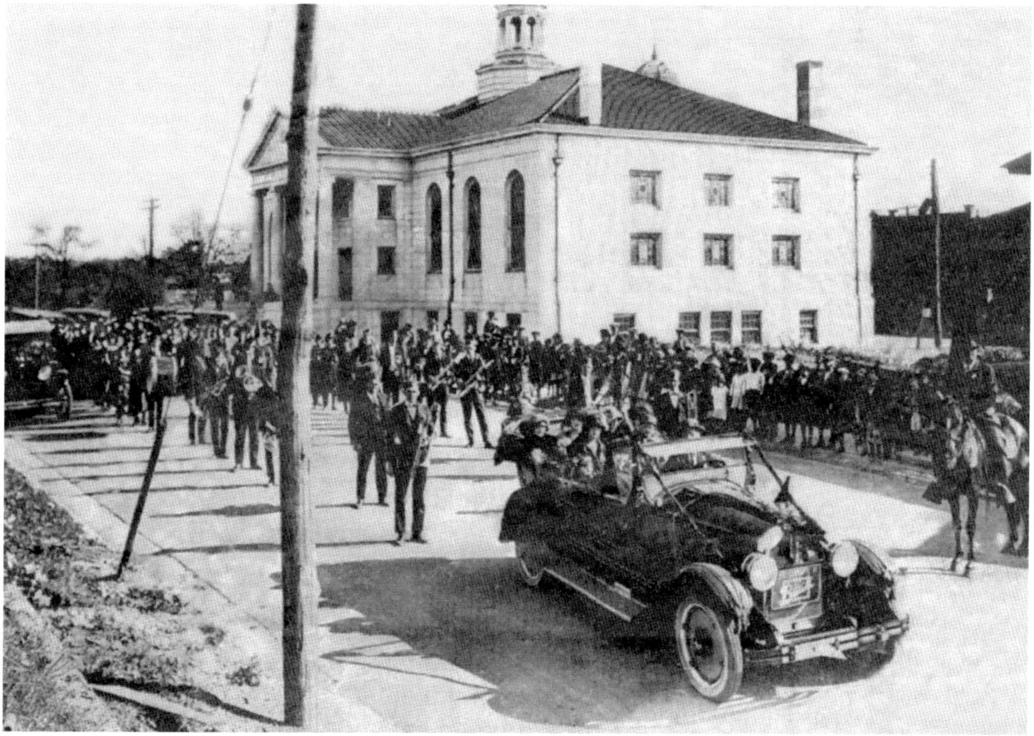

Homecoming Parade, 1923. Riding in the Buick convertible furnished by Sidney Preston are football sponsor Hazel Butler and her maids, Eva Musgrove and Eula Brele Broom. Mayor Jack Cranford, on his horse, watches the parade go north on Third Avenue past the United Methodist church in downtown Jasper. That evening, Walker played its first game in the new Ki-Ro Field stadium against Fayette, winning by a score of 7-0. Previously, games had been played at Cranford Field, affectionately known as Cranford's Cow Pasture.

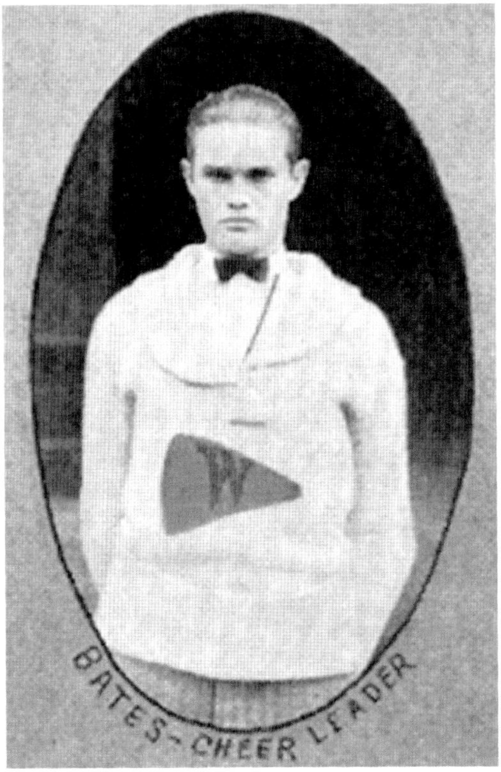

WALKER'S FIRST CHEERLEADER, 1924. Jesse Bates was Walker's first cheerleader in 1924. Unlike modern cheerleader squads that are usually made up of 8 to 20 members, early teams usually had only one or two cheerleaders who actually lead cheers. There were no routines, stunts, gymnastics, or dance competition, so they blended into the crowd, periodically surfacing to lead a cheer.

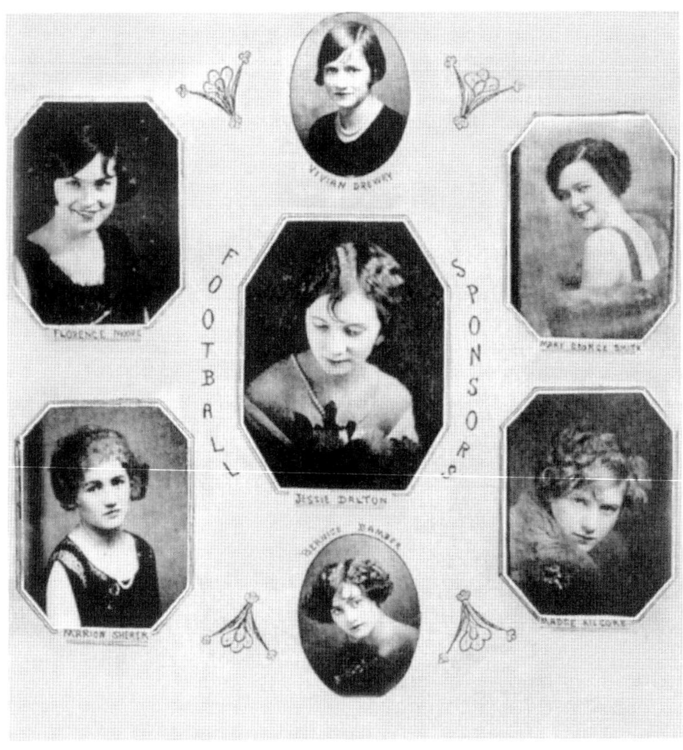

SPONSOR AND HER COURT, 1925. Pictured at right (center) is 1925 football sponsor Jessie Dalton; in the outside circle clockwise from top are court members Vivian Drewey, Mary George Smith, Madre Kilgore, Bernice Bamber, Marion Sherer, and Florence Moore. These young ladies were chosen by the student body in much the same fashion as today's homecoming queen and her court.

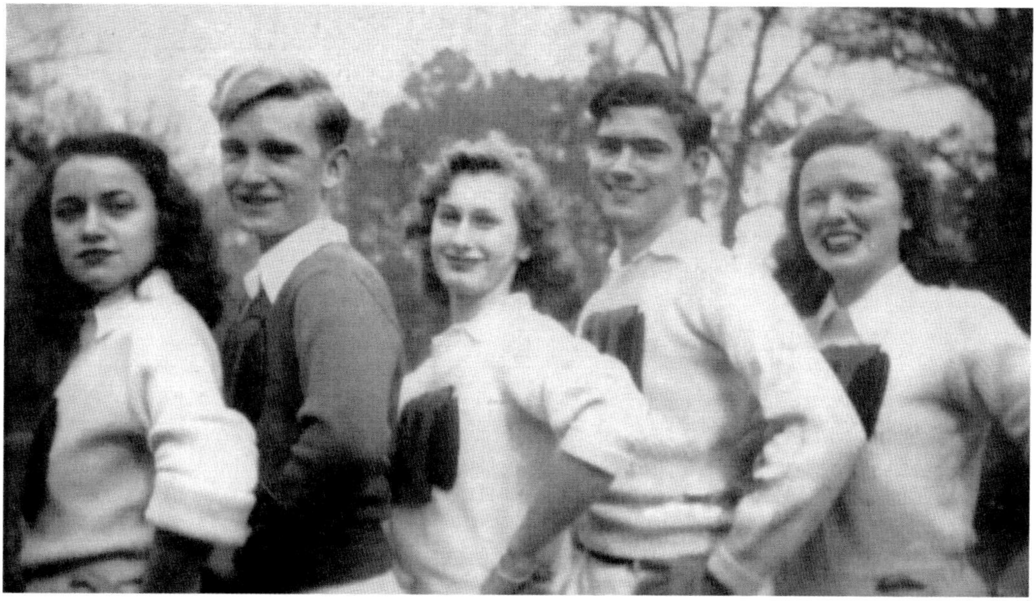

CHEERLEADERS, 1945–1946. Cheerleaders are always a big boost for the team, and this group was evidently effective, because their football team, coached by Harry Erwin, posted a 7-2-1 record. Pictured above from left to right are Nancy McConnico, Hayden Price, Mildred Wilson, Charles Rollins, and Hallie Brown. Hallie was selected homecoming queen and married T. D. Norris, later a Walker Hall of Fame member.

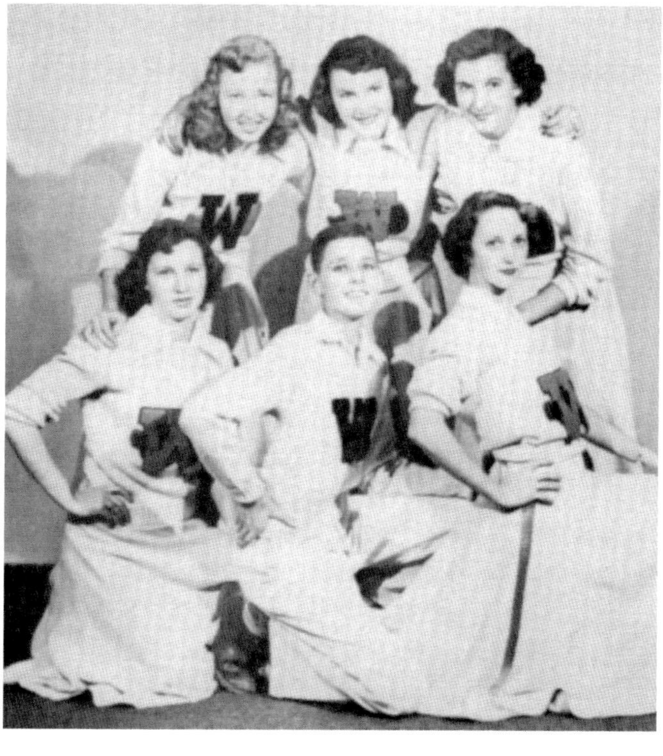

CHEERLEADING SQUAD 1950–1951. Walker had a down year in football, making a tough year for cheerleaders, but with their support and spirit, the basketball team came back with a 20-win season and captured the Walker County championship. Cheerleaders for 1951 are, from left to right (first row) Vinita Burton, J. W. Ellis, and head Billie Ruth Deason; (second row) Lula Mae Cagle, Eleanor Ashmore, and Betty Winters.

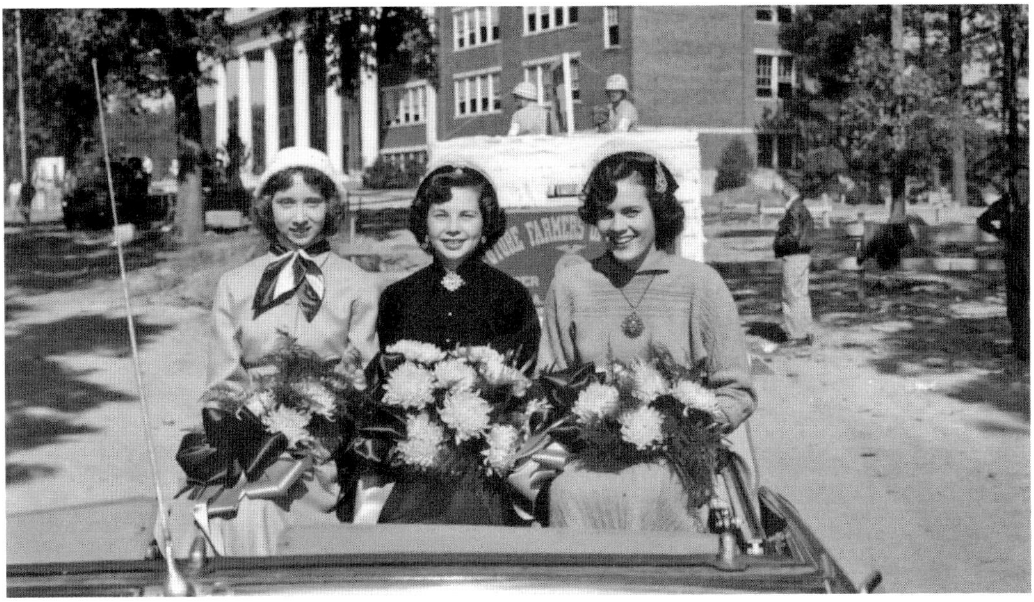

FOOTBALL SPONSORS, 1953. Football sponsors were very special to the football players because they personally selected these girls to represent the entire team. The sponsors were on rare occasions escorted to the homecoming ceremonies by members of the football team, but they were usually escorted by popular members of the student body. Riding in the convertible are, from left to right, Sadie Best, Pat Humphries, and Barbara Drummond.

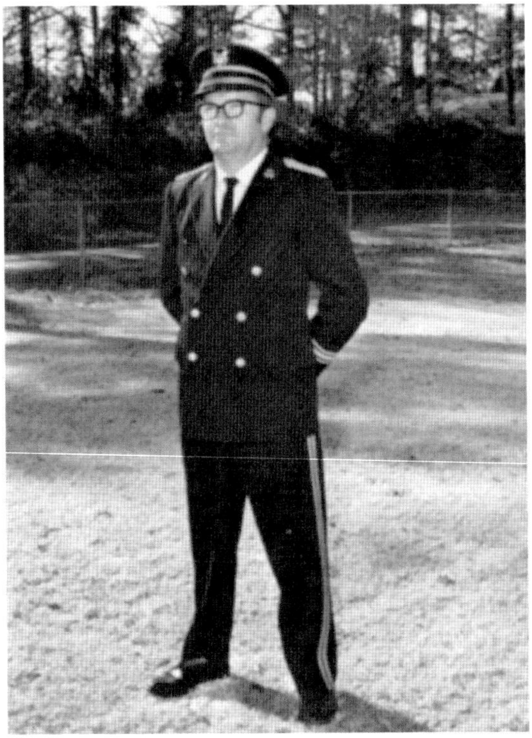

BAND DIRECTOR GEORGE PATRIDGE, 1959–1984. George led Walker's band through much of her glory days. He was that rare individual that was liked by coaches, players, band members, and parents. George loved Walker and he loved music, making him the perfect candidate for Walker band director. After retirement, he continued his love of music by playing in a professional jazz band with fellow Walker retiree Rex Brown. (Courtesy of WCHS.)

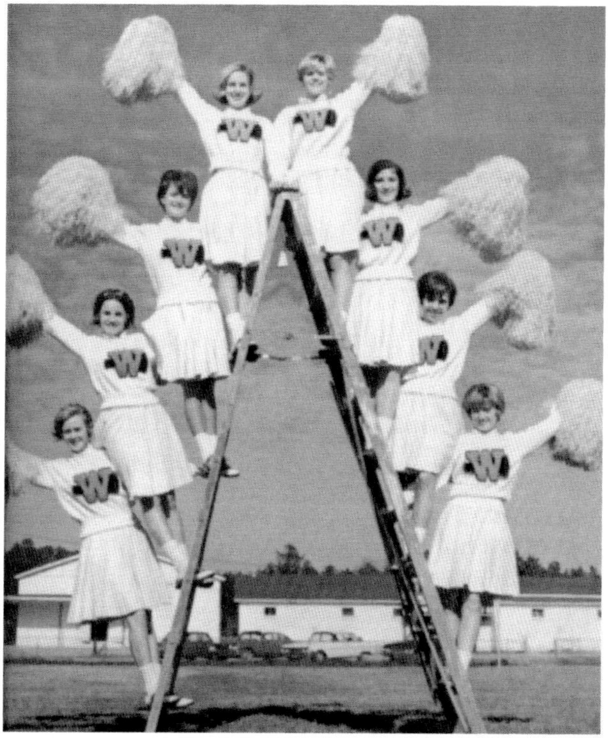

CHEERLEADER SQUAD, 1965–1966. These Walker cheerleaders are shown making the closest thing to a pyramid that the state of Alabama would allow them to perform; pyramids were discontinued because of the associated dangers. Clockwise from the bottom left of the ladder are Mary Catherine Conner, Sally Brotherton, Toni Chapman, Brenda Lewis, Cindy Caldwell, Margaret Hiller, Jeannie Lee, and Lizabeth Maddox.

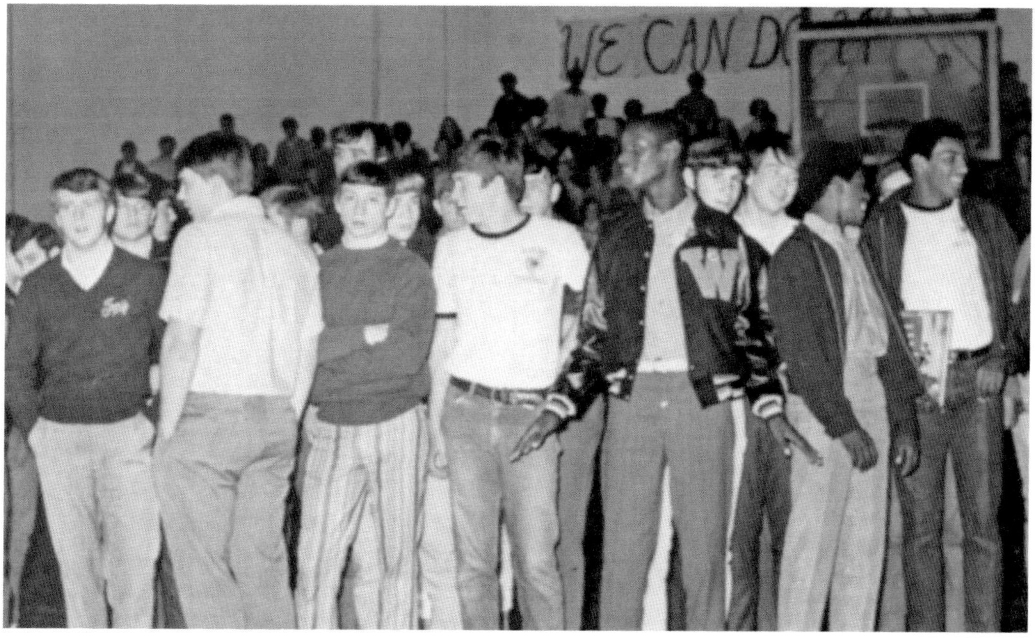

PEP RALLY, 1969. Players prepare to play the game differently. Most enjoy the Friday pep rally, when students, faculty, and parents scream at the top of their lungs to prepare these young men for battle. From left to right are Tony Swindle, Gary Akin, Jack Bankhead, Johnny Caldwell, Manley Cook, Donnie Morgan, John Jenkins, Ross Marlow, Henry Williams, and Will Fuller.

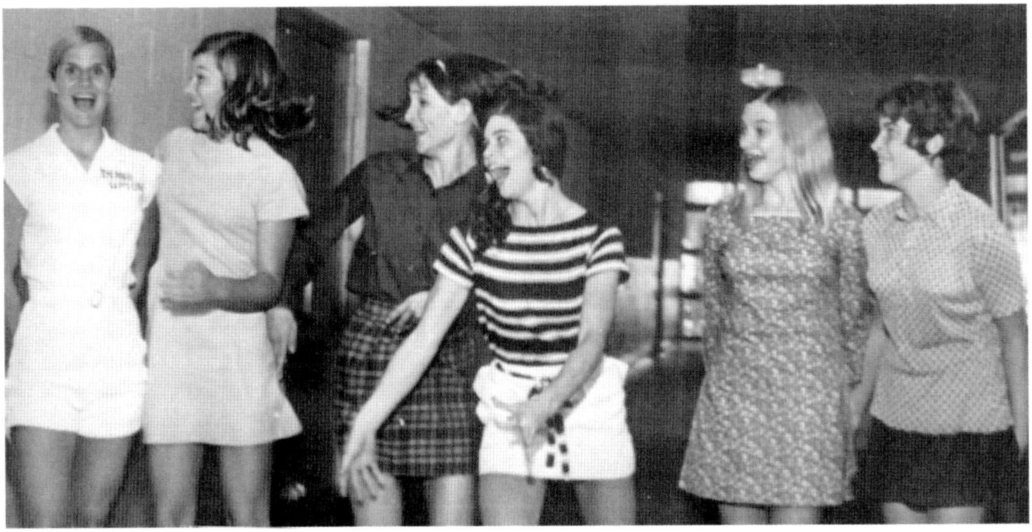

HEAD CHEERLEADER SELECTION, 1970. This group of B-team cheerleaders seems to be surprised and thrilled at the selection of Debbie Upton as the head cheerleader for the 1970–1971 season. From left to right are head Debbie Upton, Connie Lockhart, Carolyn Tidwell, Chris Cameron, Pat Brisco, and Joan Legg. Cheerleaders have to be popular with all students, be very skilled gymnasts, and possess a great work ethic.

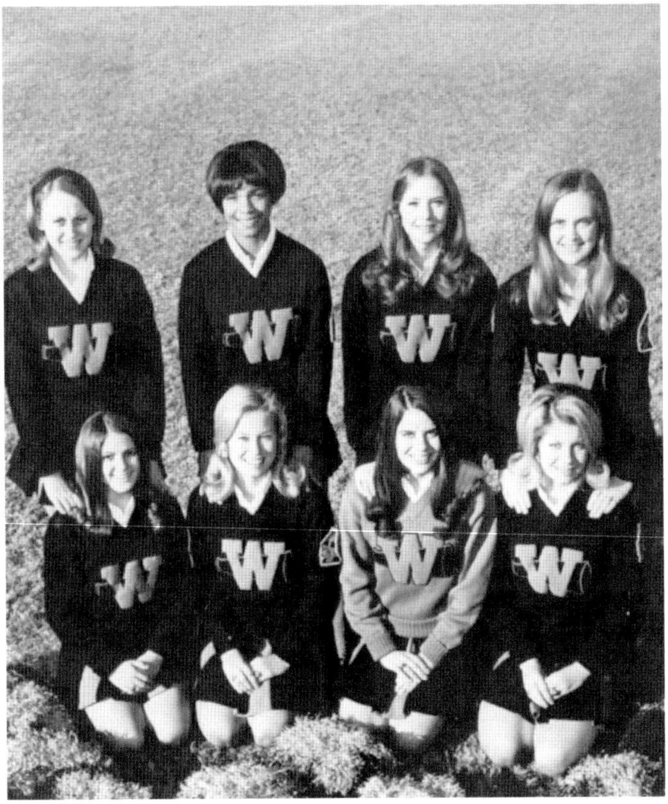

FIRST INTEGRATED CHEERLEADER SQUAD, 1970. Walker saw integration as a natural and necessary step in race relations. From left to right are (first row) Libby Brignet, cohead Debbie Young, head Vickie Lee, and Stacia Gambrell; (second row) Doris Akins, Sandra Powell, Melissa Oliver, and Marchetta Shurbitt. The credit for this smooth transition goes to sponsor Callie Sue Brakefield and the wonderful spirit of all these young ladies.

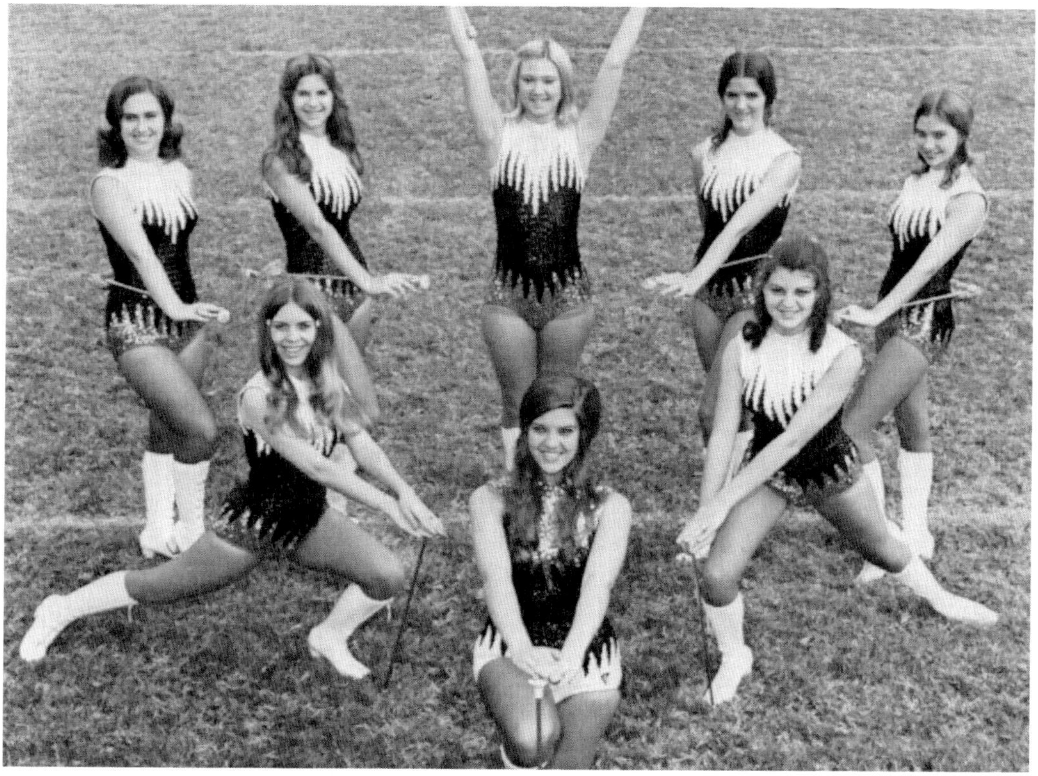

MAJORETTES, 1973. A major attraction during the halftime of any football game is the presentation of the band and especially the majorettes. No group of majorettes drew more attention than those above. In front of the group is head majorette Nancy Primm. From left to right are (first row) Pattie Davis and Carlene Key; (second row) Malea Stevenson, Linda McKellar, Susan Sims, Vicki Anderson, and Pat Briscoe.

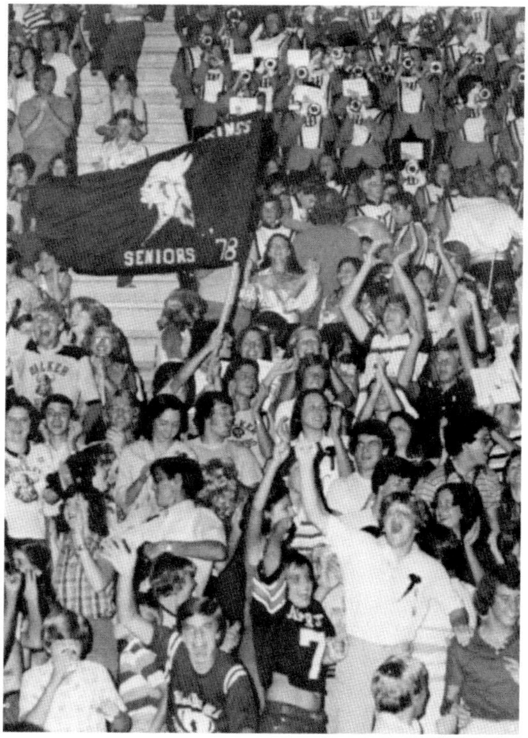

SEMIFINALS OF STATE PLAYOFFS, 1977. Fan support and enthusiasm helped Walker to become the North Alabama football champions and runners-up in the state 6-A playoffs. Walker trailed Decatur at halftime, but led by teacher James Davidson, the frenzied crowd inspired the Vikings to a brilliant double-overtime, come-from-behind victory, keeping their playoff hopes alive. These young fans enjoy the excitement.

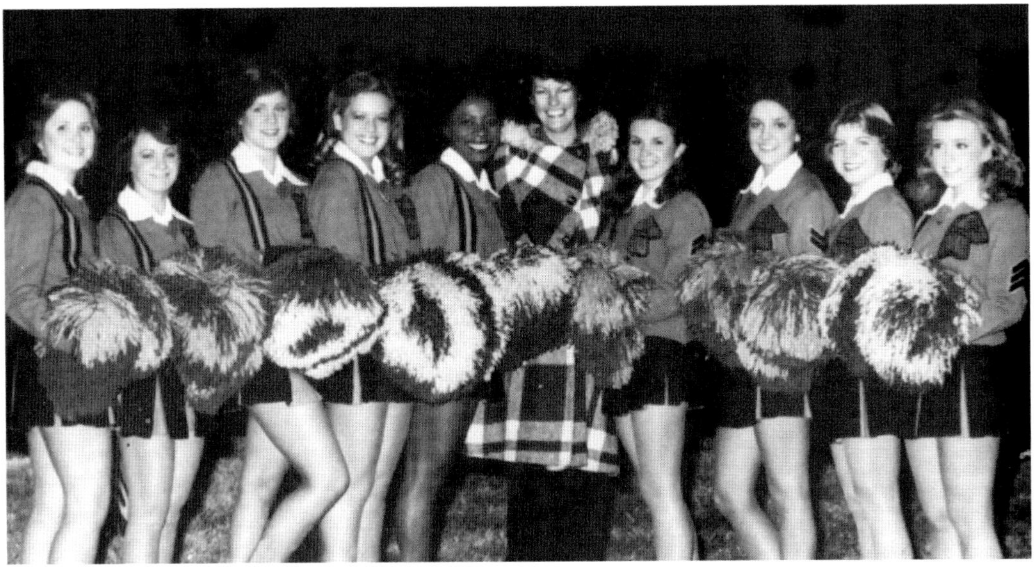

CHEERLEADERS, 1980. Cheerleading can be very rewarding, as well as emotionally draining and a lot of work and frustration. Having to cheer at games in the pouring rain can even be hazardous to your health. This group of hard-working and hard-cheering girls are, from left to right, Terri Banks, Rhonda Duncan, Regina Nuss, Donna Baxter, Sonja Elliott, sponsor Shirley Davis, Kim Guthrie, Robin Baker, Carol Richardson, and Diana Sanderson.

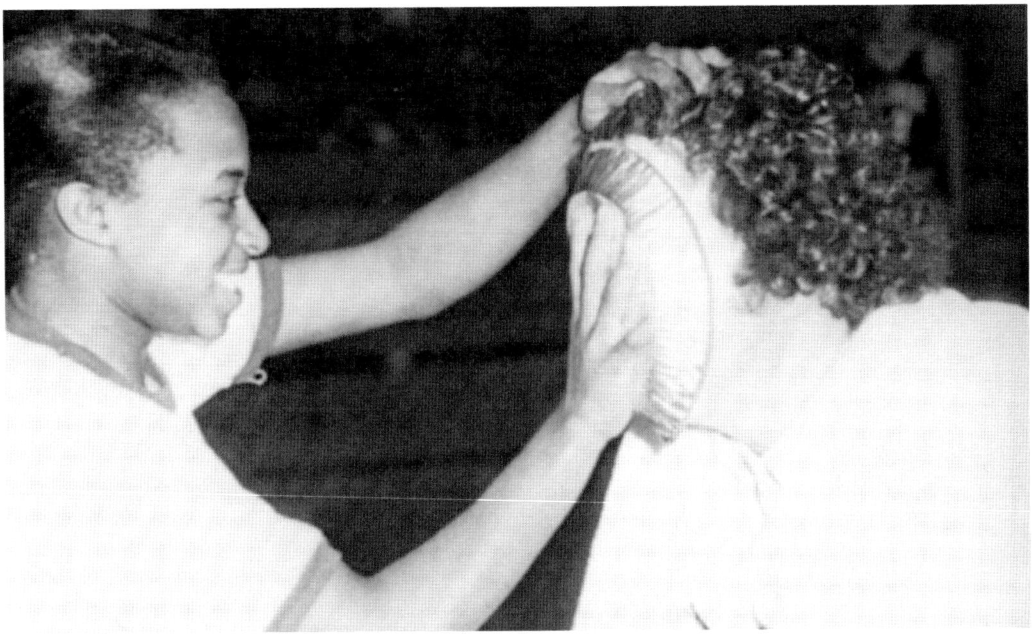

PIE IN THE FACE, 1982. Peggy Keebler seems to be enjoying paying coach David Campbell off on a bet she won. She defeated him in a free-throw contest at halftime and rewarded him with a pie in the face. Peggy won a national free-throw competition despite the fact that Walker had no girls' basketball program. She became the all-time scoring leader at the University of Montevallo.

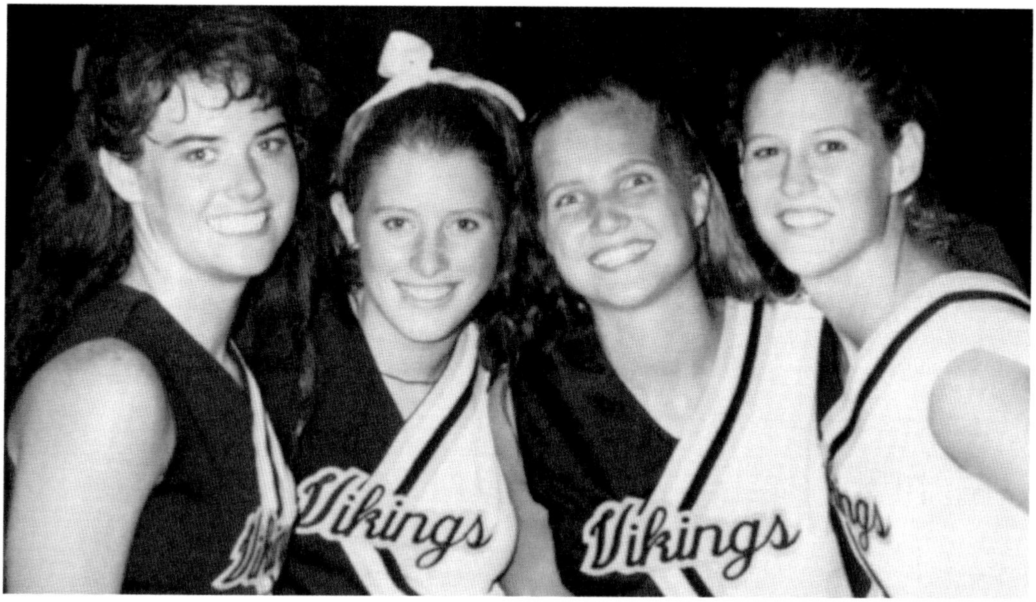

CHEERLEADING FRIENDSHIPS, 1991. Friendships formed during high school cheerleading last a lifetime because the time spent working together and the dedication it takes form bonds not easily broken. Friends formed by that lasting bond are, from left to right, lawyer Molly Williams, Dixie Lollar, Kitten Morrison, and Brandy Long—Lollar, Morrison, and Long are teachers and mothers. All four have remained close friends through the years.

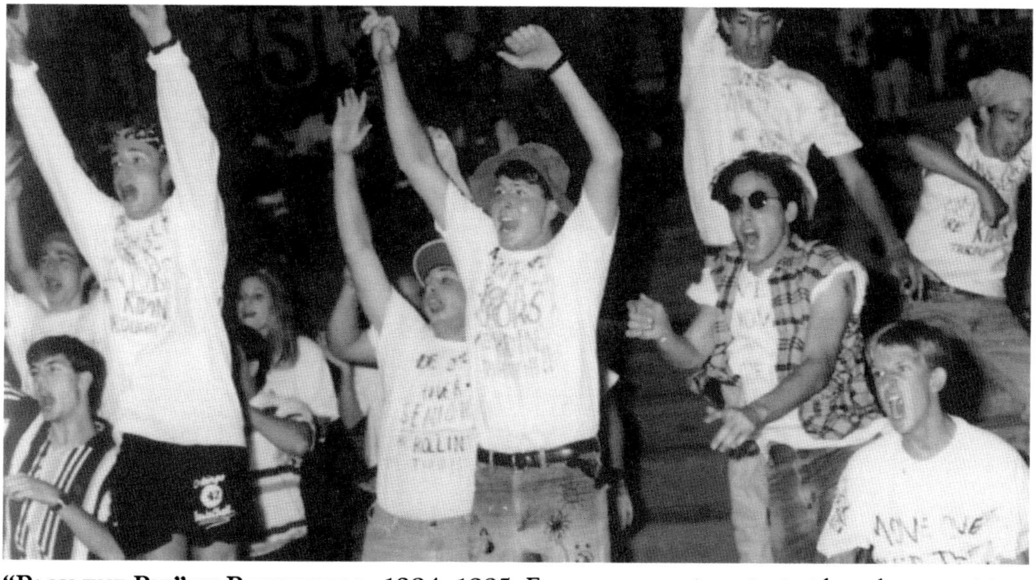

"PACK THE PIT" IN BASKETBALL, 1994–1995. Fans can sometimes intimidate the opposition, as these young Viking supporters are attempting to do. This phenomena, called "packing the pit," was instigated by Viking head coach Phil Schumacher. His teams produced some outstanding upsets at this event. Pictured from left to right are Adam Hadder, Marc Rollins, Jed Adams, Patrick Tyner, and Bryan Thompson showing that wild Viking spirit.

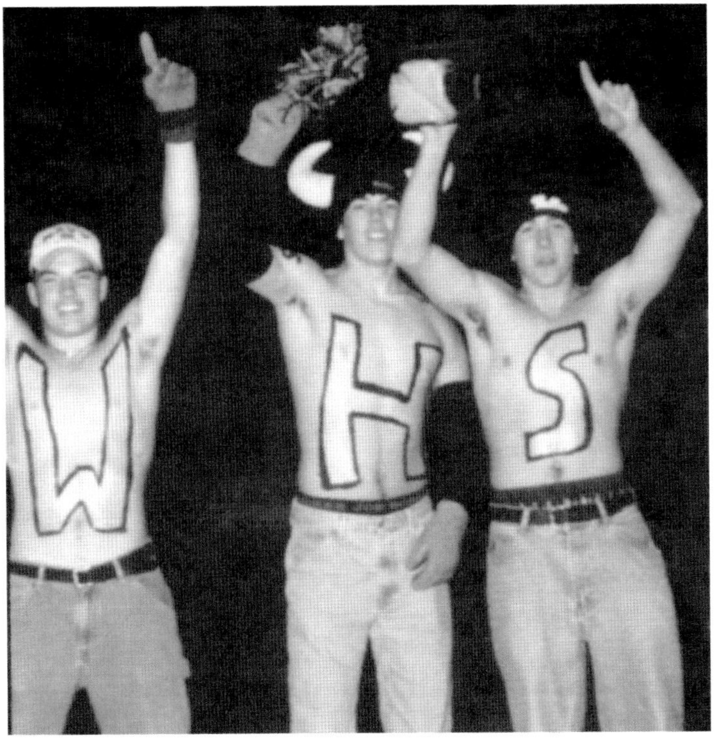

RADICAL FANS, 1999. One of the most anticipated events in recent memory at Walker was the 1999 football game with Etowah High of Gadsden, mainly because of a running back from Etowah named Carthell "Cadillac" Williams, rumored to be the best back since Walker's Linnie Patrick. Pictured from left to right showing support for their team are Walker's baseball players and fans Colby Grelle, Andy Byars, and Kyle Kilgore.

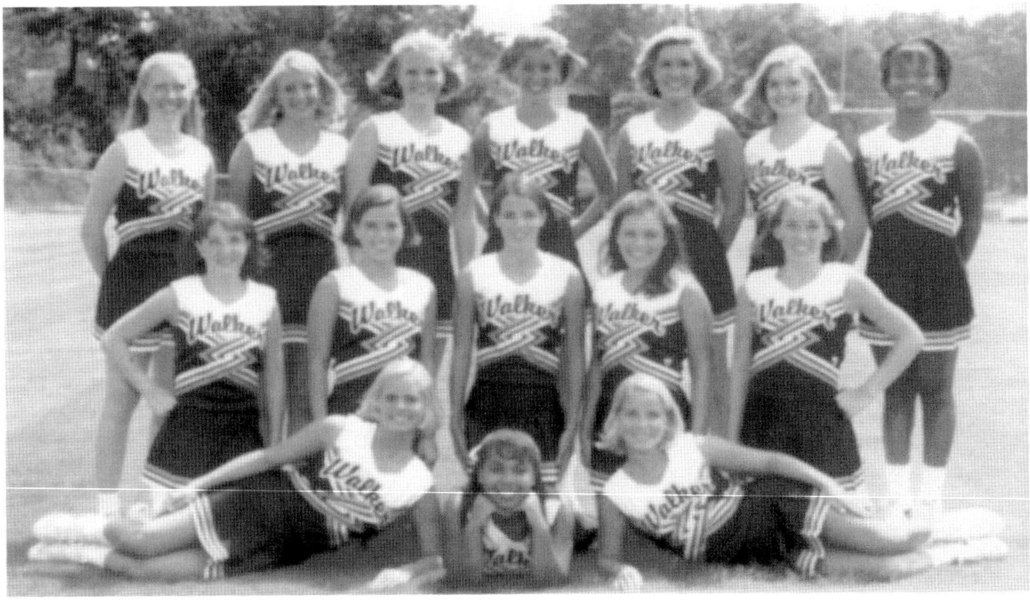

END OF THE MILLENNIUM, 2000. The last cheerleading squad of the 20th century is, from left to right (first row) Anna Kate Laskoski, Tajay White, and Ginger Swiney; (second row) Jennifer Boshell, Caroline Thornley, Julie Tracy, Haley Howell, and Kristy Beall; (third row) Laurel Price, Allison Taylor, Ashley Garrett, Katy Gambrell, Lindsey Cunningham, Lisa Gilchrist, and Lindsey McWhorter (daughter of Walker's first black cheerleader).

7

Other Men's Sports

1920–2000

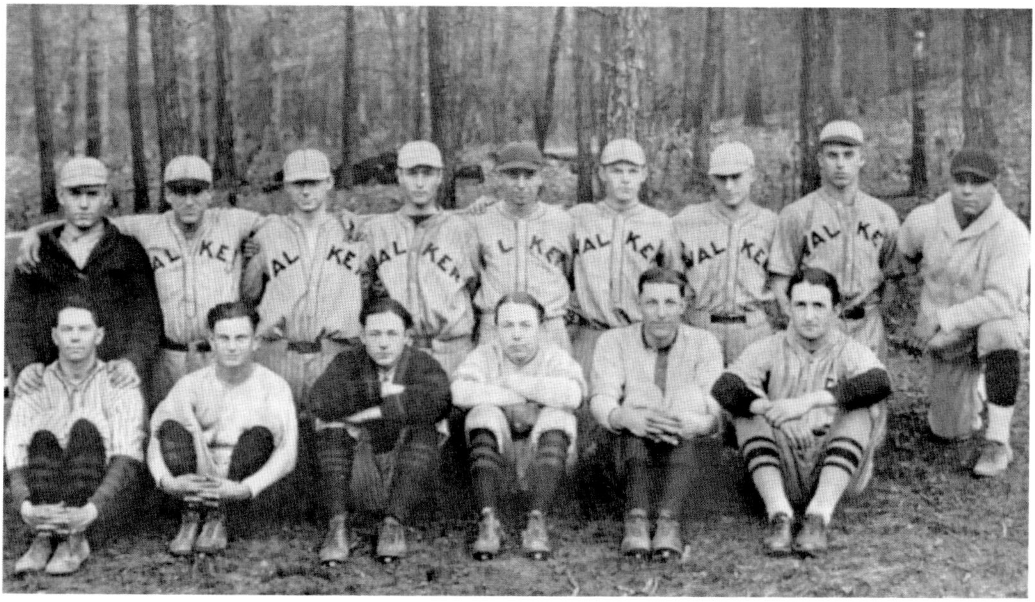

Baseball Team, 1923. This early photograph of Walker's baseball team shows (in no particular order) Ollie Staggs, first base; Joe Legg, second base; Ben Sankey, shortstop; John Roquemore, third base; George Sanderson, left field; Edgar Cain, center field; Stanley Freeman, right field; John Lollar, catcher; Criner South, pitcher; Cush Woods, pitcher; Willie Borden, pitcher; A. J. McDanal, utility; Bass Stokes, utility; and coach Eddie McLane.

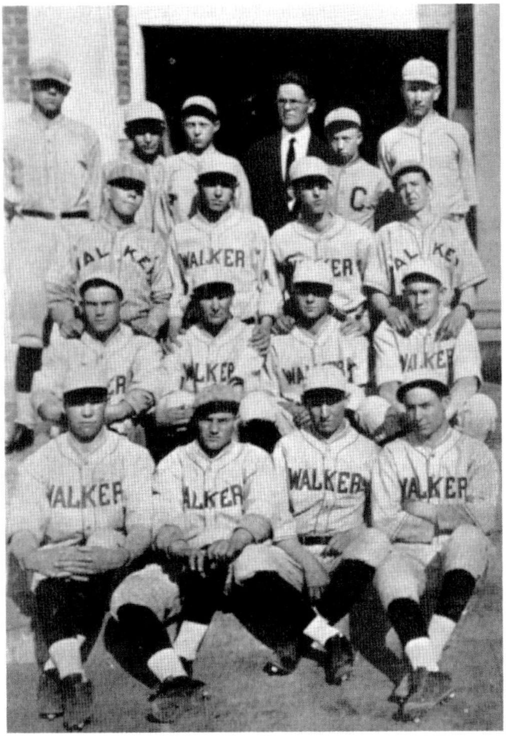

BASEBALL TEAM, 1925. Members of this power-hitting 1925 team are, in no particular order, (infield) Jess Bates, Clarence Lowell Edgil, Lowell Nichols, Jess Hudson, A. J. McDanal, Hilliard Tubbs, and Paul Smith; (outfield) Lon Richardson, George Sanderson, Leonard Hutto, and Carl Smith; (pitchers) Taylor Smith, Clarence Edgil, and Tom Grey; (catchers) Earnest Cain and Allen Pope; and head coach John C. Goodwin.

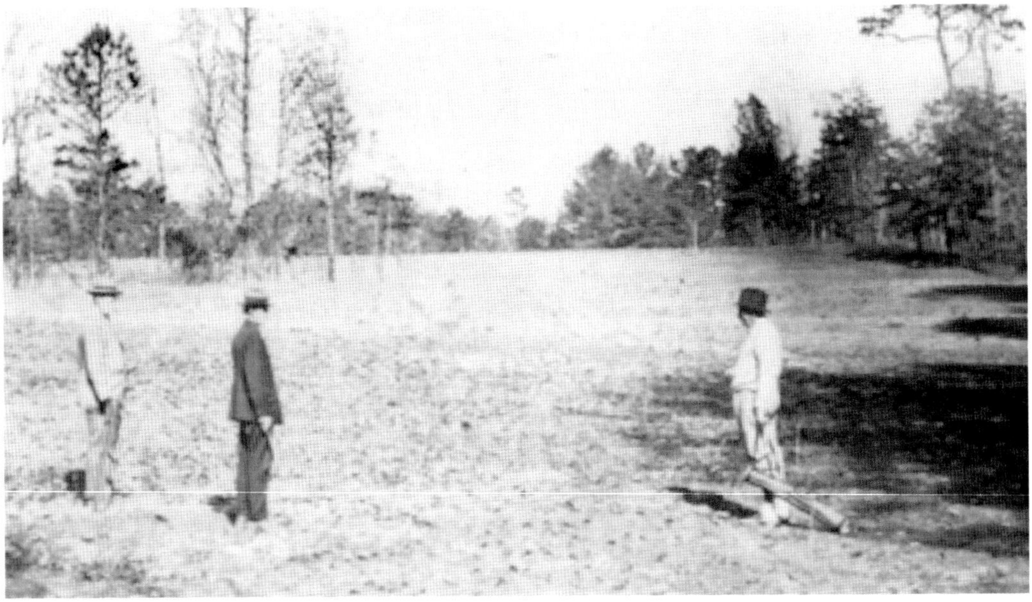

MUSGROVE GOLF COURSE, 1926. Between 1924 and 1926, local entrepreneur L. B. Musgrove built what was to become the home course for the Walker Viking golf team at his private estate in Manchester. Though it would be nearly 50 years before it was used, he laid the groundwork for Walker High School's successful golf program. From left to right are unidentified, Thomas P. Scruggs, and L. B. Musgrove.

Herbert Burton, Track, 1939. Herbert was captain of both the track and football teams at Walker. He was a four-sport letterman at Auburn University, where he captained the track team in 1943 and won five medals at the Southeastern Conference championship meet (a record at that time). He is best known as the author of the highly acclaimed children's book *The Adventures of Dixie North*. (Courtesy of WCHS.)

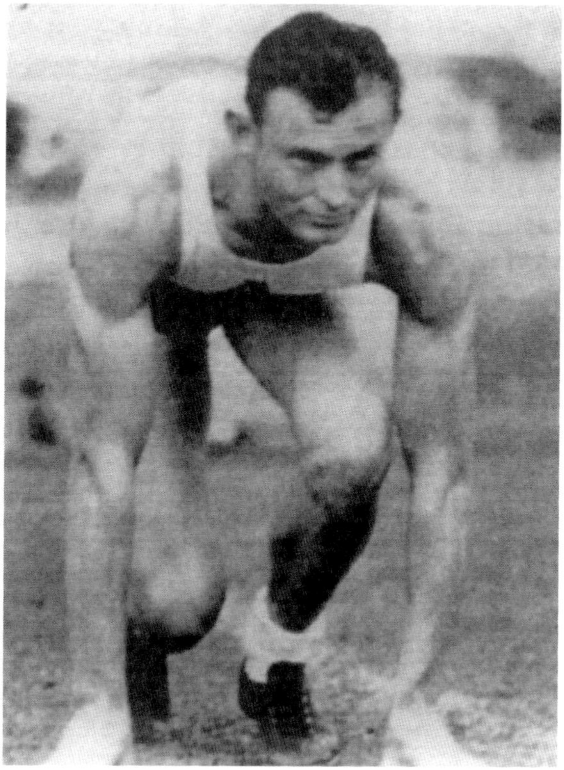

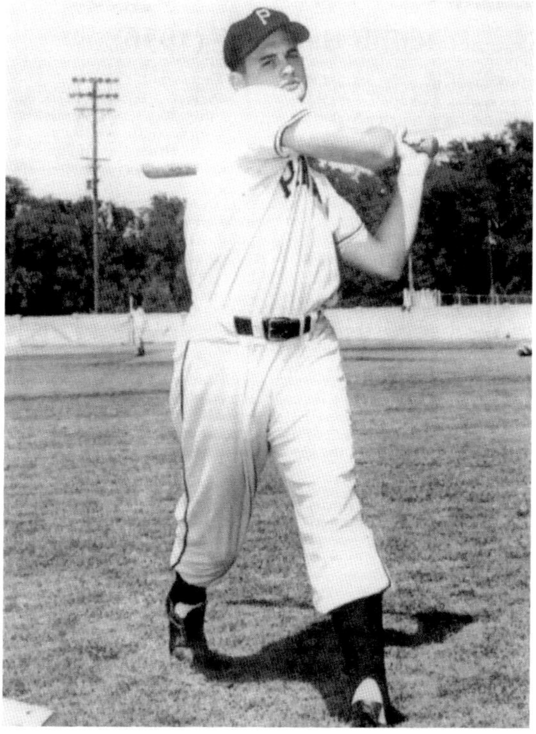

Segal Drummond, Baseball, 1949. Segal is considered one of the five best baseball players in the history of Walker County. He played in the East-West All-Star game at Rickwood Field for an unprecedented three straight years. He was picked as a prize rookie out of New Orleans along with Mickey Mantle and Billy Martin but gave up a budding baseball career to return and help shore up the family coal business.

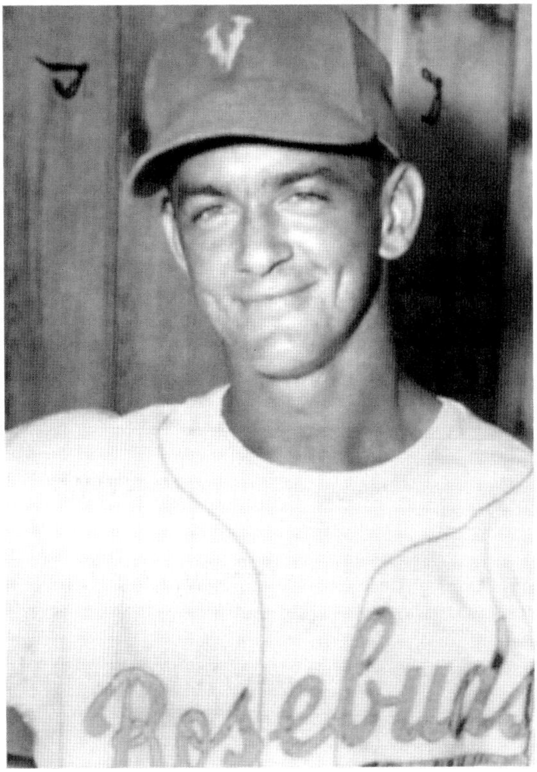

Ed Richardson, Baseball, 1951. Ed is another one of the five best baseball players in the history of Walker County. He lettered four years at Walker before going on to an outstanding career in professional baseball. He was a great glove man and a reliable hitter for many years at the AA level. Ed ended his career in the old Southern League in an age when there were only 16 major-league teams.

Walker's First Golf Team, 1963. Walker's first golf team was organized, coached, and scheduled by a young golfer named Alec Grant. Because of his love of and dedication to the sport, Walker developed into one of the most feared programs in the state. Team members are, from left to right, Bill Gwin, Richard Mooney, Bill James, Alec Grant, Sidney Reich, John Underwood, Greg Coons, Pat Martin, John Fite, and Jimmy Carmichael.

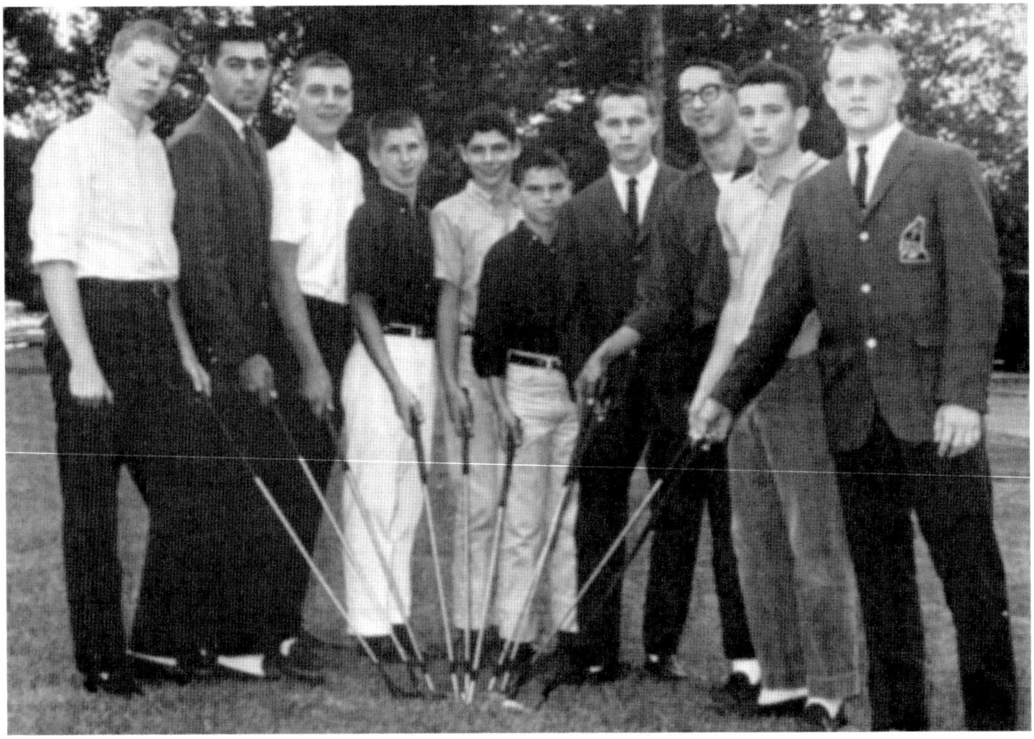

GENE RABURN, TRACK, 1963. Gene was a four-sport letterman at Walker, being selected All-State in both football and track. He played in the Alabama State All-Star Classic in football and set the state record in the long jump at the state track meet. Gene was awarded a scholarship for both football and track at the University of Alabama, where he was a member of two Bear Bryant–coached National Championship teams.

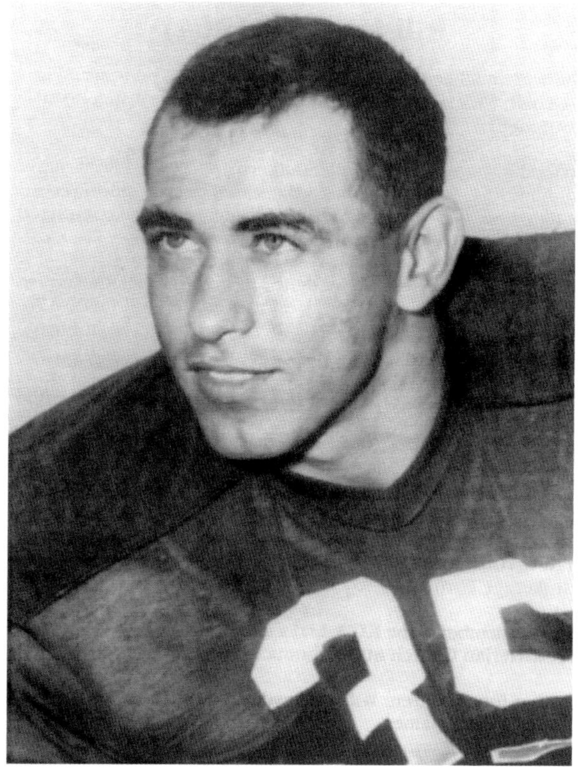

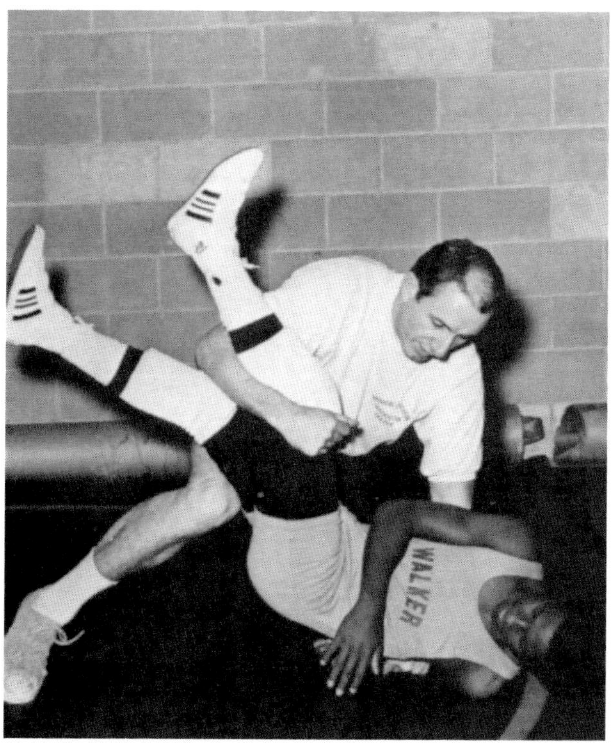

COACH VIC KARABASZ, 1968–1976. Coach Karabasz was hired in 1968 as the head football coach for the Vikings and immediately began developing a wrestling program. He became known across the state as the most knowledgeable wrestling coach in Alabama. He proved this by winning the Alabama State Championship in only his third year at Walker. His teams became a power to contend with across the South.

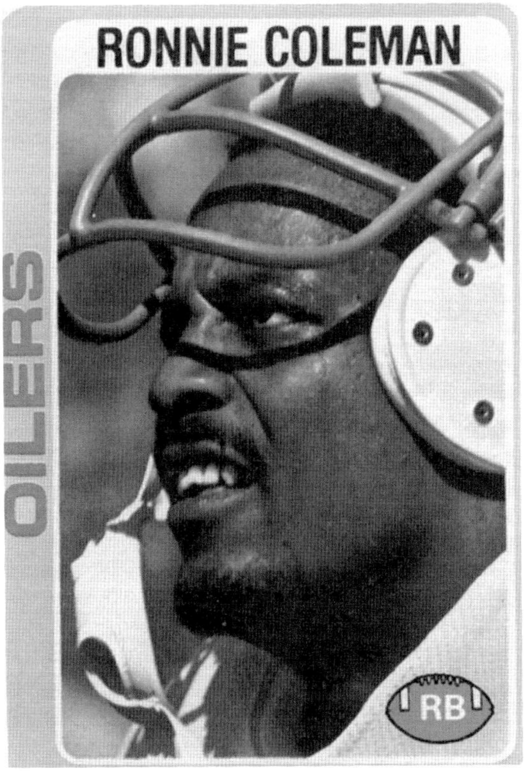

RONNIE COLEMAN, BASEBALL, 1969. Ronnie is best known because of his eight-year career as a running back with the Houston Oilers of the National Football League, but he is best remembered by Walker fans as a power-hitting clean-up batter with blazing speed on the baseball team. Ronnie was a legendary athlete at Walker County Training School, and after integration closed that school, he came to Walker to finish his senior season. He was to go on to star at Alabama A&M University.

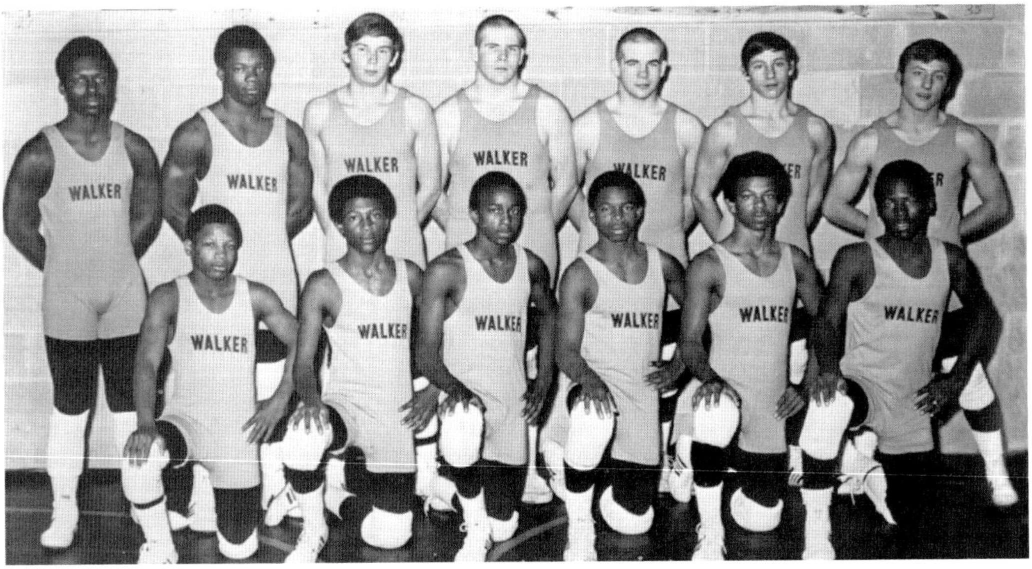

STATE WRESTLING CHAMPIONS, 1971. The Vikings were the Alabama state wrestling champions in only their third year of competition. From left to right are (first row) Bobby Colbert, James Walker, Steve Watkins, Clarence Dickerson, Melvin White, and Roosevelt McCain; (second row) Bert Rodgers, Henry Williams, Manley Cook, Roy Neighbors, Ray Neighbors, Johnny Caldwell, and Robbie Duggar. Colbert, McCain, and Duggar were individual state champions.

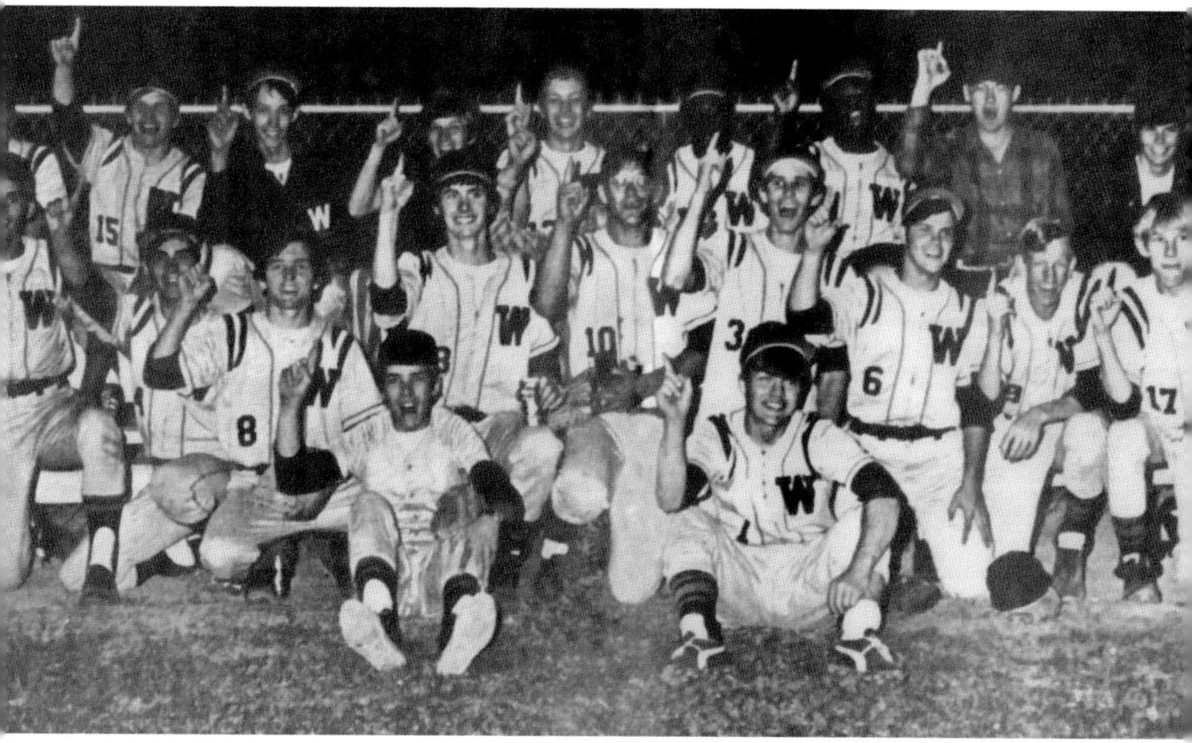

AREA BASEBALL CHAMPIONS, 1972. This was the first team in Walker High School baseball history to qualify for the Alabama state playoff system. They are shown above after winning the area championship with a come-from-behind victory over Haleyville 13-12. From left to right are (first row) unidentified and John Ed McDanal; (second row) Lamar Ingram, Mike Burton, Mark Hendon, Tony Price, David Burton, Bobby Stillman, Terry Grantham, Buddy Woodley, and Randy Panter; (third row) Sammy McGee, Joe David Gray, Jack Naramore, Daniel Craven, Mike Hendon, Ronnie Cummings, Roosevelt McCain, manager Mike Stokes, and Chuck Justice. Justice came in late in the game and got the win in his first outing as a pitcher at Walker.

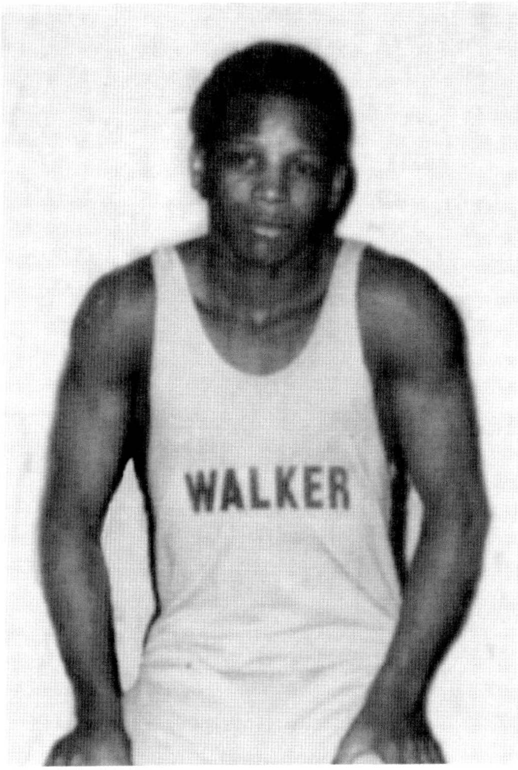

Bobby Colbert, Wrestling, 1972. Bobby was second in the state as a sophomore, captain of the wrestling team, and Walker's only two-time state wrestling champion. He holds the distinction of being the only Walker athlete to ever appear in the U.S. Olympics, where he wrestled in exhibition against Japan. He was also a member of the only Alabama state wrestling championship team at Walker.

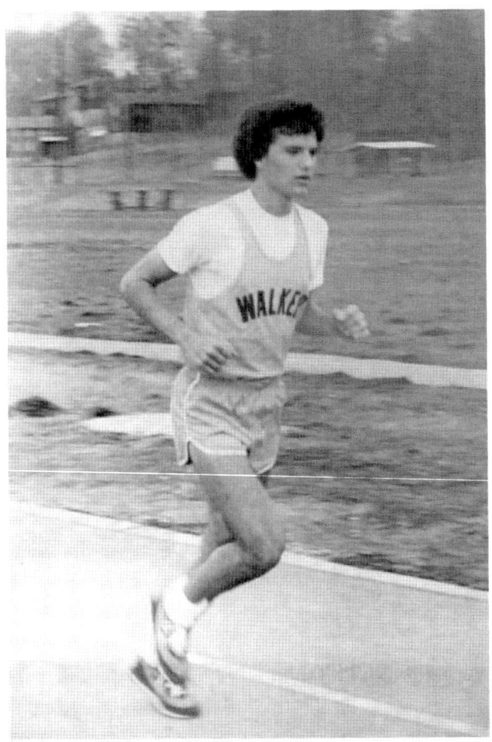

Paul Beersdorf, Cross-Country, 1981. One of the earliest cross-country runners for Walker was an energetic young man named Paul Beersdorf. Track runners ran a maximum of one mile, but cross-country required a grueling three miles. Paul became Walker's first really dedicated long-distance runner, and as other young men became interested in participating, the Walker cross-country program was born.

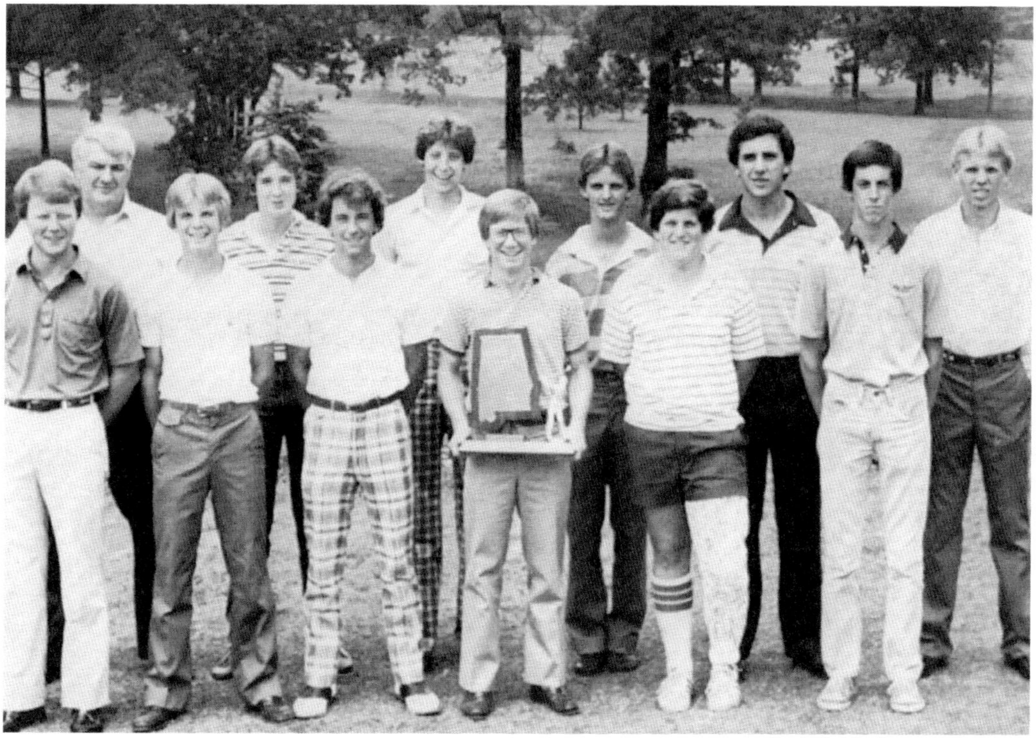

State Championship Golf Team, 1981. The year 1981 became an important one in the history of Walker's golf program, as they won the first-ever Alabama state championship trophy. From left to right are (first row) Mike Prince, Mark Richardson, Sammy Drummond, Todd Lee, Carl Elliott III, and George Lum; (second row) coach Omar Faucett, Lonnie O'Rear, Glen Clem, Rusty Brantley, Phillip Hudson, and Alan Pope.

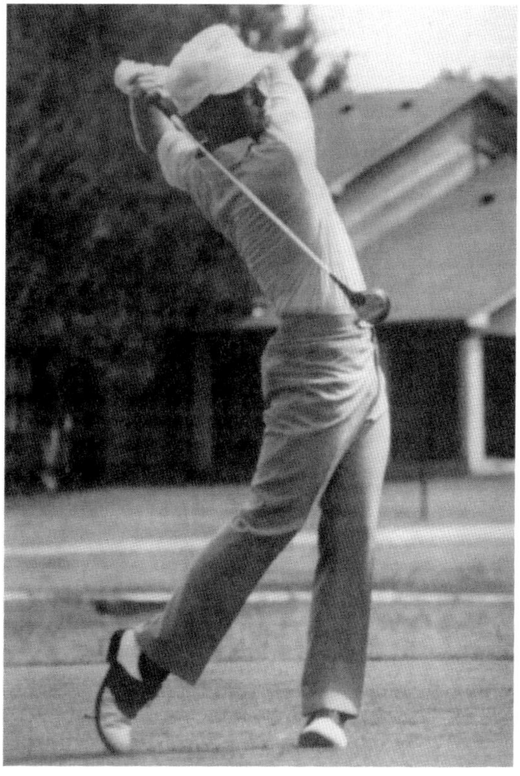

Todd Lee, Golf, 1984. Todd was an outstanding individual golfer and a member of the 1981 and the 1984 state championship teams at Walker. He received a scholarship to play for Alexander City Junior College, where he was All-American and team captain. He then played for the University of Alabama, where he won the Spirit of America Golf Classic. He is also the third all-time money winner on the Forrest L. Woods Bass Tournament fishing tour.

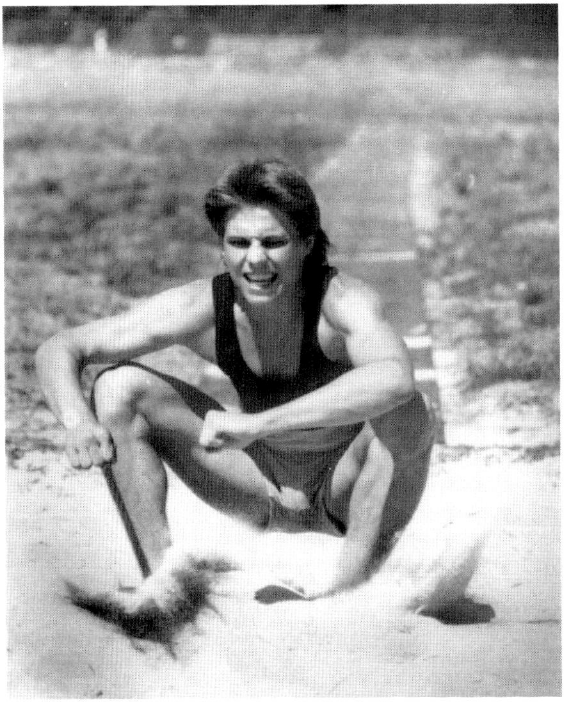

STEVIE MOSELY, TRIPLE JUMP, 1986. Stevie was one of the best all-around athletes to play at Walker. He was an outstanding basketball player, a skilled wide receiver with blazing speed, and an extremely gifted jumper. He shattered the triple-jump record held by Vince Medlock, which stood for over 15 years. Stevie signed to play football at Livingston University and now is a minister of the Gospel.

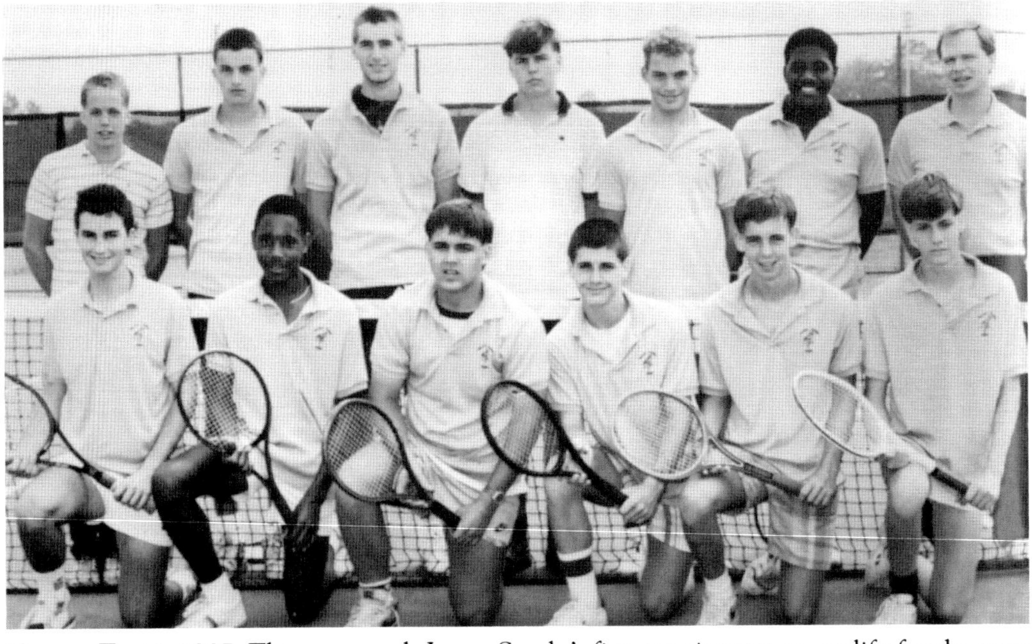

TENNIS TEAM, 1987. This was coach James Sparks's first tennis team to qualify for the state playoffs and perhaps his best. From left to right are (first row) Matt Allison, Kevin Reed, Dewayne Wigington, Shannon Johnson, Jody Barber, and Shane Wilson; (second row) Allen Baxter, Jason Selman, Brian Kelly, Casey Goeman, Bjarne Andersson, Russell Lee, and Coach Sparks. Bjarne was an exchange student from Sweden and was undefeated in 1987.

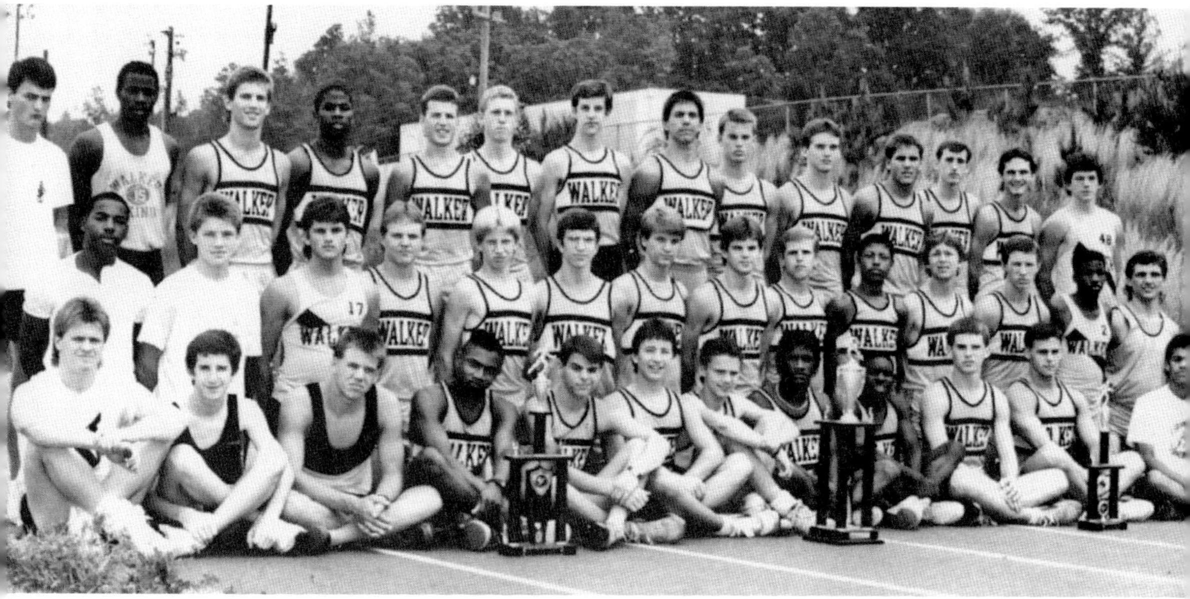

WALKER TRACK TEAM, 1987. Walker's largest and most successful track team is pictured above. They were undefeated in dual meets, won the Briarwood Invitational and the Cullman Invitational, set nine school records and five invitational meet records, and had five All-State players and one state record holder. From left to right are (first row) Chris Hanvey, Andy Laird, Jeremy Brown, Robert Stewart, Charlie Hill, Scott Dill, Jerry Smith, Mark Waldrop, Craig Smith, Wayne Myers, John Farley, and Dion White; (second row) Joe Jenkins, Larry Alexander, Todd Rogers, Chris Morrison, Brandon Chambliss, Phillip Rogers, Sam Hudson, Ben Hudson, Keith Bennett, Oliver Hembrick, Jim Sheridan, Jason Morris, Robbie Williams, and Jeremy Whitley; (third row) Ronald Richardson, Chris Cummings, Michael Abner, Obie Williams, Barry Brakefield, Gary Wolf, Ben Wall, Harry Padbury, Craig Borden, Freddie Franks, Mark Adkins, Chris Segars, Shane Calvert, and Phil Hill.

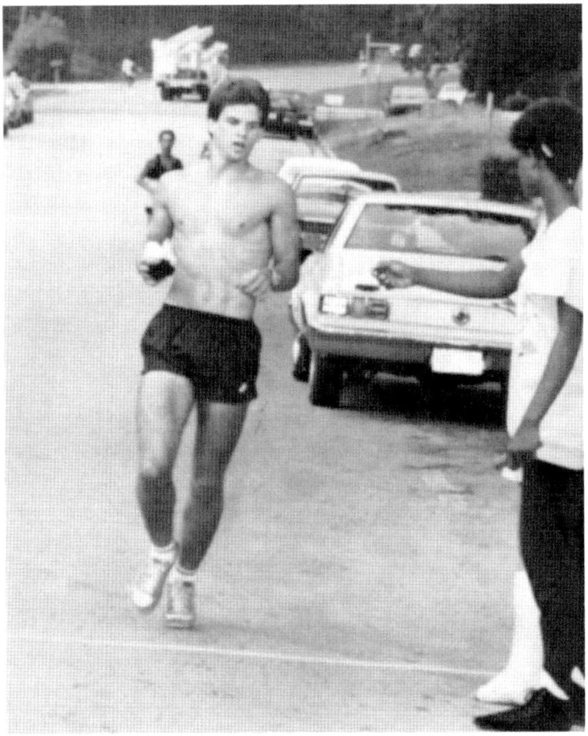

SUPER DISTANCE RUNNER BEN HUDSON, 1987. One of Walker's most unusual distance runners was Ben Hudson, a standout on both the track and cross-country teams. His biggest accomplishment was holding the Walker County and the Alabama state record in the 50-mile run. Ben was one of those unique individuals who could run 50 miles at the same pace he could run one mile.

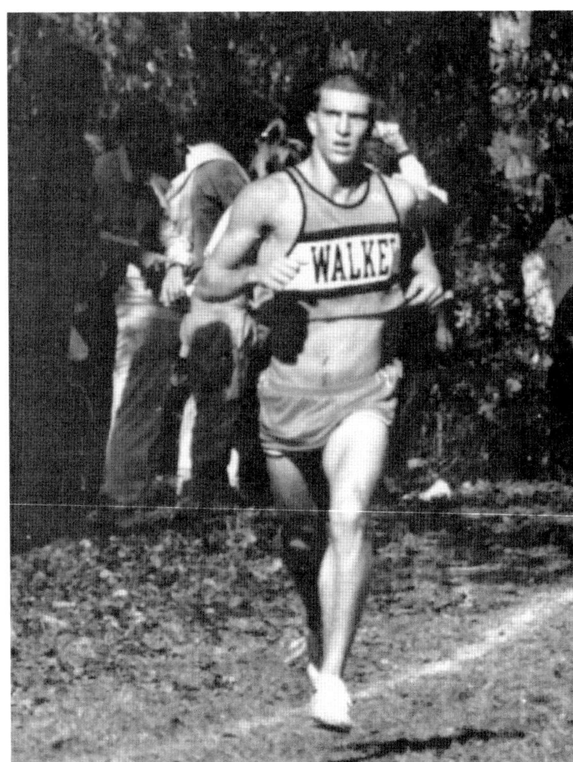

DISTANCE RUNNER PHILLIP ROGERS, 1991. Phillip Rogers was the first All-State cross-country runner in Walker history and arguably the best distance runner ever. He was a two-time All-State cross-country runner as well as an All-State distance runner in track. He was a very successful basketball player until he decided to concentrate on running his junior year. Phillip was also a top scholar with numerous academic honors to his credit.

ANDRE HOUSLEY, WRESTLING, 1992. Andre Housley (shown on the bottom) won more letters than any other modern-day athlete at Walker. He played football, ran track, and was All-State in cross-country and state champion in wrestling. In an era when athletes specialize in one sport, Andre excelled in all four. There were weekends that he would play a football game on Friday night, go to a cross-country meet Saturday morning, and practice wrestling Saturday evening.

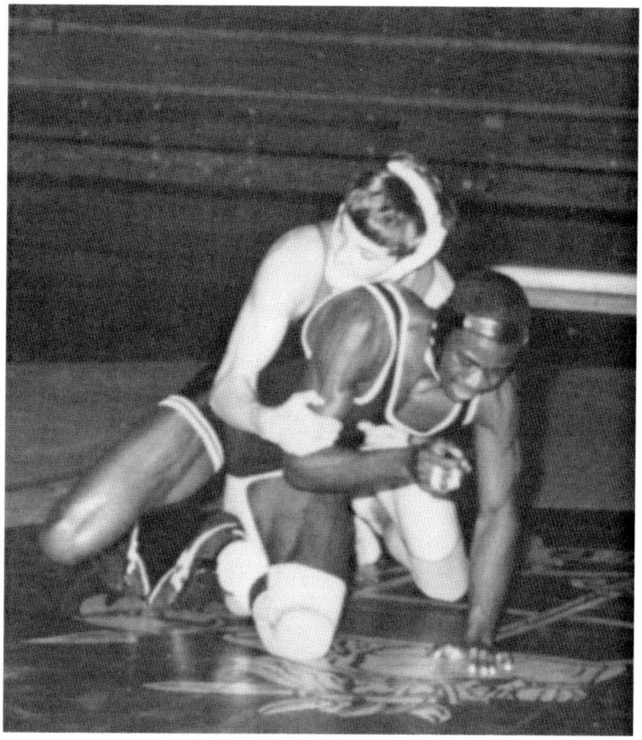

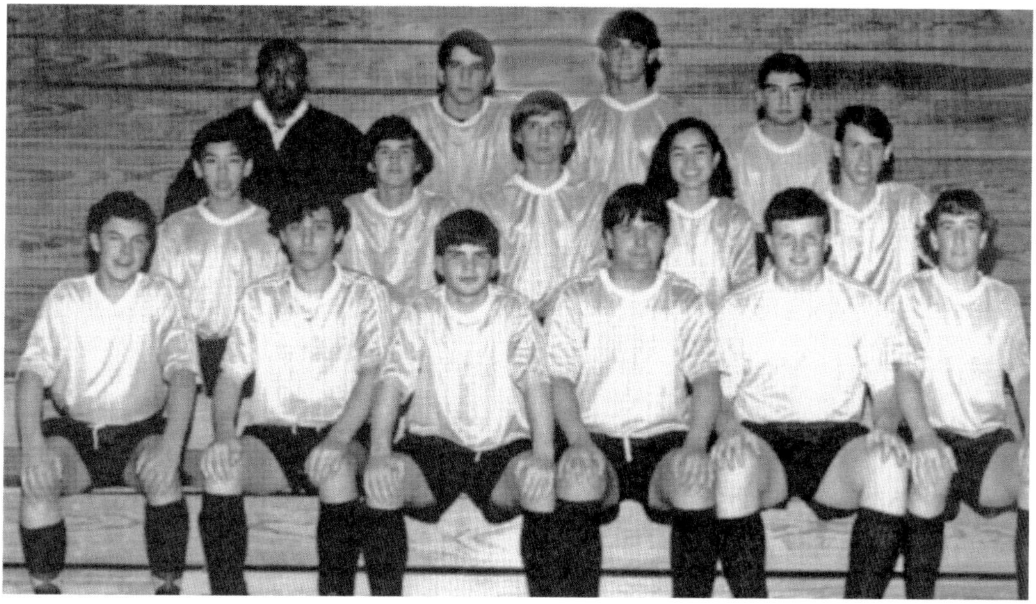

FIRST SOCCER TEAM AT WALKER, 1993. The first soccer team ever to take the field at Walker was under the guidance of coach Eric Smith. From left to right are (first row) Phillip Sanders, Patrick Tyner, Brad Vickers, Patrick Morrison, Lanue Jones, and Andrew Ellis; (second row) Chris Posey, Matthew Laird, Matt Estes, Lisa Jones, and Clay Hendon; (back row) coach Eric Smith, Kevin Anderson, David Norman, and Zac Lollar.

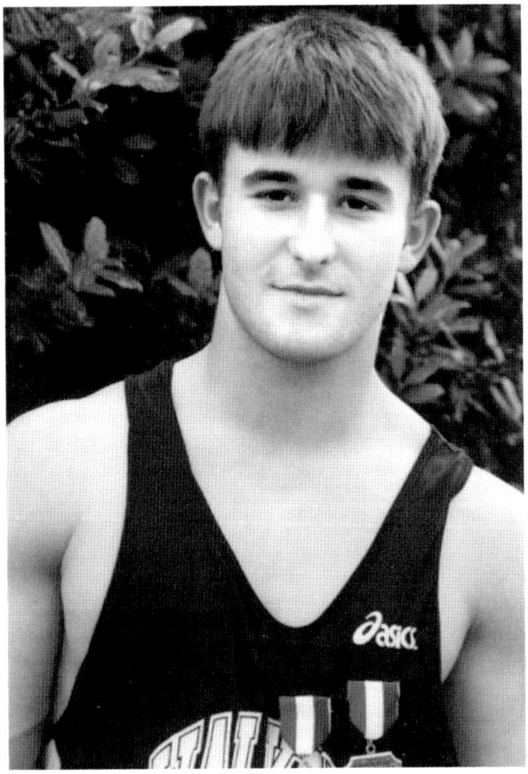

PATRICK WILSON, TRACK, 2000. Patrick was a great athlete who played multiple sports at Walker. With his blazing speed, he was an outstanding back and receiver for the Vikings. He won the 100-meter dash and was a member of the 4-by-100 gold-medal relay team, becoming the first dual state champion in track history at Walker. He was a four-year letterman at receiver and return man for the University of North Alabama.

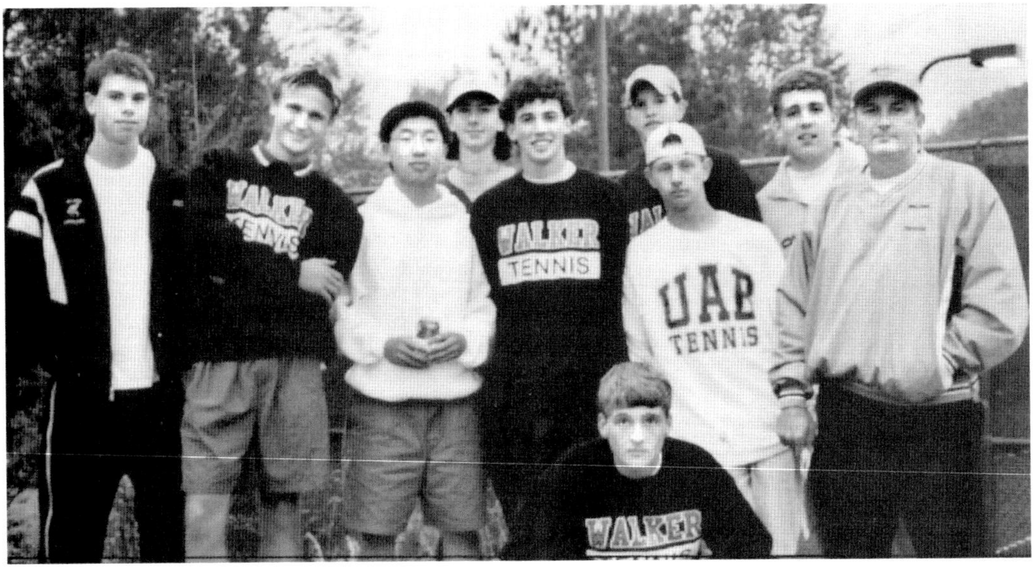

REPEAT TENNIS STATE CHAMPIONS, 2000. The 2000 tennis team won its second straight Alabama state championship and was destined to capture a third. From left to right are (first row) Bebo Dutton; (second row) Adam Sparks, Alexander Wiegelmann, Lee Kai Tai, David Donaldson, Cody Wall, and National Coach of the Year Gary Pilling; (third row) Jay Brock McCoy, Matt Dover, and Michael Matthews.

8

WOMEN'S SPORTS

1920–2000

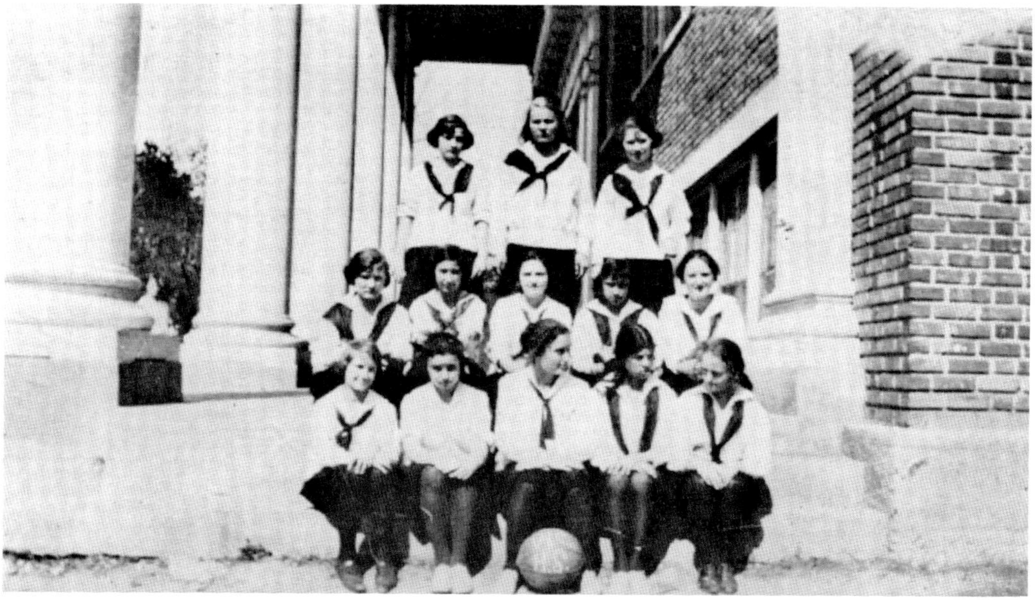

GIRLS' BASKETBALL CLUB, 1922–1923. This was the first attempt Walker made to form a girls' team. The program was short-lived. This photograph is from the 1923 annual of Walker County High School, the first one published. Bertie and Lydia Box, Esther Tallant, and Rosa Crow were members of this club.

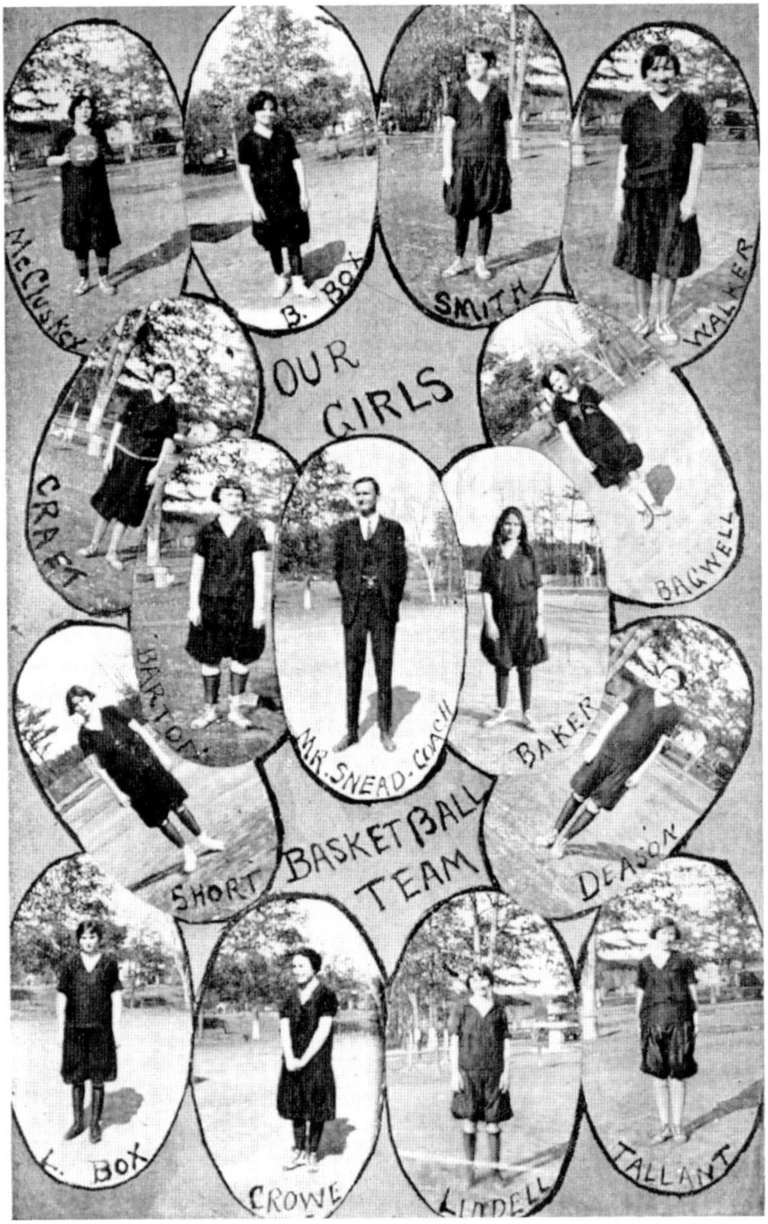

GIRLS' BASKETBALL TEAM, 1924–1925. The first girls' basketball team at Walker is this 1924–1925 team coached by Judson Snead and captained by Lorene McKlesky. Clockwise from the top left corner are Lorene McCluskey, Bertie Box, Gladys Smith, Bertha Walker, Jennie Baker, Ozella Deason, Esther Tallant, Mary Lee Lidell, Rosa Crowe, Lydia Box, Mary Short, Gertrude Barton, and Mary Craft; in the center is coach Judson Snead. Notice the uniforms, which are quite different from today. Girls' competitive athletics were discontinued in the late 1920s for almost 40 years at Walker, as well as most other Alabama high schools. It was deemed too strenuous for the "fairer sex" to participate in these interscholastic sporting events. Some junior high schools continued to have girls' teams. The next girls' basketball team was not to appear at Walker until 1988.

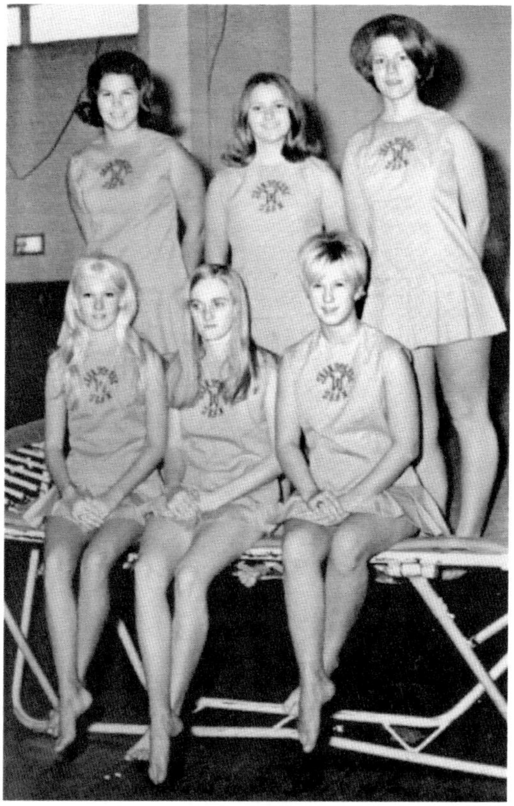

TRAMPOLINE TEAM, 1970. June Hudson started what was the first girls' athletic team of any kind in almost 45 years at Walker. These young athletes were selected for the trampoline team, mainly performing at boys' athletic events, but it was the beginning of something much bigger. From left to right are (first row) Donna Pardon, Sherry Alexander, and Shelly Harris; (second row) Kaye Salmon, Libby Brignet, and Stacia Gambrell.

CHEERLEADERS, 1972–1973. Many of the best athletes in the school were on the cheerleading squad, and almost every team was composed of at least one or two of them. Excellent examples of this are, from left to right, (first row) Shelia Morris, Brenda Clark, Jo O'Rear, Chris Cameron, and Ellen Powell; (second row) Karen Kiefer, Shelia Allred, Sharon Allred, and Connie Lockhart; (third row) Joan Legg and Debbie Upton.

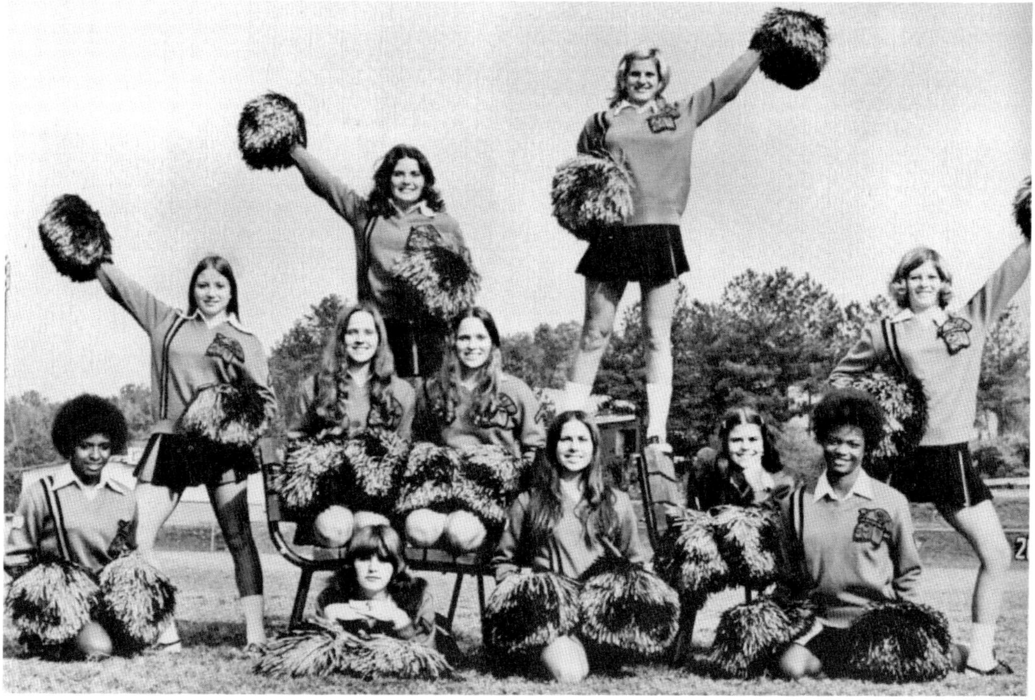

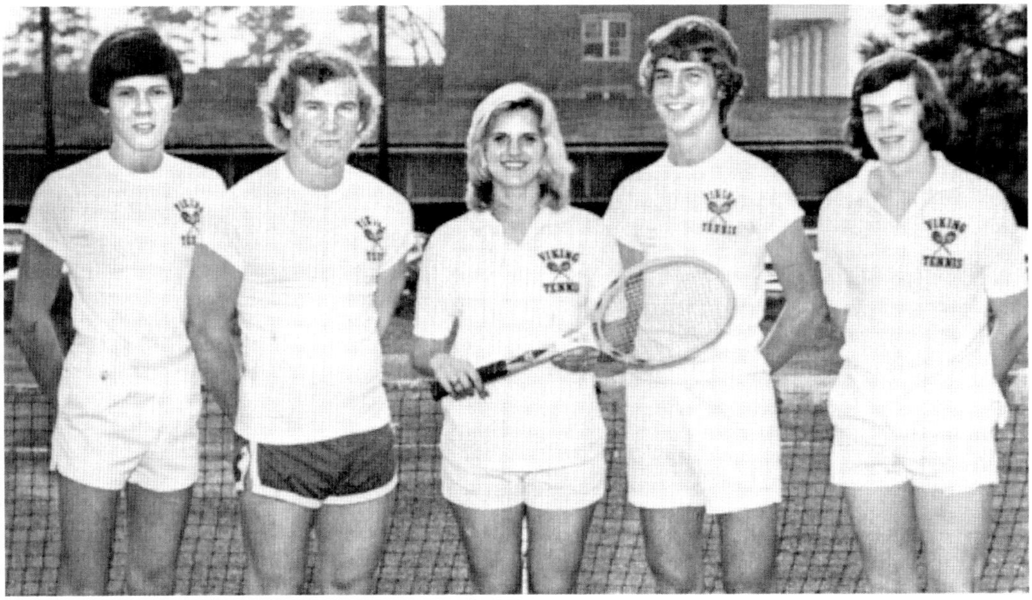

Debbie Upton, 1973. Debbie was unique among Walker athletes. She was a starter on the boys' tennis team and could hold her own with anybody, as her male opponents soon found out. Debbie had all the attributes of a great athlete: strength, quickness, and intelligence. From left to right are the returning lettermen for 1973: Hoyt Elliott, George Cook, Debbie, Phillip Bradford, and Steve York.

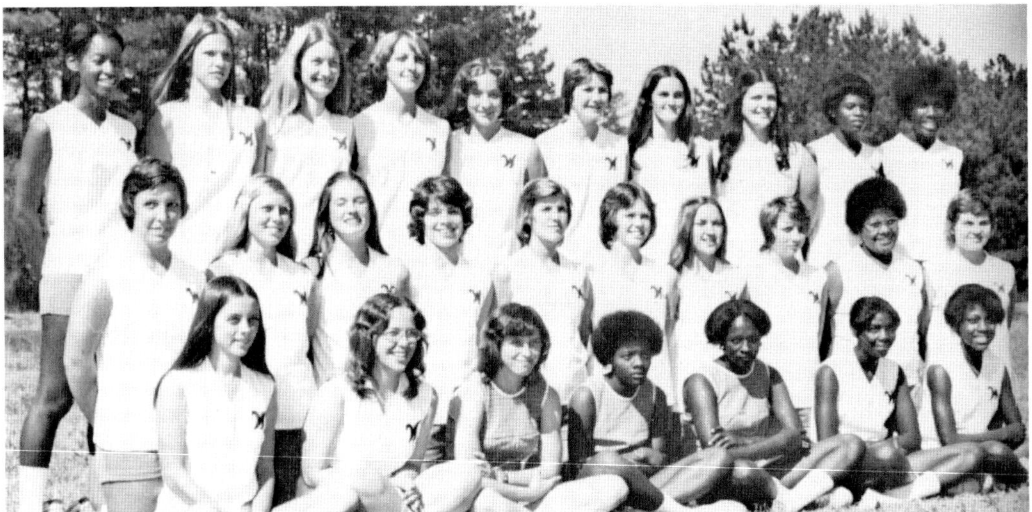

First Ladies' Track Team, 1974–1975. From left to right are (first row) Tina Carr, Judy Ferguson, Carolyn Jenkins, Josephine Harton, Sherry King, Bea Lavender, and Shelia Tatum; (second row) Beth Wynn, Kathy Powell, Marie Brown, Lynn Jones, Joy Key, Cindy McPoland, Deborah Clayton, Rosie McLean, Terrie Lee, and Kay Kimbrell; (third row) Janice Morgan, Sally Wilson, Linda Gardner, Diane Ingram, Tanya Sanderson, Chaney Clark, Dina Brakefield, Windsu Kelly, Theatrice Turner, and Pam Shaw.

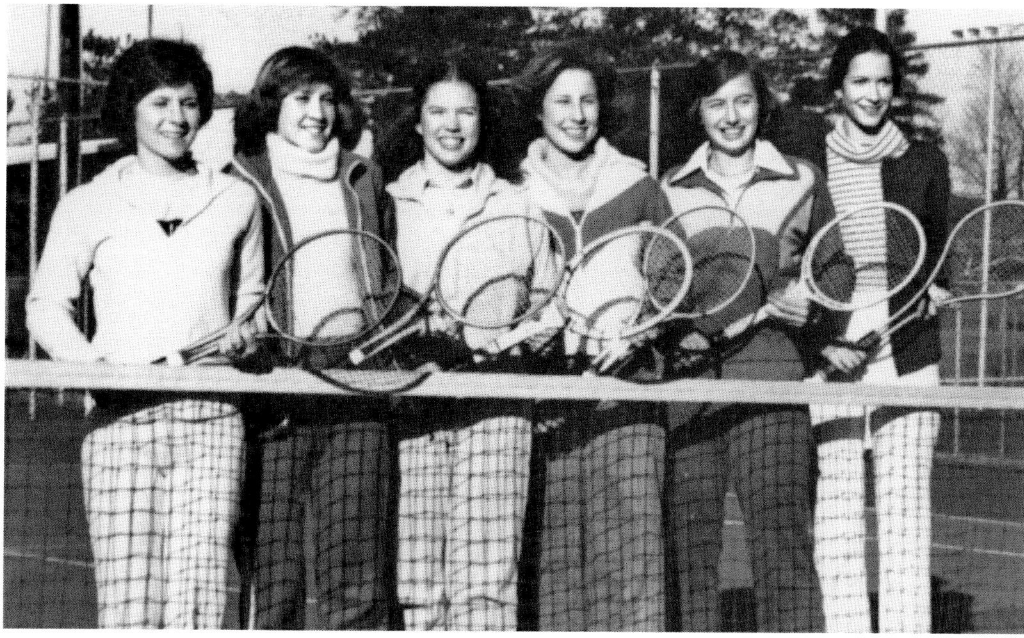

GIRLS TENNIS TEAM, 1978. These girls were on the Pat Upton–coached tennis team that won the 1977 sectional championship, qualified for the state, and came back in 1978 with another stellar year. From left to right are Jenny Brown, Lisa Harrell, Susan Wilson, Marnie Birdsong, Laura Faught, and Alice Wilson. Not shown is team member Febra White.

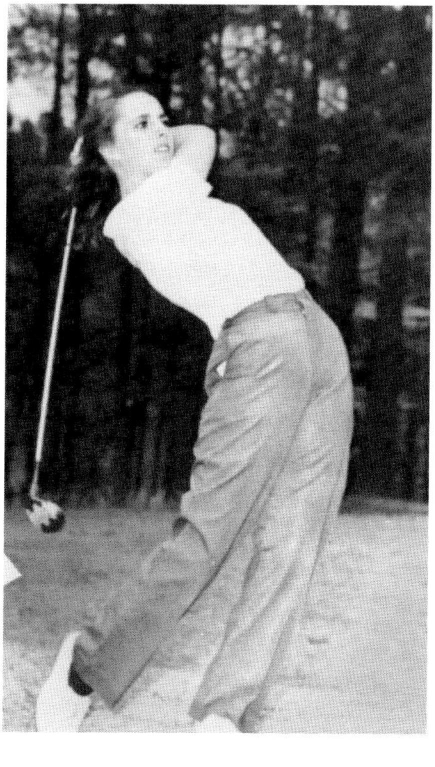

ELIZABETH LUM, GOLF, 1982. This photograph shows the form that made Elizabeth Lum a force to reckon with in girls' golf. Walker placed third in the state tournament, with Elizabeth being the low scorer for the Lady Viks in the area and state tournaments. Denise Pharris scored second lowest in both tournaments. Other members of the team not pictured are Terri Drummond, Mimi Hudson, Leigh Ann Crump, and Jill Kimbrell.

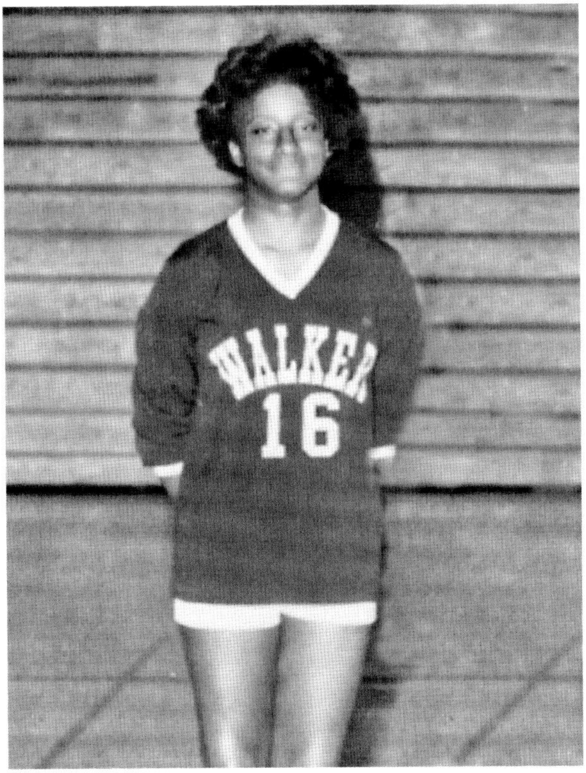

PAM KEEBLER, VOLLEYBALL AND TRACK, 1982. Pam was a top female athlete in the early 1980s. She possessed amazing speed in track, where she won numerous honors for Coach Hudson as a sprinter and jumper. Her quickness and natural ability made her one of the top volleyball players in coach Vicki Borden's volleyball program. Pam was a great athlete, but more importantly, she was an outstanding scholar and a quality young lady.

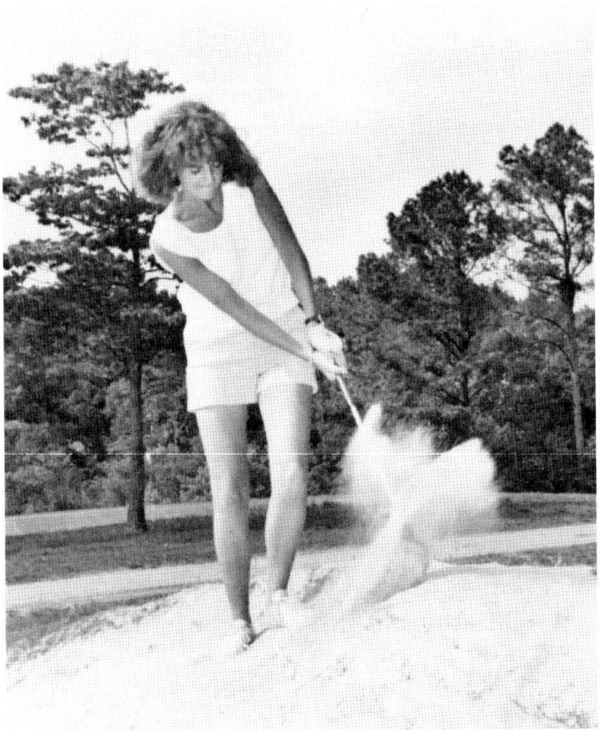

JENNIFER HILL, GOLF, 1982. Jennifer, showing great form as she hits out of a sand trap, led the girls' golf team to an undefeated regular season. At the state match held in Gulf Shores, they finished fourth overall in the state. The most exciting moment in the state tournament was when Jennifer scored a hole-in-one. She was a three-year letterman on the golf team and also served as a varsity cheerleader.

COACHES JUNE HUDSON AND VICKI BORDEN, 1985. June (right) came to Walker in 1967, developing a multifaceted girls' program that had been dormant since the late 1920s. Vicki was hired to strengthen the volleyball program. These two ladies formed a close bond, with each helping to develop the other's program—thus developing a stronger overall girls' program at Walker. Both these women are synonymous with girls' sports at Walker.

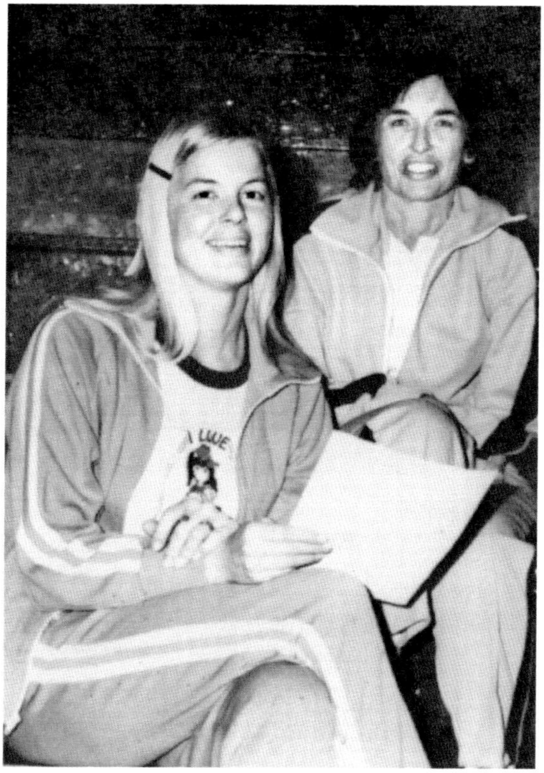

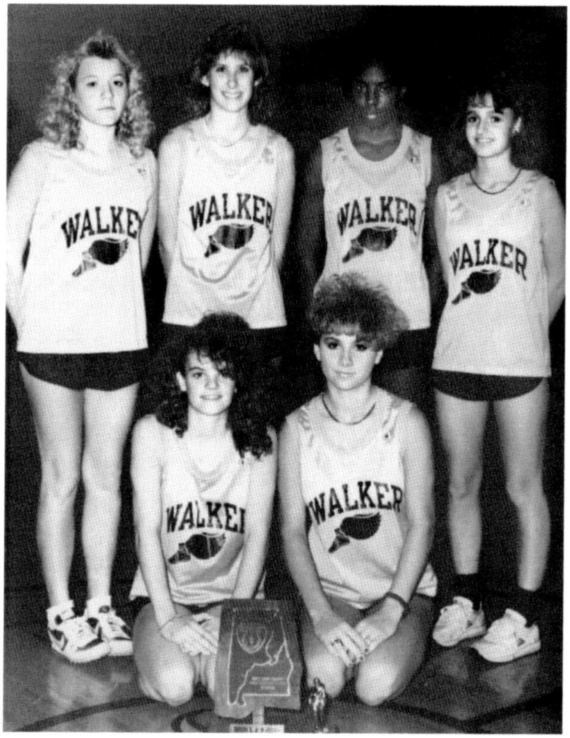

FRESHMEN CROSS-COUNTRY STATE CHAMPIONS, 1987. June Hudson's lady freshmen made their presence felt in cross-country at the state level in 1987 as they won the junior high state championship trophy. This was the first state championship girls' team ever at Walker. From left to right are (first row) Rebecca Hudson and Sandy Winsett; (second row) Monica Pyron, Bev Coggins, Aretha Smith, and Melanie Key.

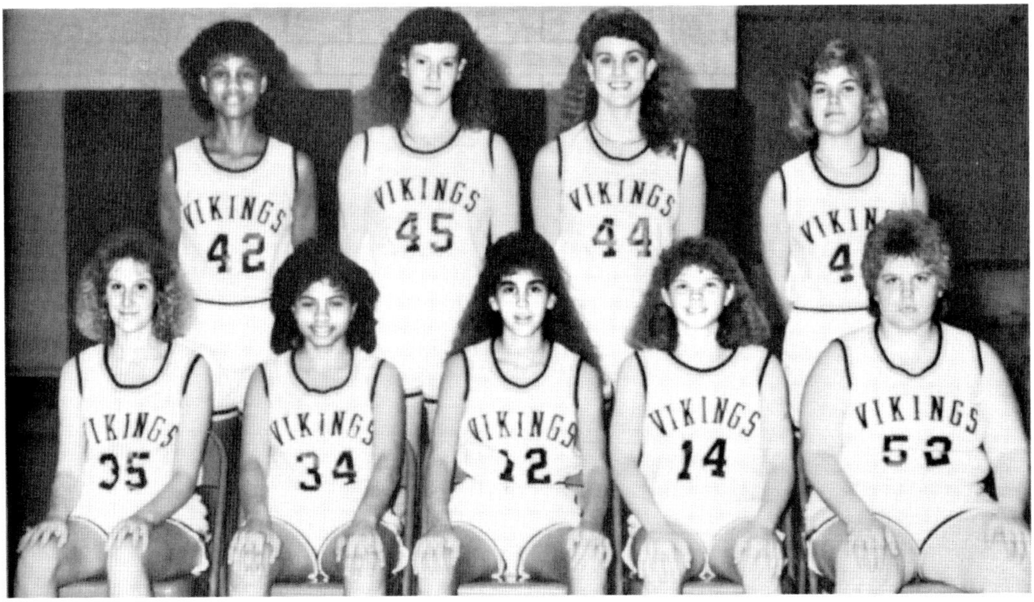

FIRST GIRLS' BASKETBALL TEAM, 1988. Paul Barker, an ex-Viking, was hired as the first girls' basketball coach at Walker since 1927. He immediately began developing a competitive program with girls who were willing to work hard to win. From left to right are (first row) Tina Langley, Tammie Terrell, Katie White, Wendy Lollar, and Kristie Gregory; (second row) Shayla Johnson, Lisa Evans, Melissa Woodley, and Lori Sherer.

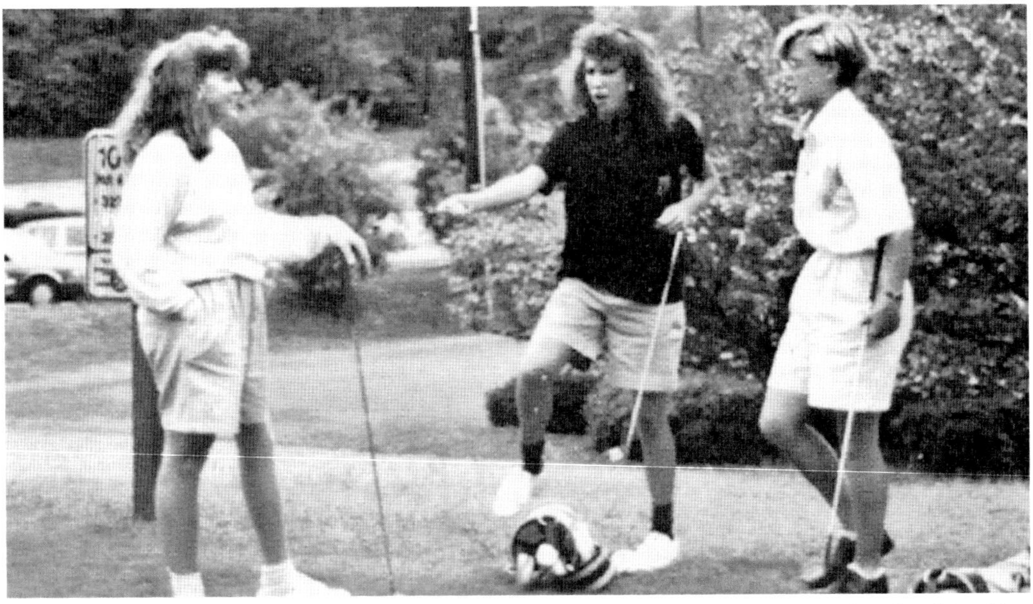

GOLF STATE CHAMPIONS, 1989. This was a great year for girls' sports in general and girls' golf in particular at Walker. The 1989 Lady Vikings were the Alabama state golf champions for the first time in history. Preparing to tee off are, from left to right, Stephanie Fowler, Rachel Stephens, and Lori Sherer. Not pictured is fourth member Laura Martin.

JOETTE KELLEY, STATE CHAMPION, 1989. Joette was the first cross-country state champion in the history of Walker. She won the freshman title by covering a two-mile course through sheer determination in the time of 14 minutes and 50 seconds. Joette was one of the most aggressive and competitive runners to ever compete at Walker. Strangely enough, her specialty was not distance running but hurdling.

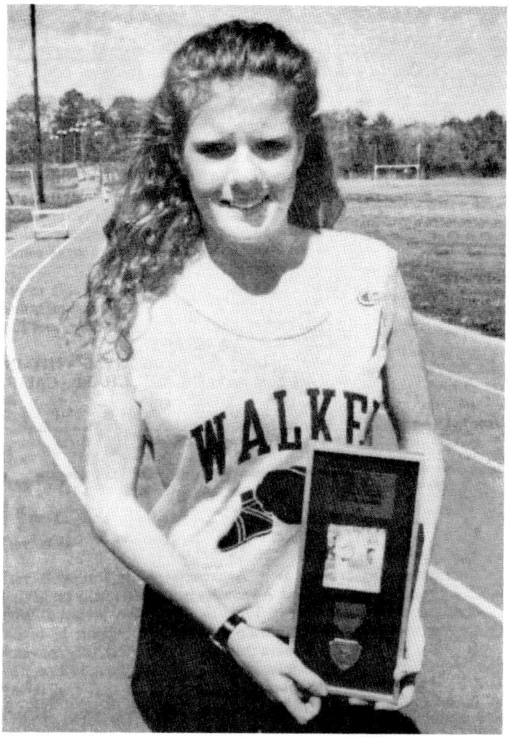

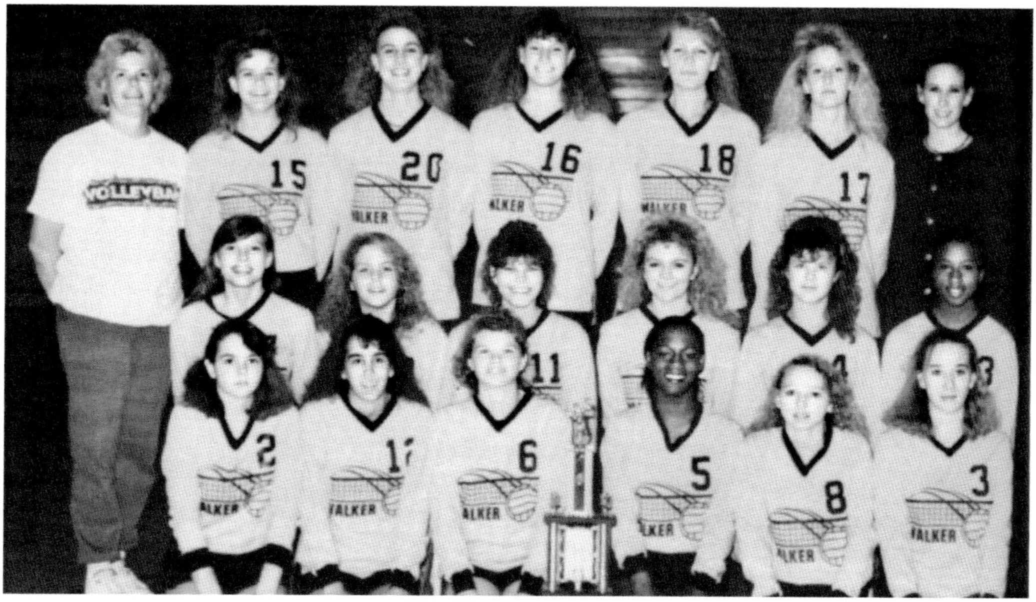

VOLLEYBALL REGIONAL CHAMPIONS, 1991. Vicki Borden's first Region 8 championship team is, from left to right, (first row) Laura Hudson, Kati White, Wendy Lollar (MVP), Shea Blair, Kelly Hendon, and Angela Elkins; (second row) Lynn Watkins, Juli Holderfield, Kristi Burton, Kristi Peak, Angie Kitchens, and Tai Keebler; (third row) Coach Borden, Misty Diehl, Melissa Woodley (All-Tournament), Lisa Evans, Evelyn Guthrie, Tina Langley, and Bev Coggins.

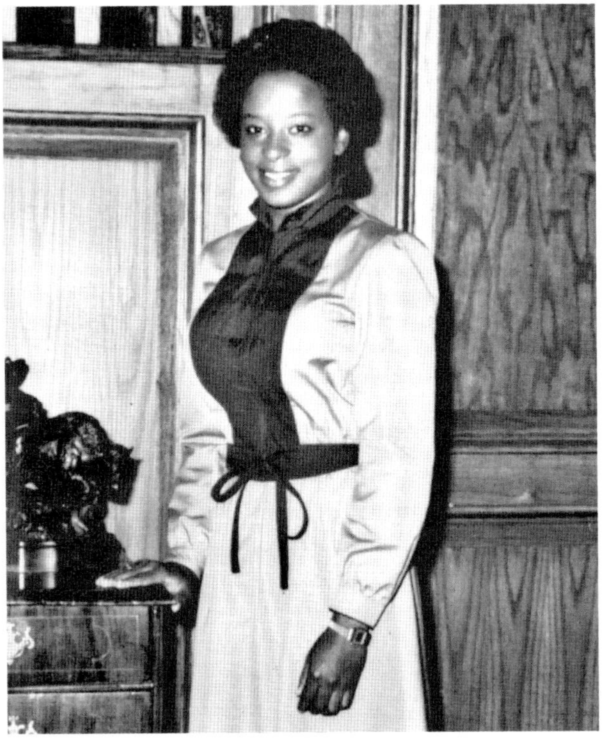

PEGGY KEEBLER, BASKETBALL COACH, 1991. Peggy graduated in 1985 from Walker and attended the University of Montevallo on a basketball scholarship, even though Walker did not have a girls' basketball team. In 1990, she broke Montevallo's scoring record, set the NAIA single game scoring record, was player of year, made the Kodak All-American team, and had her jersey retired. She was later selected head coach at the University of Montevallo.

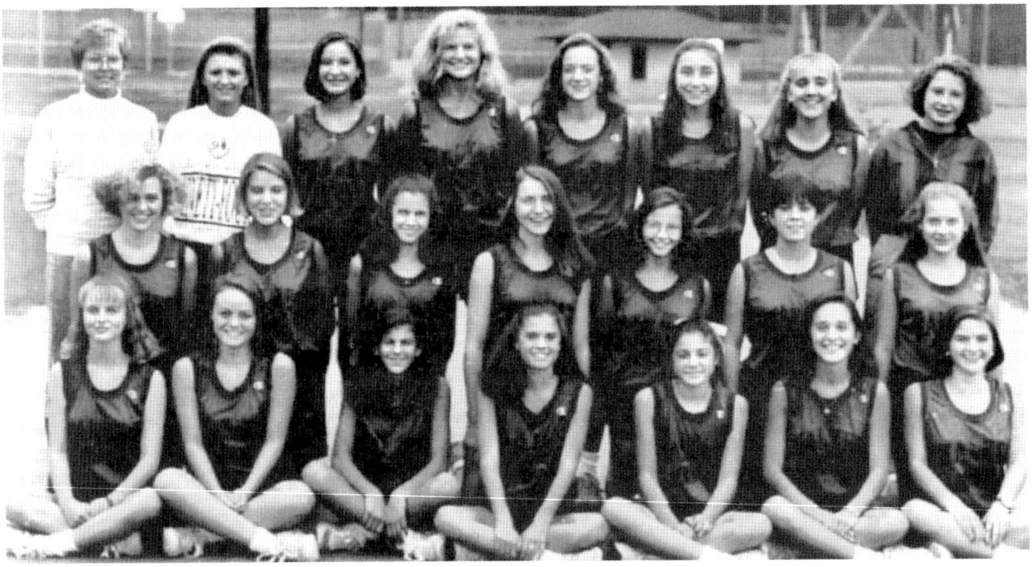

CROSS-COUNTRY TEAM, 1993–1994. One of Walker's most successful cross-country teams is, from left to right, (first row) Kim Crews, Emily Tapley, Tasha Parrish, Mary Beth Roland, Andrea Kiker, Terri Myers, and Natalie Brown; (second row) Shannon Reed, Brandy Corbell, Mary Catherine McCulloch, Megan McClendon, Jannell Canerday, Julie Parrish, and Shana O'Rear; (third row) coach Helen Morrison, Amanda Wade, K. D. Jent, Amy Gilbert, Alicia Kelley, Aimee Best, Kendra McLemore, and Keeva Patton.

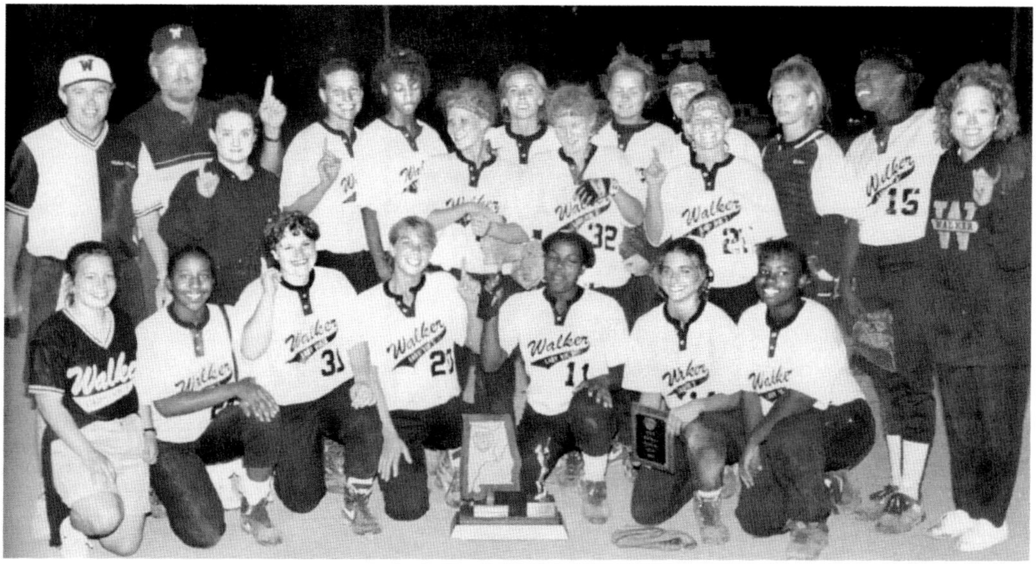

FIRST SOFTBALL STATE CHAMPIONS, 1994. Celebrating their victory at state are, from left to right, (first row) Jennifer Guthrie, Latish Ogbeide, Stacy Barnette, Ginger Lollar, Sonya Harris, Malia Bailey, and Shayla Rogers; (second row) coaches Ronnie Kilgore and Ronnie Brown, Sherry Parrish, Amber Thomas, Shawn Medlock, Mandy Brown, Lora Martin, Brandi Brown, Melanie Barton, April Walker, Dana Burton, Heather Slagle, Synesha Smith, and coach Shelia Kilgore.

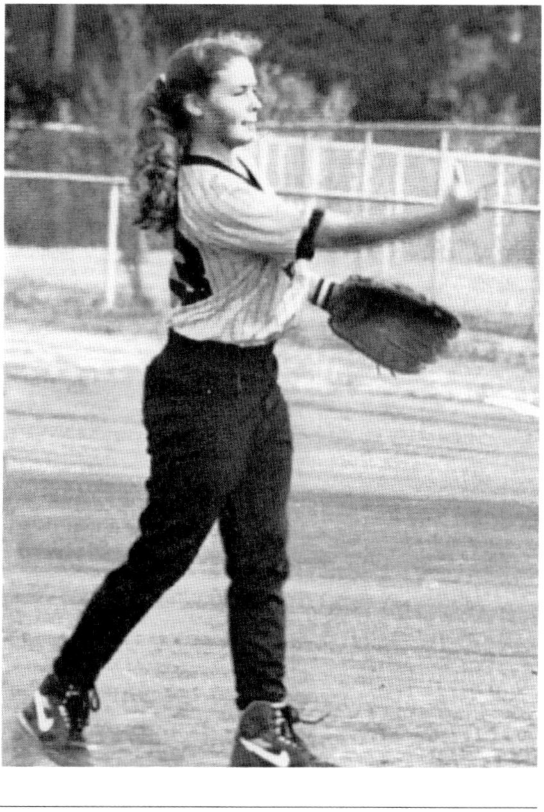

MELANIE BARTON, SOFTBALL, 1994. Melanie played for Walker from 1993 to 1995. She was a pitcher for Shelia Kilgore's Lady Vikings and was a member of two state championship teams, finishing second the other year. She set an Alabama high school record for most victories by a pitcher by winning 245 games over her career. This record still stands 11 years later. She played softball for Bevill State College.

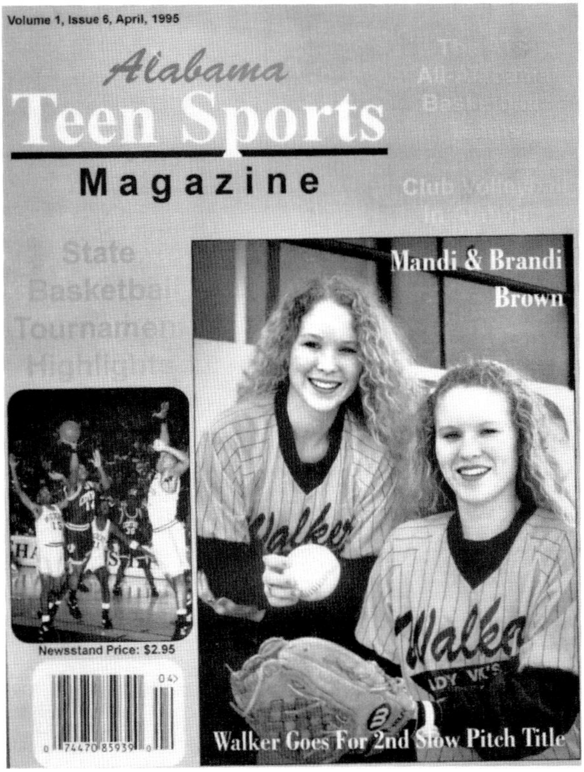

COVER GIRLS, 1995. The Brown twins were featured on the front of the April issue of *Alabama Teen Sports Magazine*. Mandy and Brandy were both outstanding athletes on Coach Kilgore's squad at Walker in the mid-1990s and were featured in this article on Walker's run for a second straight Alabama state title in softball. Not only did they win this year, but they also went on to win an unprecedented three state championship trophies. (Courtesy of WCHS.)

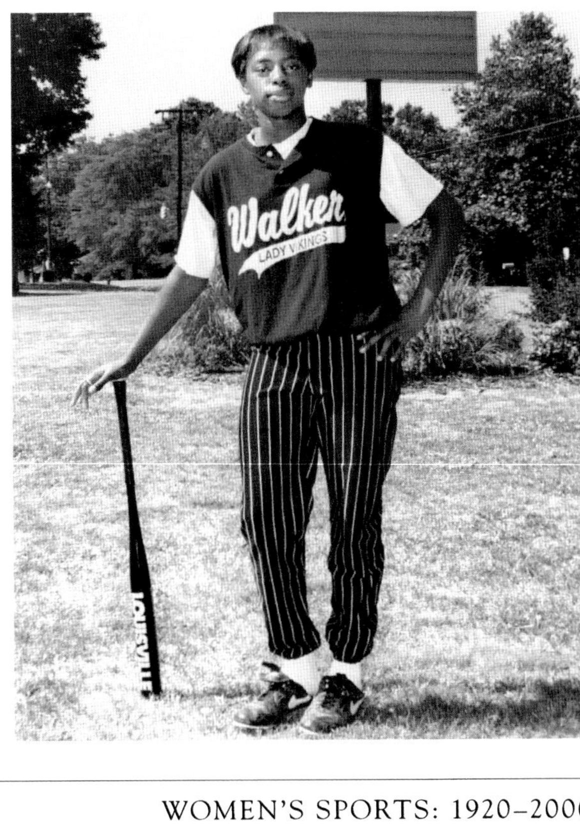

SYNESHA SMITH, SOFTBALL, 1996. Synesha "Neicey" Smith was a two-sport letterman for Walker in the late 1990s. She is arguably one of the best basketball players ever to play at Walker. Neicey could hold her own in street ball with most guys, but she was even better in softball. Neicey played on back-to-back state championship teams and set the single-season Alabama state home run record her senior year with 36.

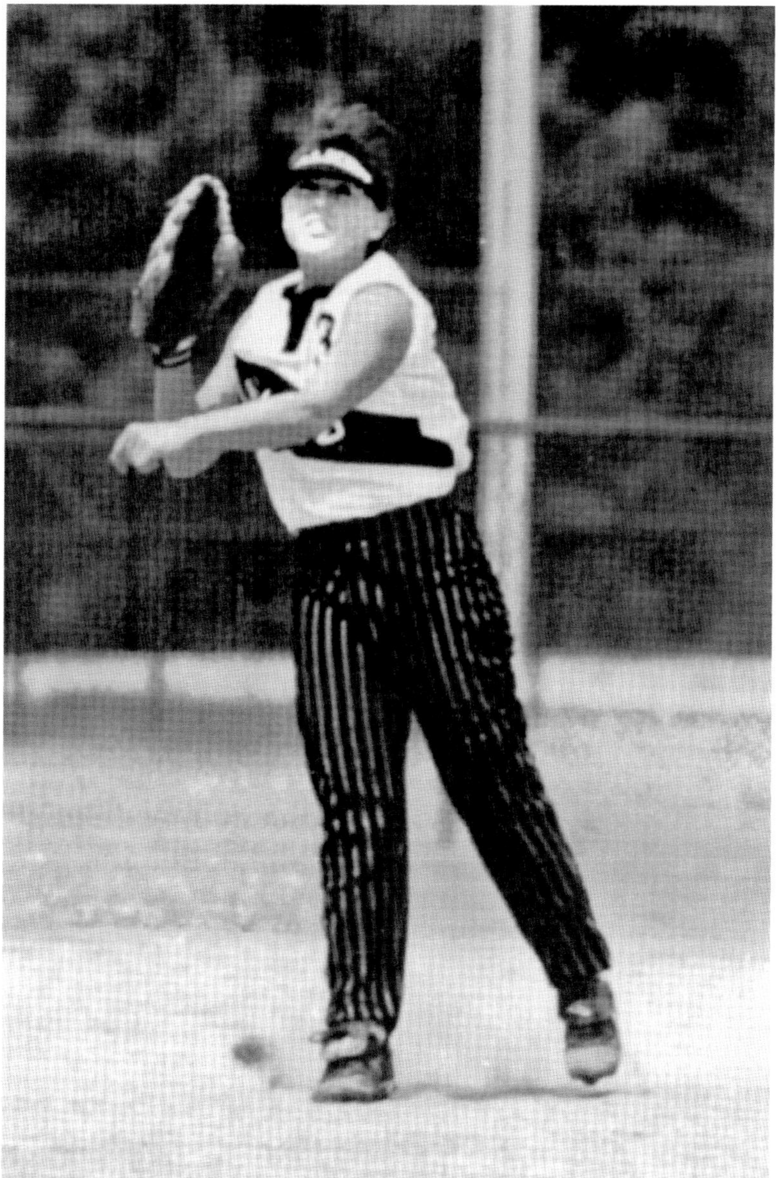

First Fast-Pitch Softball, 1998. After an unbelievably successful stint as a state power in slow-pitch softball and three straight state championships to her credit, Shelia Kilgore made a tough decision to switch from slow-pitch to fast-pitch softball. This was a totally different sport, and she knew it would probably cost her a couple of state championships. All the colleges were going to fast-pitch, and she knew it would benefit the girls to make the change at the expense of her own record. She made the decision unselfishly, and to everyone's surprise but hers, the girls won sub-state and finished fifth in the state that first season, a monumental achievement. Pictured above is Cassidy Anderson, a member of that first team and also a member of the 1996 state championship team. Cassidy was an outstanding player who holds a share of the state record for batting average percentage at .665. This is still one of the top 10 averages in the state today.

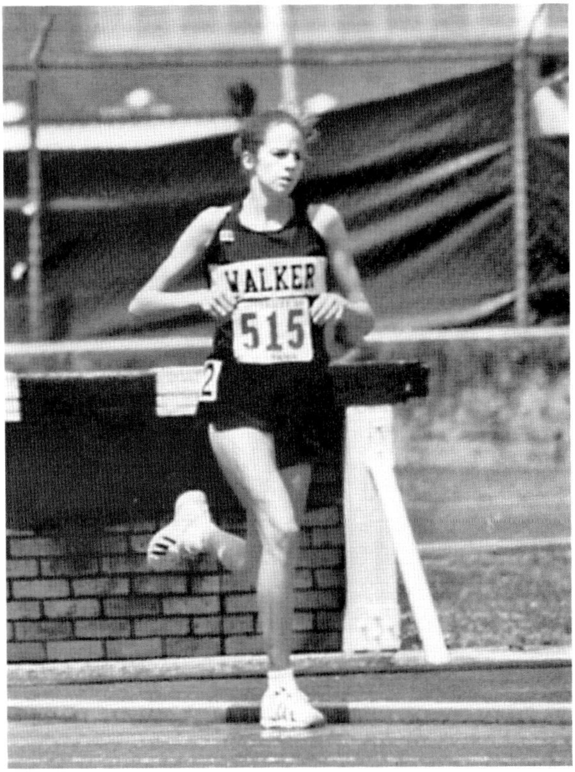

MARY CATHERINE MCCULLOCH, TRACK AND CROSS-COUNTRY, 1998. Walker's most successful distance runner and arguably the school's best runner in history was Mary Catherine McCulloch. She was All-State three years at Walker in track and cross-country before going on to a successful career at Auburn University. She was a coach's dream and a true scholar-athlete. Nobody could outwork her on the playing field or in the classroom.

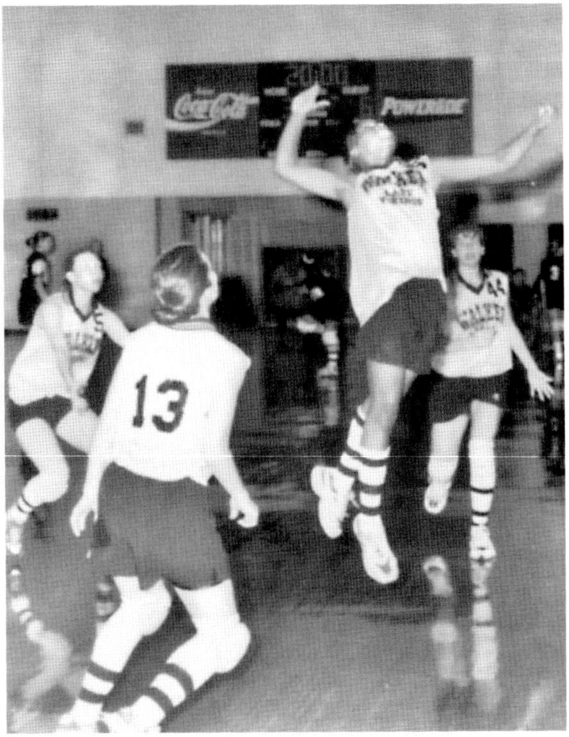

KILL IN VOLLEYBALL, 1998. The 1998–1999 volleyball team was coached by Shelia Kilgore, who took over the program when Vicki Borden retired. They were a talented group of girls known for their thundering kills. Liz Wilson (25) drives home another kill after the set by Jenny Kelly (13). Looking on are Britney Maulden (5) and Christy Alexander (44).

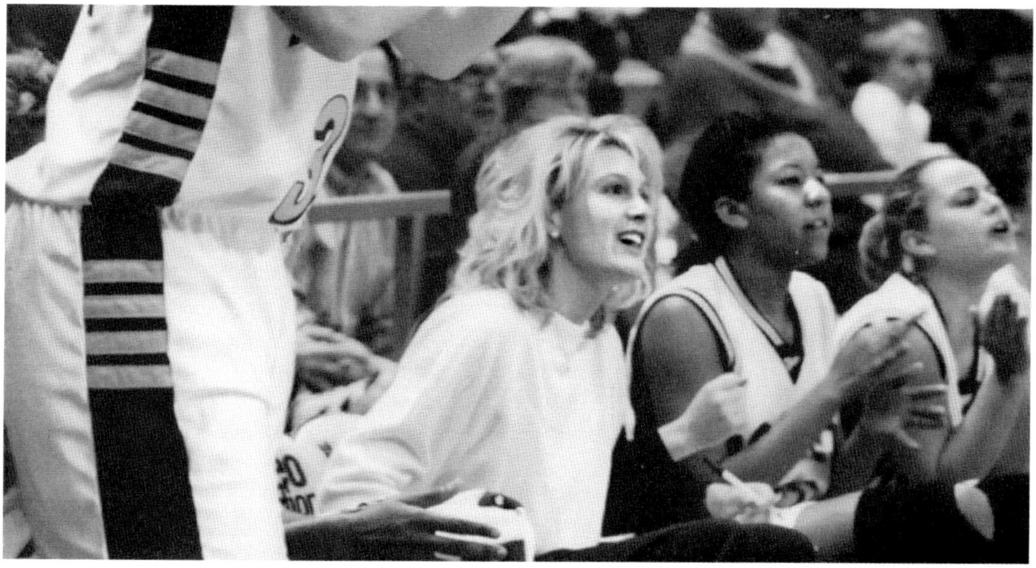

COACH TINA LANGLEY, 1999. Tina was an outstanding athlete at Walker in volleyball, softball, and basketball, graduating in 1991. She returned to Walker as an assistant coach and then accepted the head girls' basketball position in 1998. She guided the Lady Vikings for two years before moving to the University of Toledo as assistant head coach. She later coached at Clemson University and the University of Georgia.

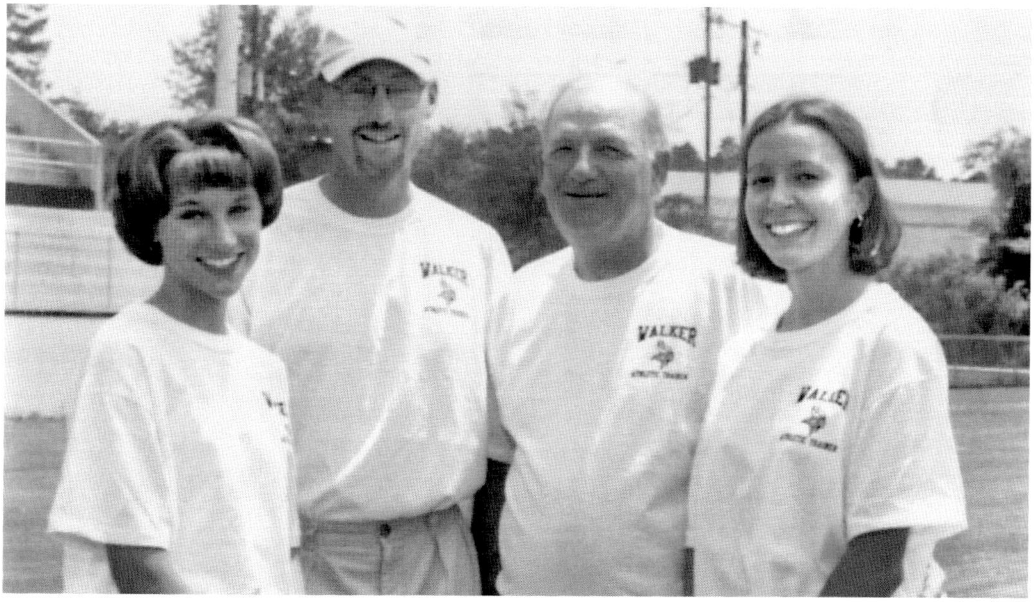

ATHLETIC TRAINING PROGRAM, 1999. Walker started only the second student athletic training program in the state of Alabama in 1996 with Amy Byars as its first student. Amy graduated and went to Auburn University, where she entered the program there. The 1999 members of the program are, from left to right, Wendy Smith, Bob White (director), Jack Lamon (trainer and director), and Andrea Kennedy.

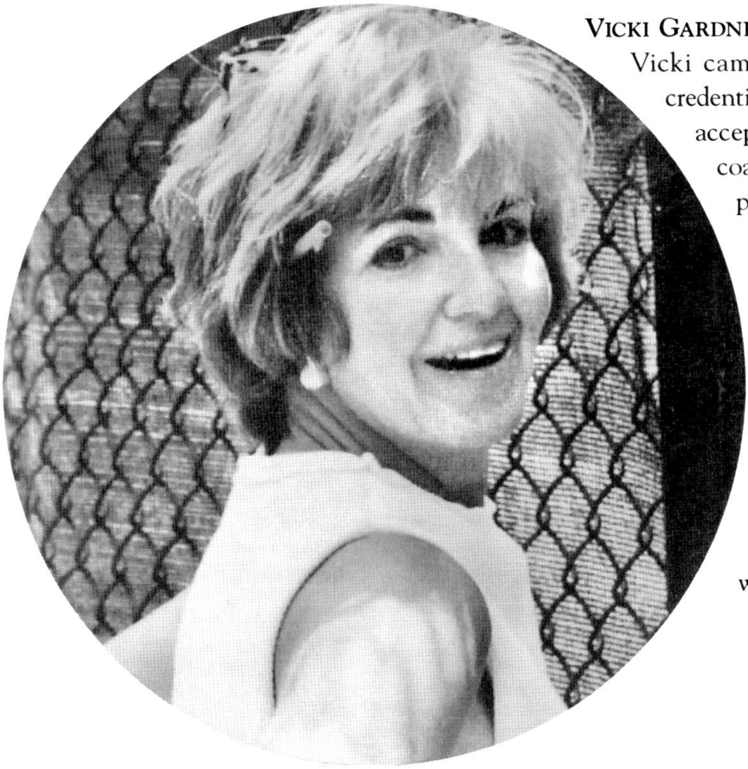

VICKI GARDNER, TENNIS, 1987–2000. Vicki came to Walker with great credentials as a science teacher and accepted the position of tennis coach. She was a competitive player with a unique knowledge of the game and immediately instilled that competitive spirit in her girls. She won the only state tennis title in the school's history. Vicki coordinated Walker's Athletic Hall of Fame, and her dinners and decorations are without equal.

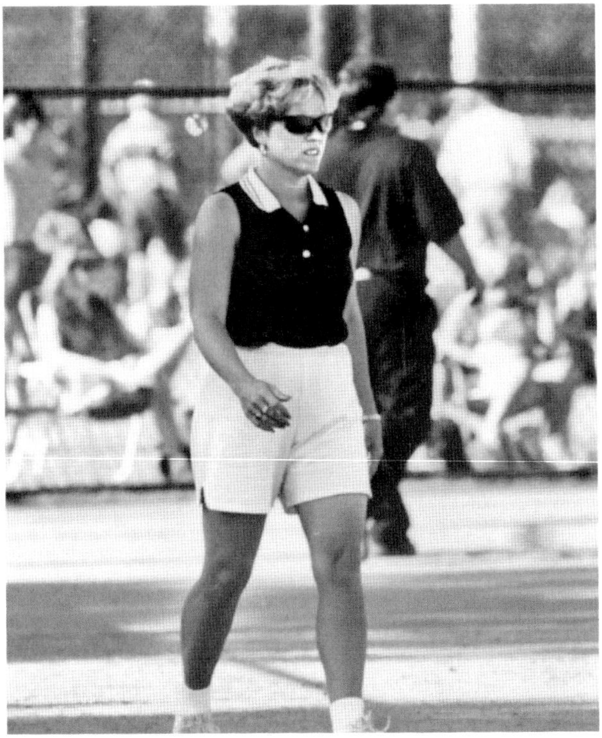

SHELIA KILGORE, SOFTBALL, 1992–2000. Shelia started her career at Walker as a cheerleader because there were no competitive sports at Walker in the early 1970s. She participated in volleyball and bowling before returning to Walker as the girls' softball coach and immediately took them to prominence at the state level. Shelia is the only coach in Walker's long and varied history to win three straight state titles in any sport.

9

MISCELLANEOUS

1920–2000

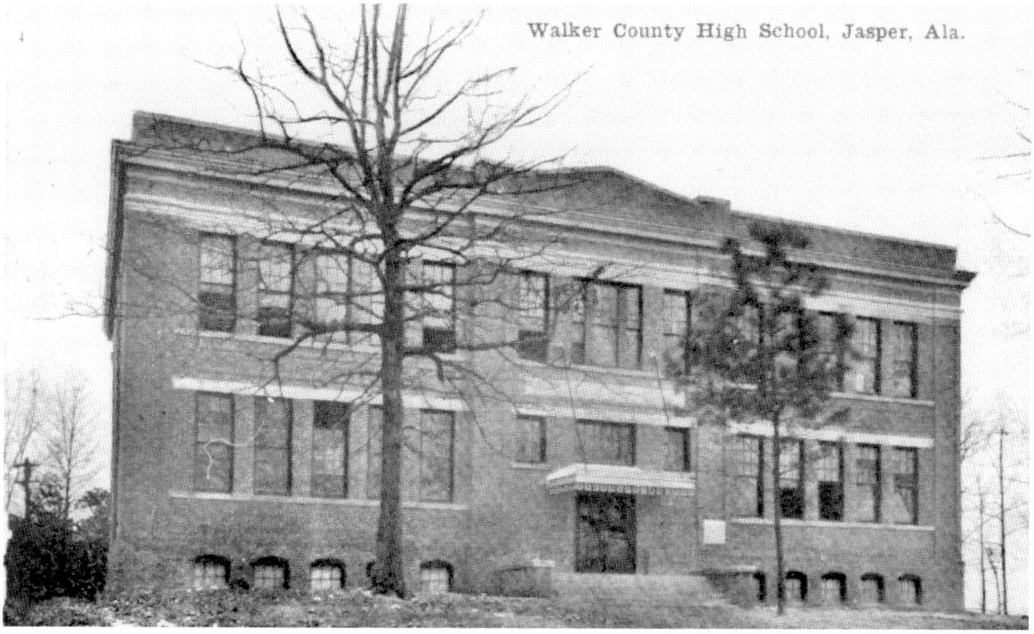

FIRST WALKER COUNTY HIGH SCHOOL, 1914. The first building with the name of Walker County High School was constructed in September 1910 on the top of Academy Hill in Jasper. On Friday night, January 28, 1916, this school burned to the ground because water could not be pumped to the top of the hill. The new Walker County High School was built at its present location in the fall of 1917.

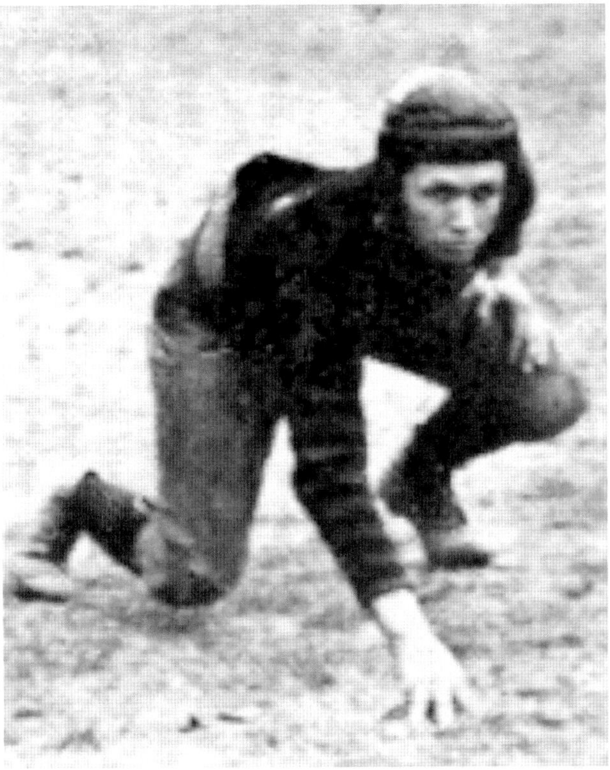

Soft Leather Helmet, 1922. By 1922, all players were required to wear the soft leather helmet pictured here. Most of the players still did not want to wear this headgear, but the rules would allow nothing less. The head was not used as a weapon in the early days; therefore, the helmet was not as important as it is today. Shown sporting the latest model of this soft leather headgear is Hugh Deason. (Courtesy of WCHS.)

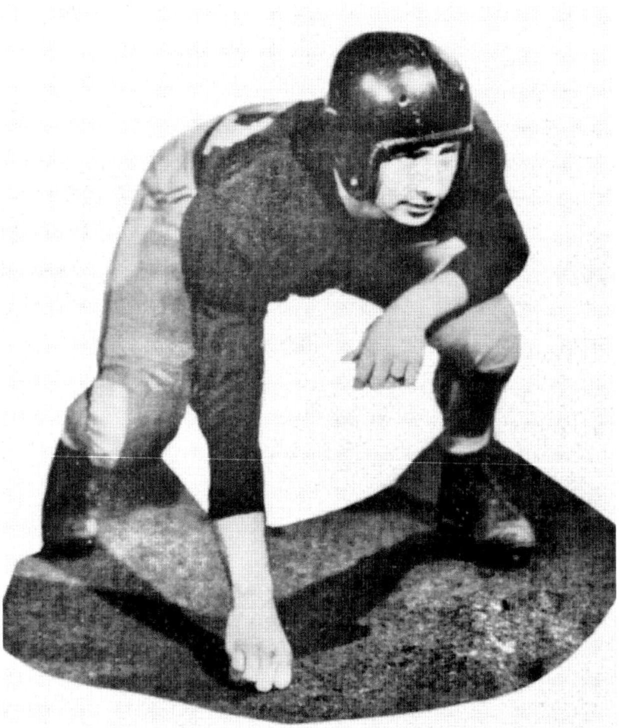

Hard-Shell Helmet, 1950. Charles Underwood models the new hard-shell helmet, which was a great improvement over the older soft helmet. The game became more scientific, and this helmet was the next step to give greater protection to the head. Notice no face mask of any type is yet being used. Charles, an All-County guard, played a hard-nosed, no-nonsense game.

FIRST CLEAR FACE MASK, 1954. After the game was played without a face mask for some 30 years, the development of the clear bar was a great improvement, especially for linemen who fought it out in the trenches with many blows to the head and the face. Billy Elkins, shown here, was a tough offensive lineman on the 1954 Viking squad. Billy served a hitch in the army and then came back to a career with the postal department.

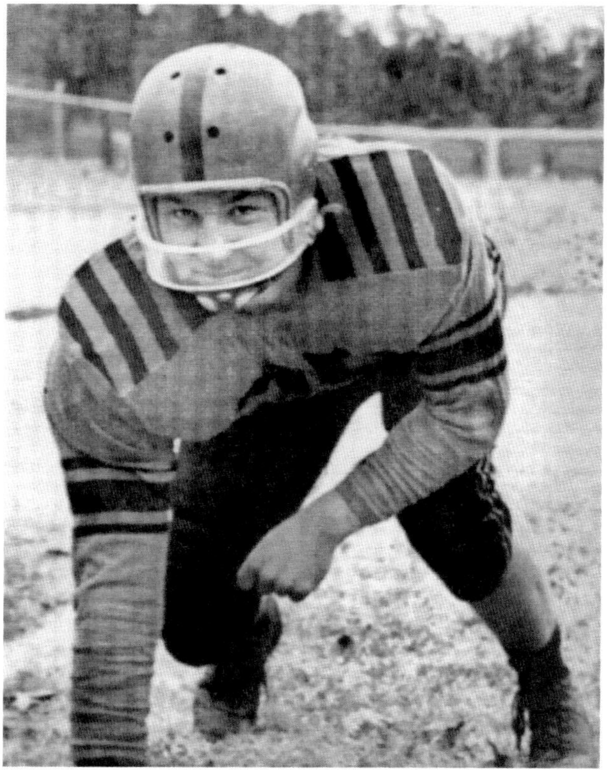

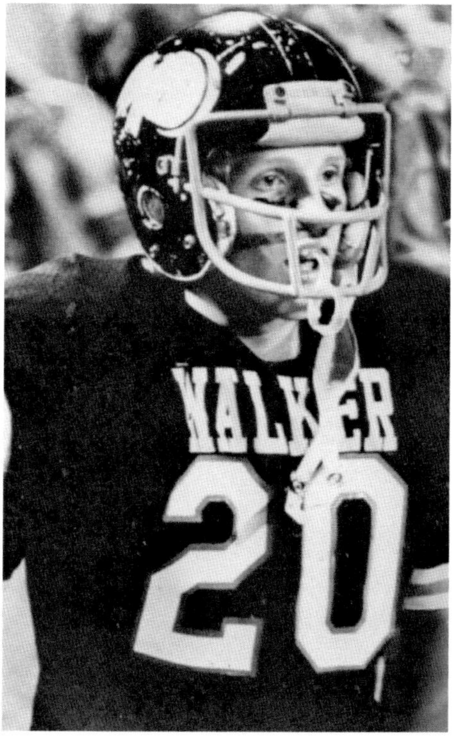

CAGE FACE MASK, 1976. Ricky Allred was a star running back and defensive back with the Vikings from 1974 to 1976. Like many backs of his day, he appreciated this double-bar style of mask because it allowed him to keep all his teeth in place. Notice the addition of the mouthpiece, which prevented chipped and broken teeth. Ricky became one of the most successful Little League and Toy Bowl coaches in Walker County.

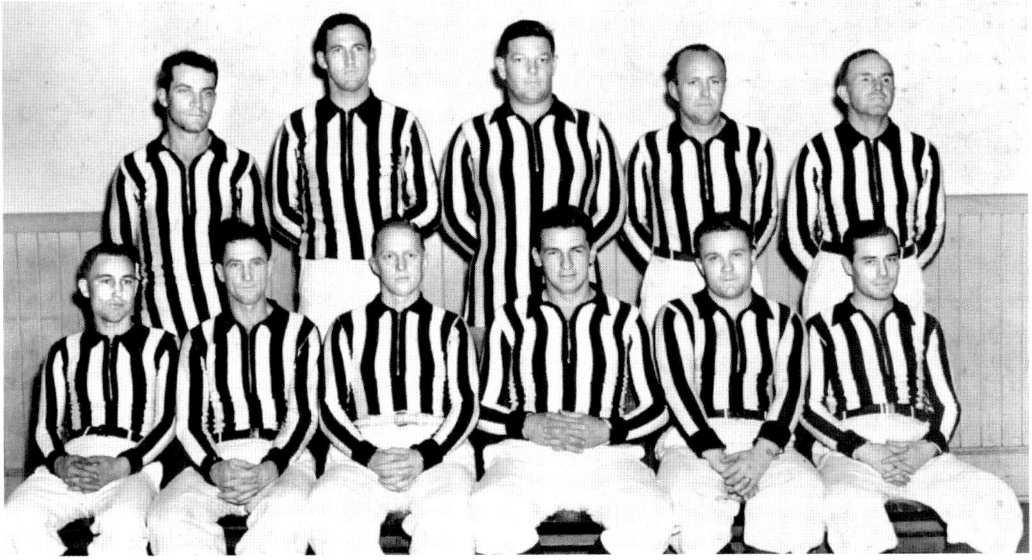

FIRST WALKER COUNTY OFFICIALS ASSOCIATION, 1939. This association consisted of, from left to right, (first row) Loyal Johnson, Parrish; Allen Douglas, Cordova; Al Blanton, Jasper; Paul Boteler, Jasper; Wilson "Shorty" Beard, Parrish; Jimmy Jones, Jasper; (second row) Gordon Craven, Parrish; Thomas Abbott, Cordova; Bruce Jones, Jasper; Harry Erwin, Jasper; Drew "Red" Gibson, Oakman. Not pictured are "Red" Franks, Cordova; Howard Clark, Carbon Hill; Cupe Perry, Goodsprings; "Red" Wright, Jasper.

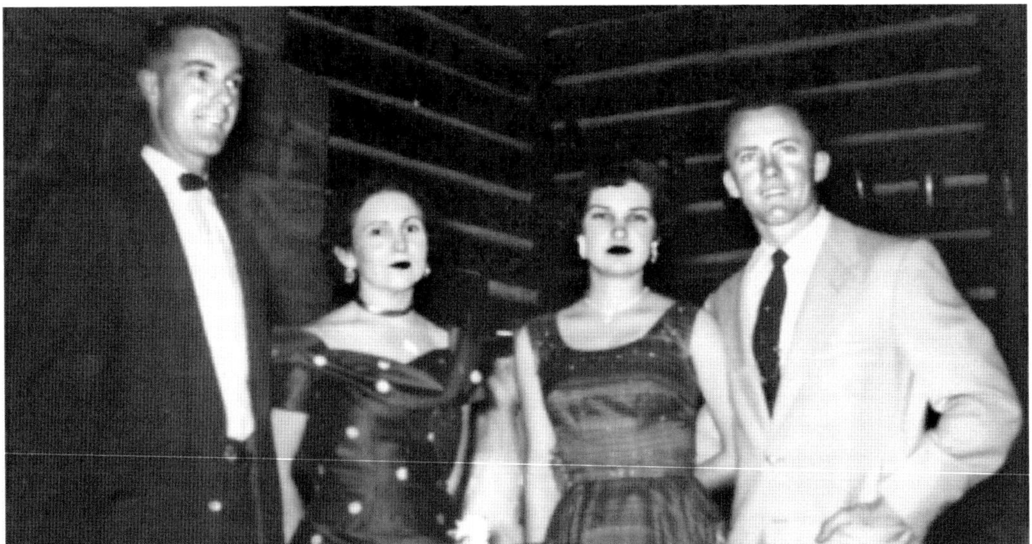

JASPER ICONS, 1960–1990. No book on athletics would be complete without the mention of these two families. From left to right are James Fowler, coach, athletic director, director of transportation for the city, and Walker Hall of Fame member; Sue Fowler, Jasper swim team director; Gail Upton, wife of Pat and sister of Walker's great Billy Richardson; and Pat Upton, longtime tennis coach and member of the Walker and the Alabama Halls of Fame.

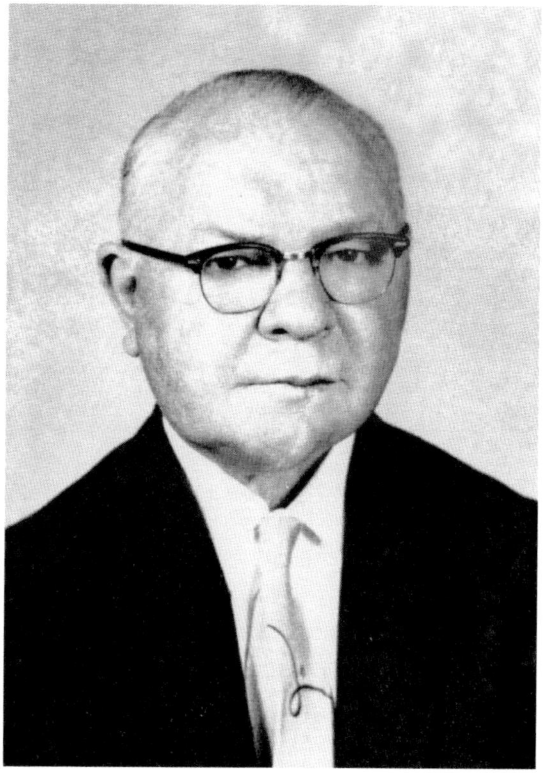

Principal Geddes Self, 1954–1968. Self embodied the true Southern gentleman in every way. He was honest, caring, and dedicated and always kept his Christian life first. A close second was his love for Walker athletics. An ex-Auburn football and baseball star known as the Babe Ruth of Auburn, Self was Walker's principal and its biggest fan. His motivational speeches and loud fight music on game day are still remembered.

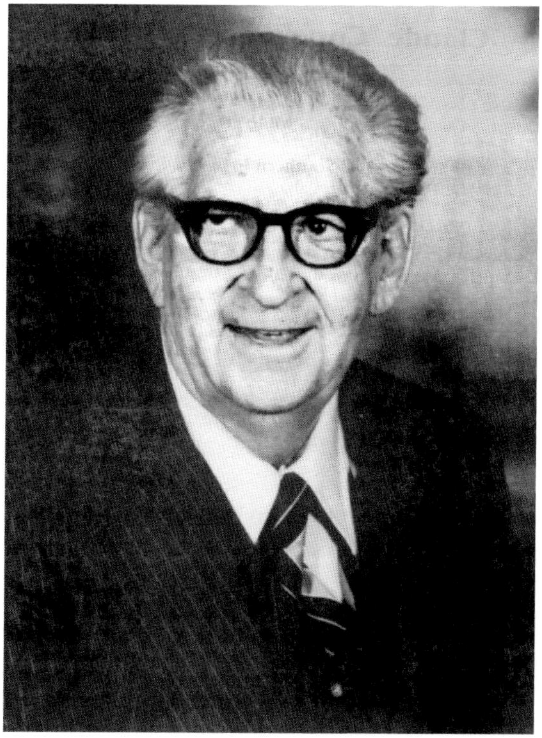

Rev. Paul W. Stewart, 1962. Reverend Stewart was second only to Geddes Self in his love of Walker athletics. In 1962, he wrote the first book on the history of Walker High School athletics, *My Beloved Vikings*. His flamboyant use of adjectives was his trademark remembered by all who knew him. Much of the research for this book would have been very difficult without his book.

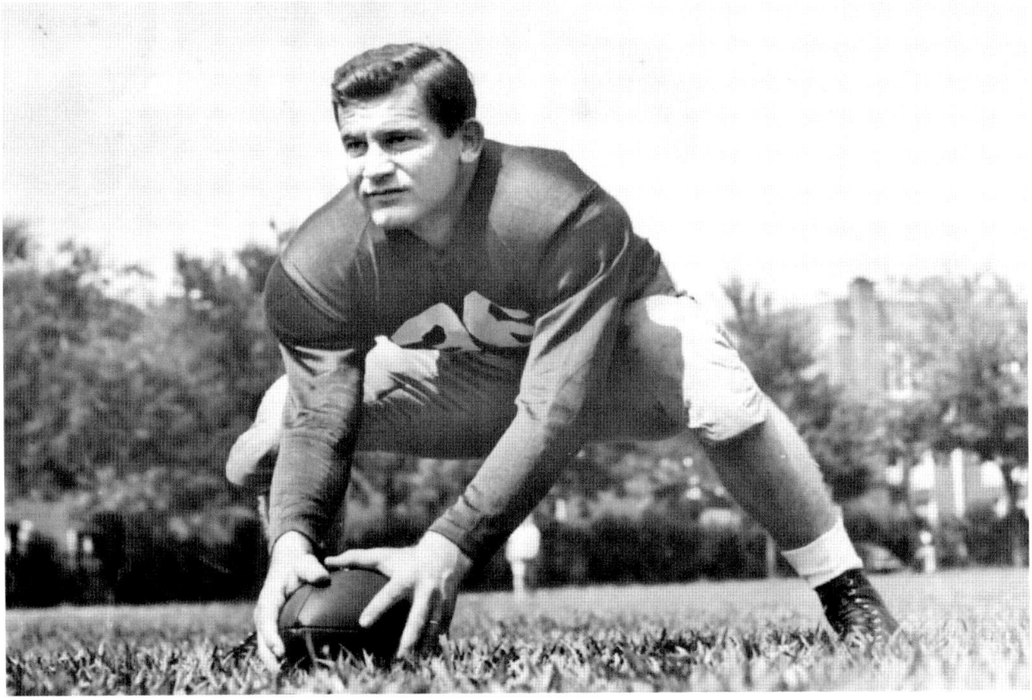

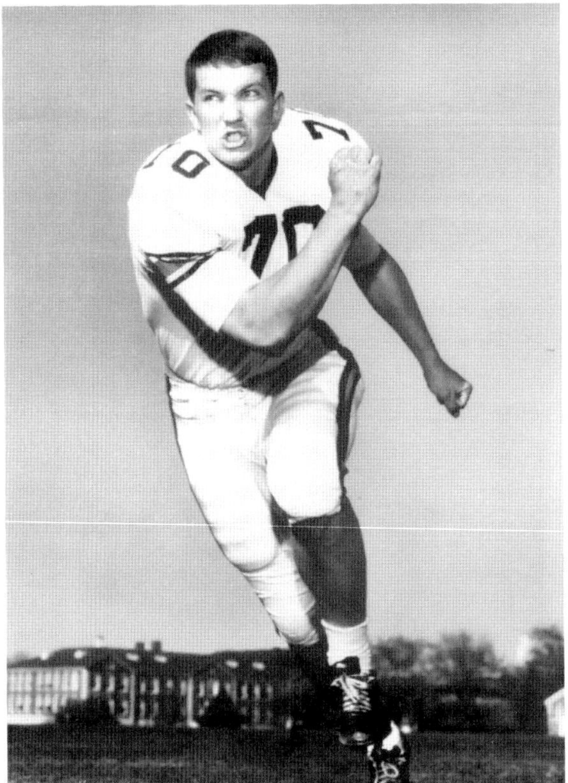

D. Joe Gambrell, 1952–1966. With D. Joe's appearance at Walker, a new era was born, bringing the football program to prominence in the state. He was one of only three coaches in Walker's 80-year history to bring home a state championship trophy in football. D. Joe had been a great football and baseball player at the University of Alabama before coming to Walker.

David Campbell, 1971–1987. David, an All-American tackle at Auburn, came to Jasper as an assistant to Larry Blakeney. He became the head coach in 1975, leading the Vikings to the finals of the state playoffs and being crowned as North Alabama champions in one of Alabama's toughest regions. He was Alabama 6-A Coach of the Year and served as the president of the Fifth District Board of the Alabama High School Athletic Association.

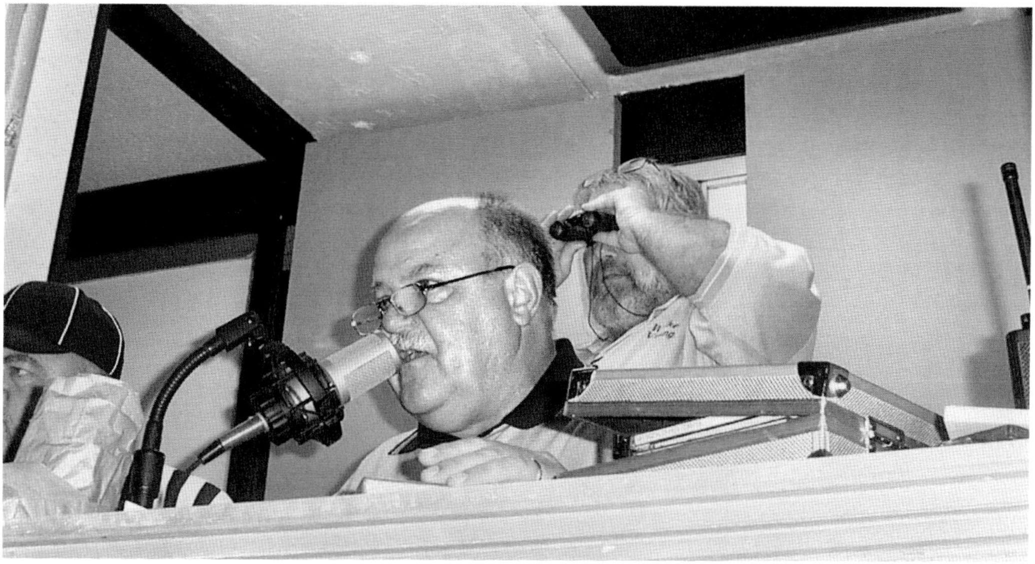

Announcer Sonny Posey, 1963–2000. For over 30 years, Walker fans have heard the voice of Sonny Posey every Friday night describing the action at the Walker High football games. He was a color man on the radio before that, working with such notables as Fred Norris and Bill Call. As public address announcer, he has been assisted since 1988 by Tommy Knight, shown behind Sonny in this photograph.

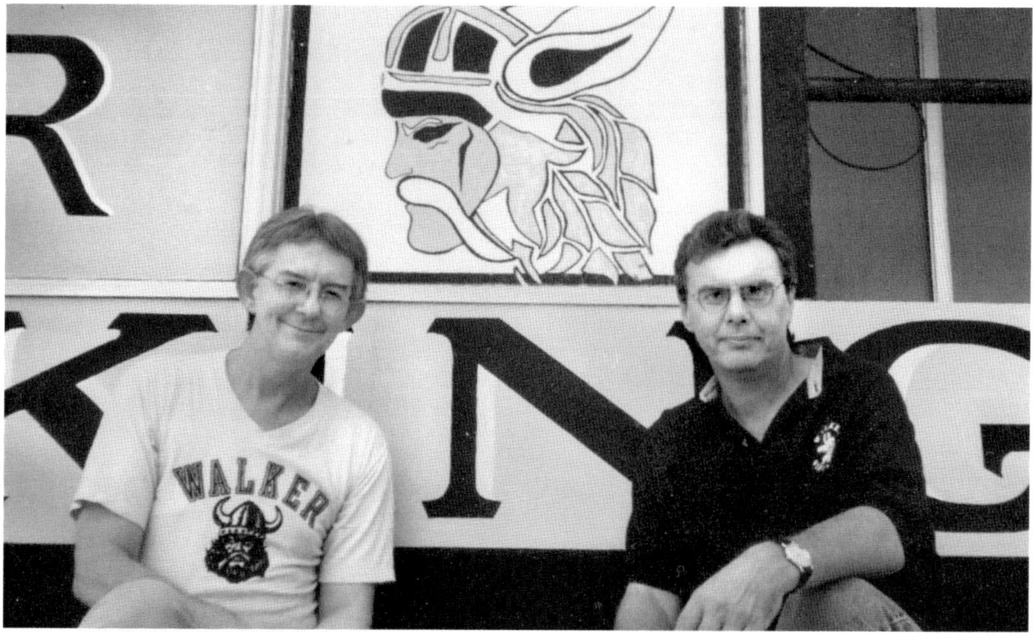

Voices of Walker Football, 1980–2000. Derwood Wilson (left) and Johnny Elmore have been the voices of Walker football on the radio for the last 20 years. Every Friday night, they announce and critique the play of the Vikings. They are upbeat and knowledgeable of not only the game, but of individual players, always making an interesting picture of the game.

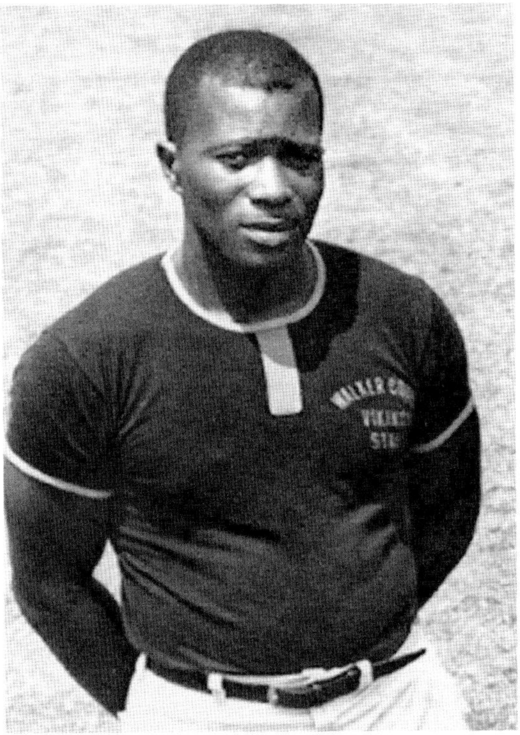

HERMAN DAVIS, FIRST BLACK COACH, 1969. Herman was the perfect man to break the color barrier in coaching. He was tough, fair, knowledgeable, and had a real love for the young men and women he came into contact with at Walker. He was the first black basketball and football assistant coach, first black head baseball coach, and first black assistant principal, as well as a great teacher and a true Christian gentleman.

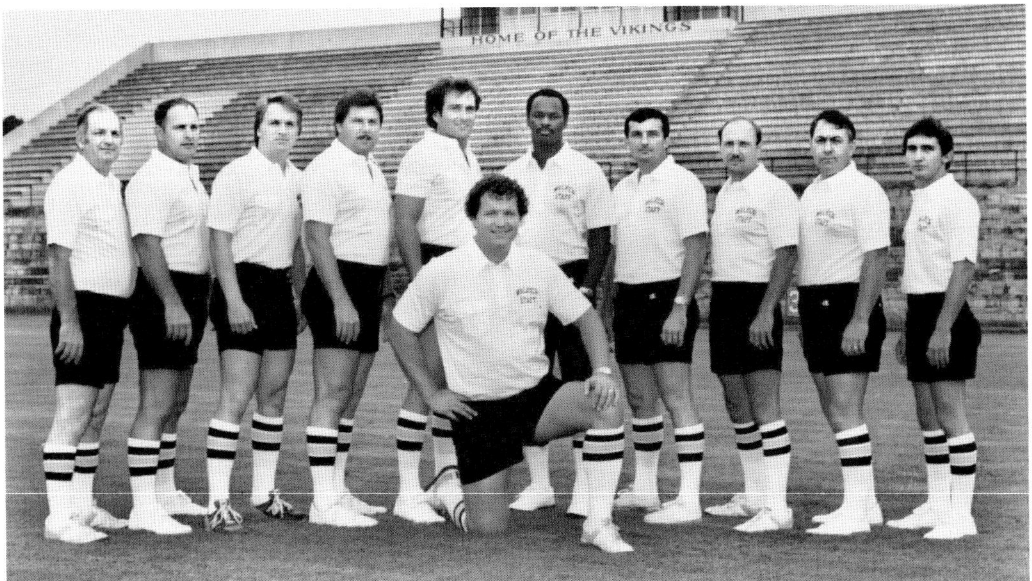

WALKER'S LARGE FOOTBALL STAFF, 1985–1986. Head coach David Campbell assembled a large staff of coaches who worked well together, efficiently handling the roles they were assigned, making for a very successful teaching environment. From left to right are (first row) head coach David Campbell; (second row) Jack Lamon, Gary Borden, Jerry Nix, John Sasser, Ricky Brown, Donnie Morgan, Gary Pilling, Pat Morrison, Blackie Lollar, and Scotty Lynn.

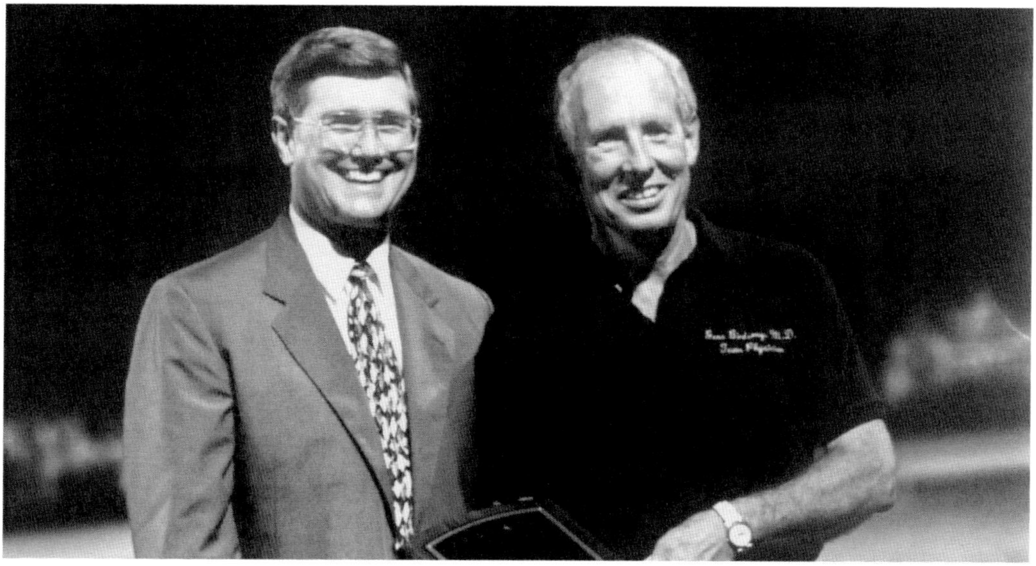

Dr. Gene Birdsong, 1996. Dr. Birdsong was a member of the first class of inductees into the Walker Athletic Hall of Fame. He was the team doctor for over 30 years and a true friend of all areas of the athletic program at Walker. He is shown on the right accepting his hall of fame plaque at the homecoming game from Dr. Bob Neighbors, the superintendent of education for the Jasper City School System.

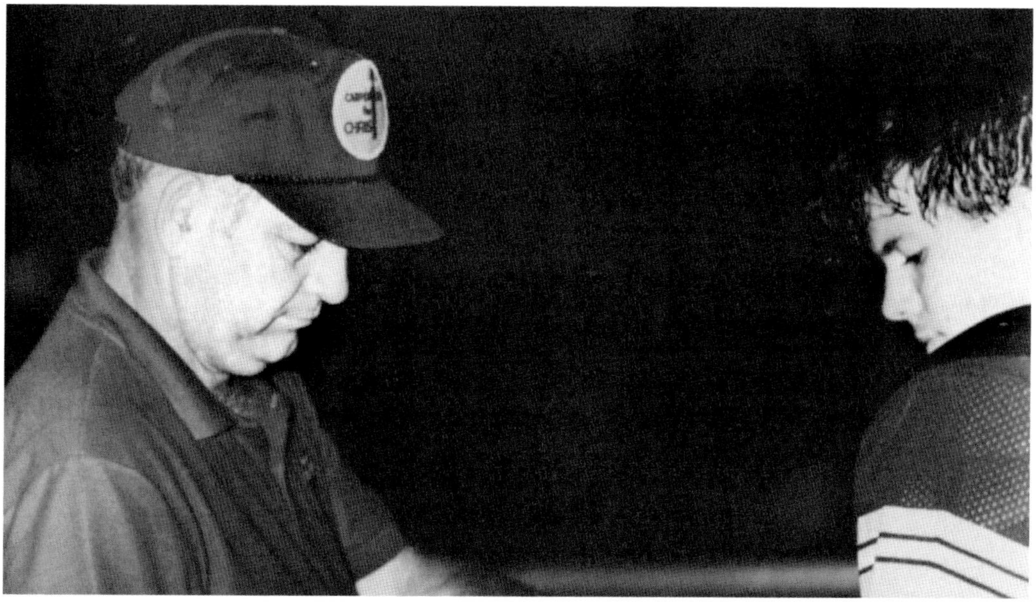

Jack Lamon, 1968–2000. Jack has been involved in Walker athletics since the 1950s, minus a stint in the U.S. military, where he was critically injured during the Vietnam War. After recovery, he returned to Walker as trainer, medic, and chaplain, where he still serves. Jack has served Walker's athletic program faithfully for some 40 years. He was honored in 1998, when the school named its training facility for him.

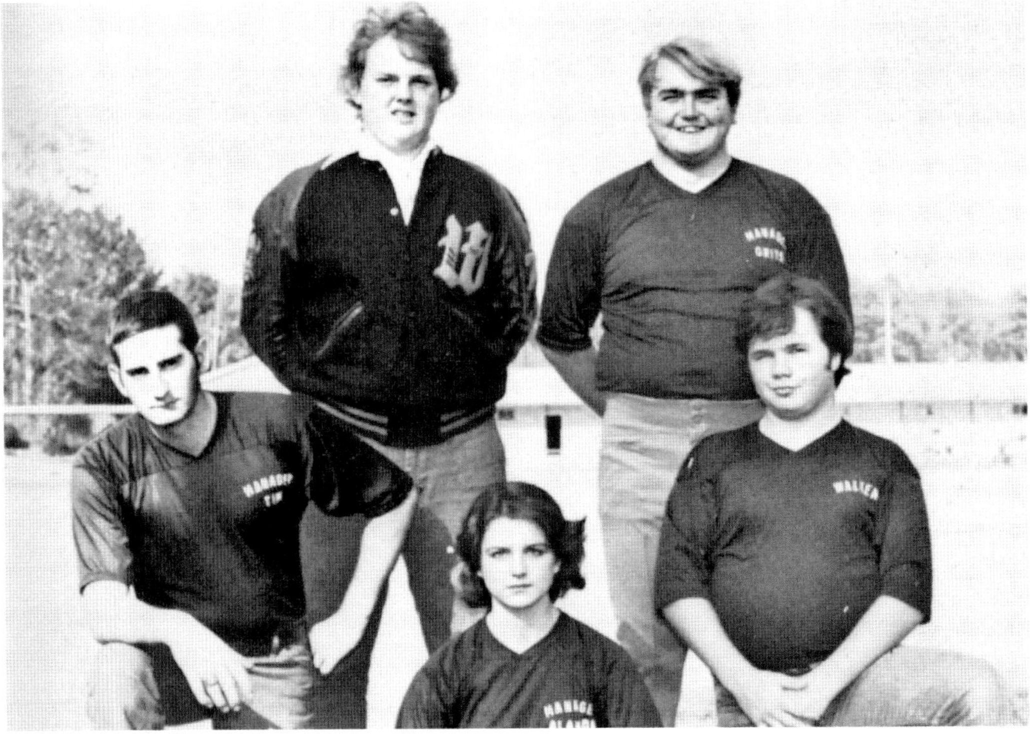

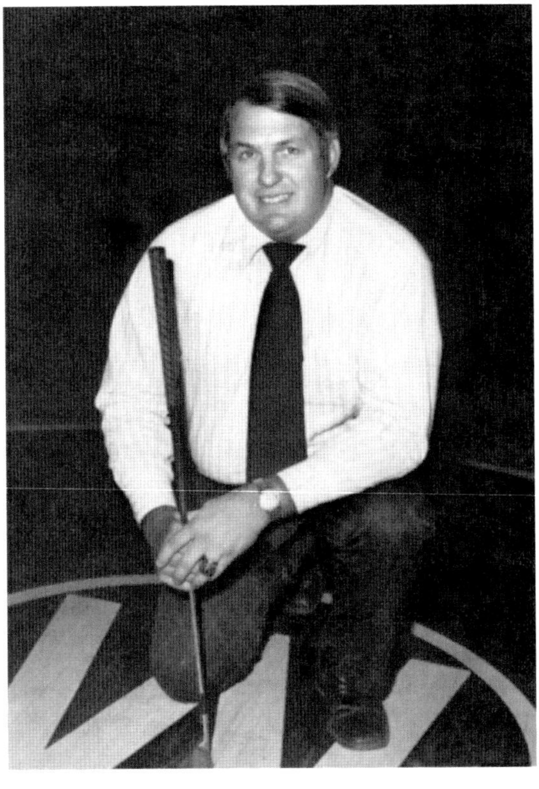

MANAGERS, 1920–2000. This picture is representative of the hundreds of managers who have served Walker over the last 80 years. Managers are the unsung heroes of the athletic world and do all the jobs nobody else will or can do. From left to right are (first row) Tim Richardson, Alanda Sims (the first female manager), and Randy Lamon; (second row) David Dennan and the legendary Randy "Grits" Green.

OMAR FAUCETT, GOLF, 1973–2000. Omar came to Walker after a brilliant career at Moundville and Mountain Brook. He was Walker's golf coach from 1973 until he retired in 2000. His teams were always competitive on the state level, winning four state titles and consistently being in the top five teams in the state during his tenure. He coached the 1989 girls' golf team to the only Alabama state championship in Walker's history.

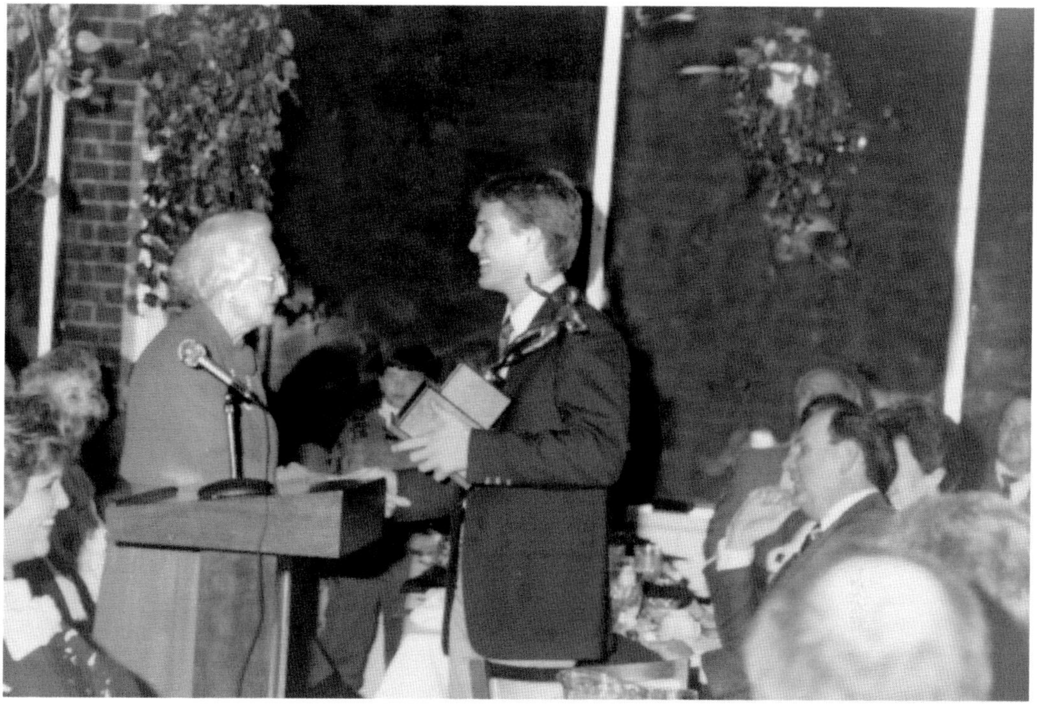

GEDDES SELF AWARD, 1988. The most prestigious award given at Walker is the Geddes Self Award. The award, given each year, exemplifies the best in Walker's young men. Football captain and academic All-State Chris Morrison is shown receiving the award. Presenting the award is Trudy Self, widow of Geddes, who celebrated her 100th birthday in 2005.

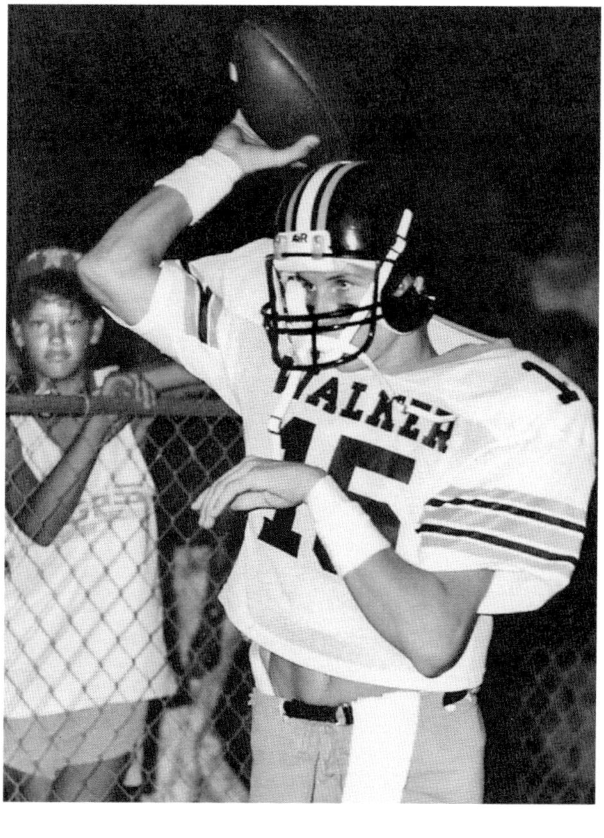

TWO FUTURE ALABAMA STARS, 1990. Griff Redmill, behind the fence, watches his hero Chad Key and dreams of playing at Walker and the University of Alabama. This dream came true for both of these Walker stars. All-State Chad Key played quarterback and wide receiver at the Capstone, while Griff, an outstanding player for Walker, developed into a 300-pound starting lineman for the Crimson Tide.

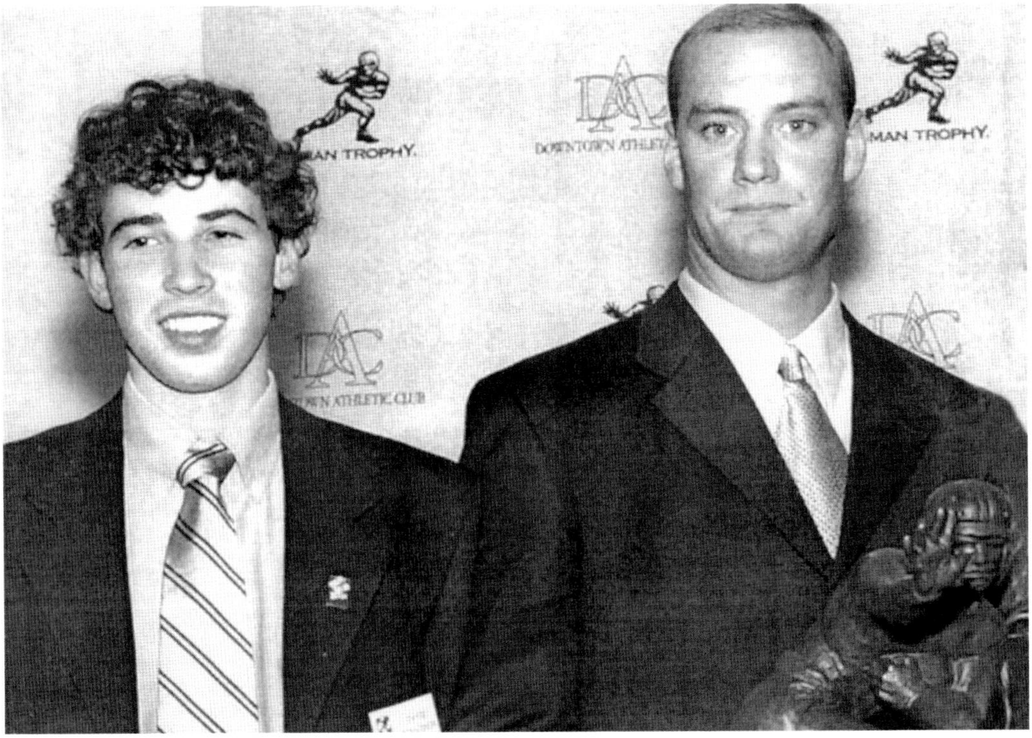

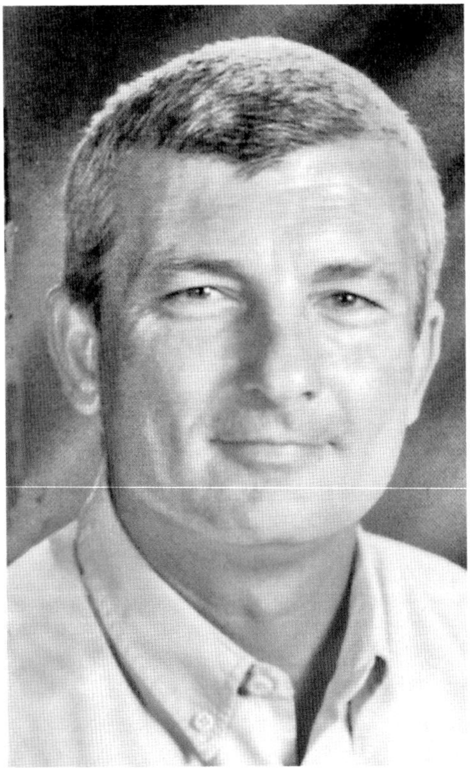

HIGH SCHOOL HEISMAN TROPHY WINNER DAVID DONALDSON, 2000. David and the collegiate winner Chris Weinke of Florida State University are pictured on the day they accepted the trophy from the Downtown Athletic Club in New York City. This is the highest honor a high school athlete can attain. David was the first Alabama winner in history and was selected as the *Daily Mountain Eagle* Sports Person of the Year.

NATIONAL COACH OF THE YEAR GARY PILLING, TENNIS, 2000. Gary, a former player, coached the 1999 and 2000 tennis teams to consecutive Alabama High School Athletic Association state championships and was honored as the National High School Coaches Association Men's Tennis Coach of the Year. He was honored at the National Sports Festival banquet in Orlando, Florida, becoming Walker's only national coach of the year. He won his third straight title in 2001.

Walker High School Hall of Fame

Walker started an athletic hall of fame in 1996 to honor those people who had made a significant contribution to the athletic program from 1920 to the present day. Below is an alphabetical list of the Walker High School Athletic Hall of Fame inductees.

Murry Argo
Elton Banks
Dr. Gene Birdsong
Larry Blakeney
Judge Al Blanton
Scott Brown
Luther Brown
Herbert Burton
Jack Caldwell
Dr. Pete Camp
David Campbell
Glen Clem
Bobby Colbert
Tommy Cole
Ronnie Coleman
Jerry Colvin
Jack Cornelius
Dr. Bubba Crump
Dr. John Crump
Pervy Dodd
Garry Neil Drummond
Larry Drummond
Segal Drummond
Billy Edge
James Fowler
Greg Farris
D. Joe Gambrell
Wayne Gillott
Alec Grant
Herbert Greene
Dr. Ben Hale
Jack Hall
Ralph Hamner
Bay Bay Harris
June Hudson
Tab Hudson
Bill James
Bruce Jones
Chuck Justice
Peggy Keebler
Chad Key
Jack Lamon
Todd Lee
Dr. George Lindsey
Doug Lockridge
Bud Long
A. J. McDanal
Pat Morrison
Rex Murray
Barney Musgrove
T. D. Norris
Linnie Patrick
Dr. T. J. Payne
Cupe Perry
Gene Raburn
Billy Richardson
Ed Richardson
Ben Sankey
Geddes Self
Bob Songer
Rev. Paul Stewart
Dr. Buddy Thorne
Charles Tweedy
Pat Upton
Bernard Weinstein
Clarence White
Goober Williams
M. A. Woodley
Melissa Woodley